Praise for *From the Navy to College*

"This book will no doubt be invaluable to sailors interested in pursuing higher education goals. It is all-encompassing, clearly spelling out the complicated options available to service members, whether their goals point toward degree completion or vocational training. The book does an excellent job pointing out potential pitfalls that may confront sailors in their educational journey and how best to avoid them." —**Edward McKenney**, former dean of military academic programs, Coastline College, Fountain Valley, California

"*From the Navy to College* is a great and practical source of information we usually don't hear enough about. It is very personable and has good practical advice. The information is relevant to all still in active duty, as well as to those who have transitioned into the civilian world." —**Elizabeth G. Beazley**, Medical Corps, U.S. Navy (Ret.)

"After reading Ventrone and Blue's book I can honestly say that it is a useful to me for all those servicemen and -women trying to navigate the waters of higher educational opportunities. This manual is indispensable in finding the way toward a higher degree. I recommend it without reservation." —**David T. Dennihy**, MD, clinical assistant professor, Emergency Medicine SUNY

"Jill Ventrone and Robert W. Blue have done an excellent job in putting this resource together and making it available to individuals interested in the continuing education of our military members. So much of the information is applicable to anyone working in military education." —**Susanne Bowles**, retired Navy campus director

"Today's sailors have more drive and more opportunities to enhance their education than any previous era. *From the Navy to College* is a magnificent one-stop reference guide for leaders throughout the Navy. It points sailors in the right direction to get factual information they need as they make the decision to commit to institutes of higher learning, whether vocational, distance learning or brick-and-mortar schools. *From the Navy to College* is a great tool to add to the deckplate leadership toolbox and a tremendous reference guide when doing one-on-one counseling or career development boards. Quite frankly, if this book had been around when I went to advance my education, I wouldn't have faced the obstacles and unanswered questions that presented a challenge to me. Bravo Zulu to Robert Blue and Jillian Ventrone for their collaboration to put this excellent resource guide together." —**David S. McArtin**, CMDCM(AW), U.S. Navy (Ret.)

"I've been earning my education with military programs since 2008 and have always had to jump through hoops or chase people who know how to do things, but Jill and Robert's book takes all the resources and methods I've been utilizing (and a lot I didn't know about) and literally compiles it all to a 'one-stop shop' book for Navy personnel. It also makes chasing individuals a thing of the past, and turns 'he said, she said' education theories into factual reality. If a Navy service member were to purchase this book, there would be no confusion how to earn a degree or where to start." —**Jeffrey D. Osborne**, BU1(SCW/EXW/MTS)

From the Navy to College

*Transitioning from the Service
to Higher Education*

Jillian Ventrone and Robert W. Blue Jr.

ROWMAN & LITTLEFIELD
Lanham • Boulder • New York • London

Published by Rowman & Littlefield
A wholly owned subsidiary of The Rowman & Littlefield Publishing Group, Inc.
4501 Forbes Boulevard, Suite 200, Lanham, Maryland 20706
www.rowman.com

Unit A, Whitacre Mews, 26-34 Stannary Street, London SE11 4AB

British Library Cataloguing in Publication Information Available

Library of Congress Cataloging-in-Publication Data

Ventrone, Jillian, 1973–
From the Navy to college : transitioning from the service to higher education / Jillian Ventrone and
Robert W. Blue Jr.
pages cm
Includes bibliographical references and index.
ISBN 978-1-4422-3995-1 (cloth : alk. paper) — ISBN 978-1-4422-3996-8 (electronic)
1. Veterans—Education—United States. 2. Sailors—Education—United States. 3. United States.
Navy. I. Blue, Robert W., Jr. II. Title.
UB357.V343 2015
378.1'982697—dc23
2014029223

∞™ The paper used in this publication meets the minimum requirements of American
National Standard for Information Sciences Permanence of Paper for Printed Library
Materials, ANSI/NISO Z39.48-1992.

Printed in the United States of America

Contents

Preface

People are driven to join the Navy for many different reasons; often education and career skills are at the top of the list. Service in the Navy can offer either option, but why not consider pursuing both at the same time in order to maximize promotion power while in the service and career potential upon leaving the service? *From the Navy to College: Transitioning from the Service to Higher Education* was written to help guide sailors through their higher education journey before, during, and after their military service. Sailors have many education and career opportunities available to them because of their service, but they are often hard to find and navigate correctly. *From the Navy to College* simplifies this process by disseminating necessary information and teaching readers how to manipulate available resources.

Introduction

From the Navy to College: Transitioning from the Service to Higher Education is an education and career reference guide for sailors looking to join the Navy, already on active duty, or transitioning into the civilian sector. The information offered within the book will enable sailors pursuing higher education and vocational training to navigate and understand all possible options. The book is meant to serve as a long-term support guide for sailors who are actively seeking to improve themselves through education and training. From getting started to degree completion, all available funding resources to help cover costs and Navy-based program options are detailed for the reader in order to assist throughout the course of an individual's chosen pathway.

The Navy offers numerous programs for its service members to participate in while on active duty, but very few sailors are aware of the options. No main Navy manual exists that demonstrates these programs, outlines eligibility parameters, or details the admissions process. *From the Navy to College* aims to correct this problem by disseminating the needed information in one easily accessible place for sailors to reference. If a sailor is interested in expanding upon his work credentials through education or training, this book offers him the chance to prepare appropriately because it arms readers with the information needed to find success.

Today's service members are resilient, dedicated, motivated, and undeterred in their pursuit of higher education opportunities. They are diehard in their service, especially considering the sacrifices they have made over the past twelve years while our country has been at war. As the service branches face budget cuts and draw downs, active-duty personnel are looking for outlets to help make them more competitive for promotion or more credible for potential civilian-sector employers. *From the Navy to College* fills this need.

The Navy gives its members numerous chances to fulfill these goals through the programs it offers, but sailors must first learn how to navigate the maze. Very little guidance is available for sailors who desire information pertaining to available programs. Together the authors of this book have worked with thousands of sailors who have already taken their advice and found success. Compiling this book enabled them to disseminate the knowledge they have used to assist these sailors to a greater audience. Readers will feel more capable planning and executing the necessary steps to begin their transitions.

Some of the information delivered in this book is reprinted from the Marine Corps version, *From the Marine Corps to College: Transitioning from the Service to Higher Education.* Much of the information provided is applicable to service members from each of the different military branches. It is also highly relevant to individuals considering entering the Navy who might be looking for more information regarding the available benefits specific to this branch of the armed forces.

Chapter One

Get Going on Your Education

Oftentimes sailors who visit my (Jillian's) office tell me they have been interested in starting college for a long time but are unsure how to get going. Many have received mixed advice about how to take the first step and are now nervous that they will make a mistake. This chapter will help you prepare properly to take your first step with confidence.

GET GOING ON YOUR EDUCATION

Getting started on higher education is usually the most difficult step a service member will take. Higher education is often a foreign environment for active-duty or veteran sailors. Once that initial hurdle is overcome, the rest will begin to fall into place. That is not to say that it will be smooth sailing. But the fear factor will have dissipated, and you will learn to understand the rhythm of your classes. If you follow the directions outlined in this chapter and reference this book along the way, your trip down the higher education road should be much less stressful.

If you are still on active duty, Navy College offices are available on most bases to assist in your decision-making process. After reading through this book, make an appointment with an academic counselor at the base where you are stationed. He or she will help guide you through the process of getting started. The counselor can also act as your guide along your educational pathway. If you ever feel that your chosen pathway is not progressing properly, the counselor should be your first go-to individual.

If still on active duty, there is a specific pathway to be eligible for Tuition Assistance (TA). The section on TA in the "Cost and Payment Resources" chapter (chapter 6) will cover the steps to receive funding through this program in an in-depth manner. If you are preparing to transition off active-duty service, make an appointment with a counselor to receive assistance in understanding your GI Bill benefits and how you can activate the benefit process. The counselors can also help you prepare for your new mission: higher education.

If you are a veteran and located close to a military base (any branch), contact the base education center for assistance. If you are not located near a military base, call the veterans' representative at the school you are thinking about attending. He or she should be your initial point-of-contact for everything at the school. These individuals are often veteran students at the school and have already been there and done that, so they know how to get you started along the proper pathway.

The following checklist will help you structure an educational plan. Take the time to write down your answers and review the information.

1. What do you want to be when you grow up? (This is still a difficult question for many of the career service members whom I counsel.)
2. What type of school should you attend—traditional or vocational?
3. Do you need a two-year or a four-year institution?
4. Have you picked a school already?
5. What are the institution's application requirements?
6. Have you collected your required documents?
7. Have you applied to the institution?
8. How will you pay for your schooling?

Let's sort through the list to help you start making decisions.

WHAT DO YOU WANT TO BE WHEN YOU GROW UP?

If you know which career you would like to pursue, you are already a few steps ahead. If not, try a self-discovery site such as CareerScope (http://www. gibill.va.gov/studenttools/careerscope/index.html) or O*NET OnLine (http:// www.onetonline.org/). Both sites are free and might help narrow down possible career fields to fit your personality type. Researching different career possibilities including income levels, job openings, and required education levels usually helps sailors begin to develop interest in a specific pathway. More information on these sites can be found in chapter 3, "Research Tools."

If you have no idea which career pathway to take, starting at the local community college is often the best bet. Attending a community college may help you test the waters. Declare for an associate degree in general studies and use the elective credits to try different subjects. Elective credits are built into degree plans and offer you freedom to pursue topics outside your declared major. Many community colleges offer vocational classes; if you think that might be a viable pathway, you can add some of these classes as well.

WHAT TYPE OF SCHOOL SHOULD YOU ATTEND: TRADITIONAL OR VOCATIONAL?

If you have chosen a specific career, you also need to decide upon the type of school necessary to achieve the appropriate degree or certification. Education that is traditional in nature, such as criminal justice, engineering, or business, will require a traditional degree path at a regionally accredited institution of higher learning.

Education that is vocational in nature might require a nationally accredited vocational school. The different types of schools you can select for your educational pursuits are discussed in chapter 4 of this book. Always check at your local community college to see if it offers the vocational education you are interested in pursuing. Oftentimes, community colleges have apprenticeship or on-the-job training (OJT) programs attached to their vocational training options.

DO YOU NEED A TWO-YEAR OR FOUR-YEAR INSTITUTION?

Does your educational pathway require a two-year or four-year degree? If in doubt, check O*NET OnLine, or contact the schools in the area to inquire about the level of degree offered for that particular field of study. O*Net demonstrates the different educational levels along with corresponding wages nationally or for a selected state.

Most vocational pathways require either a one- or two-year certification, and oftentimes an associate degree is required. Most career fields that are traditional in nature (think white-collar work) require a four-year bachelor's degree or a graduate-level degree.

HAVE YOU PICKED A SCHOOL ALREADY?

If you have a school (or schools) that you are interested in attending, check to see that it is accredited and offers the degree you would like to attain. If so, the first phone call you make should be to the veterans' representatives. They should be able to answer all of your questions. If not, they will direct you to the appropriate individuals. Accreditation, which is covered in chapter 4, can be extremely important for career viability.

Here are a few questions to ask the veterans' representatives:

- What are the admissions requirements? Are they flexible for veterans? Do you need an SAT or ACT? What are the admissions deadlines?
- Will the school accept military transcripts (Joint Services Transcript)?
- Is the institution a member of Servicemembers Opportunity Colleges?
- Which GI Bill is best for the school: Montgomery GI Bill (MGIB) or Post 9/11?
- Will you have to pay out of pocket for tuition or fees above the amount the GI Bill will cover?
- Does the school approximate how much money books will cost yearly?
- Where are veterans buying their books? Through the bookstore or online? Is there a book exchange or rental program for veterans on campus?
- What veteran services are offered at the institution or nearby?
- How far away is the closest VA center (http://www.va.gov)?
- How many veterans attend the school?
- Does the institution have a student veterans' organization?
- How can you find other veterans who need roommates (if applicable)?
- Does the school have a veterans' center, and what resources are available in the center?
- What helpful hints can they offer pertaining to your attendance at the school?

If you are trying to decide between two schools, the answers to these questions may offer additional guidance.

If you do not know where to go to school, read on for more advice. College Navigator, which is discussed in the "Research Tools" chapter (chapter 3), can be incredibly helpful for conducting school searches. Remember, when in doubt, the local community college is a safe bet, and getting started should be the goal.

If you narrow your search to a few schools but are still unsure which one to choose, make a quick campus visit, check the application process, and review the time-line restrictions. Oftentimes, settling on a school requires a leap of faith, but many small, often overlooked, factors can help guide your decision. For example, if you are about to deploy and are indecisive about choosing between two different schools, the school that offers the smoothest registration process might be a better choice. Service members have to consider time spent and mission demands because pursuing education while on active duty remains an off-duty benefit.

WHAT ARE THE INSTITUTIONS' APPLICATION REQUIREMENTS?

Depending upon the type of school you choose, it might have stringent application requirements, or it might be quite lenient. Application requirements can help you eliminate schools if you missed deadlines or do not possess the materials required for submission—for example, an SAT or ACT score, or letters of recommendation.

If you choose a four-year university or college, most likely the institution will require SAT or ACT scores and a formal application process. If you opt for community college, you can avoid a long application process and transfer to a university after acquiring a predetermined amount of college credit. The amount of credit you will be required to finish prior to being eligible for the transfer process will be based upon the transfer requirements of the institution where you are trying to finish your bachelor's degree. If you are pursuing a vocational degree or certificate, these types of schools typically have open admissions similar to community colleges.

If your transition from active duty to veteran is quick, the open admissions process with a local community college can be a less stressful transition into higher education. As long as you follow an appropriate course of study, dictated by an academic counselor at your school, you should not need to worry about the transfer process until a later date. The counselors will tell you which classes you are required to take to be eligible for transfer, and they will be listed on your academic degree or transfer plan.

HAVE YOU COLLECTED ALL REQUIRED DOCUMENTS?

Prior to applying, verify with your school of choice which documents you will need to provide. If an ACT or SAT is required, have you tested? Do you have proof of residency? Have you applied for your GI Bill and received your Certificate of Eligibility (COE)? If you plan to attend a university, you might need a completed application, submitted test scores, letters of recommendation, an application fee, and transcripts. Open admissions institutions such as community colleges and vocational schools usually require a completed online application and proof of payment such as the COE for GI Bill or a TA voucher for active-duty personnel. Visit the "Cost and Payment Resources" chapter of this book (chapter 6) to learn how to apply for your benefits.

HAVE YOU APPLIED TO THE INSTITUTION?

Complete the required application process using all applicable documents. This process is usually online and can take quite a bit of time. Most sites will save your information for a certain number of days if you are unable to finish in one sitting. The admissions process chapter of this book (chapter 4) offers detailed guidance for this area. Many of the sailors whom I (Jillian) counsel request help with this process, especially because a personal statement essay section often appears in one of the steps.

HOW WILL YOU PAY FOR YOUR SCHOOLING?

This is the time to pay good attention to your funding possibilities! When discussing funding options for education, GI Bills are best for veterans and TA is best for active-duty service members. MGIB and Post 9/11 are not the same. Both help with academic funding, but the two bills work in sharply different ways. Veterans who use either bill will find that a great many expenses are still left uncovered.

Active-duty service members and veterans can apply for Federal Student Aid (FSA) for extra help. Veterans also have unemployment as an option. Check out your state's Department of Labor for more information on unemployment eligibility and possibilities. Many of the active-duty service members I work with are awarded Pell Grant money through the Free Application for Federal Student Aid (FAFSA), and Pell Grants do not need to be repaid.

The "Cost and Payment Resources" chapter (chapter 6) offers detailed information about funding your education.

To recap the checklist above in an abbreviated format:

- Choose a career.
- Find a school.
- Organize your finances.

If you are undecided upon a career, get started on general education classes at the local community college. Exercising your brain is never a mistake.

Chapter Two

Active-Duty and Veterans' Educational Concerns

Active-duty and veteran sailors usually have special needs regarding higher education, and these needs can vary drastically depending on their service status. Finding an institution that can fulfill these needs prior to starting down the education pathway is important. To accomplish this task, sailors must consider what types of flexibility they are looking for in an institution and vet the schools using all available resources before settling on one institution.

ACTIVE-DUTY AND VETERANS' EDUCATIONAL NEEDS

Active-duty and veteran sailors should consider the types of needs they might have while pursuing higher education prior to determining which institution will best suit them. Typically, these needs are considerably different from the civilian population. Considering issues such as the position you currently hold, the amount of free time you have, location concerns, learning styles, Internet availability, and personal needs while searching for a school will save you much heartache down the road. You can always transfer schools if your first choice does not work out, but you run the risk of losing credits in the process.

Just as not all our personal needs are the same, not all schools are the same. School offerings will vary by the levels of education, resources, or support systems they can provide. Picking the right institution for you is a personal process and, in most cases, will require quite a bit of research.

During counseling sessions, most active-duty sailors tell me (Jillian) that flexibility is their number one concern. Often, they need a school that offers a wealth of online courses and degree offerings, fast-paced semesters, military familiarity, understanding professors, and an academic counselor who will always be available. Each of these items is necessary in order for the population to achieve academic success. Just be careful if you are not a solid online learner. I have worked with sailors who decided to pursue online school even though they considered themselves hands-on learners, and they struggled through their classes.

If you need to attend school in a face-to-face setting because it is better for your learning style, check to see that the school you choose maintains the flexible classroom offerings you need to be successful. Does the institution offer weekend, evening, or hybrid classes? Does it offer classes on your base? What are the professors' contact policies regarding their active-duty students? Lastly, what can the school offer in the way of support services?

Military students require high levels of flexibility by both the institution and its professors. Between deployments and PCS moves, sailors need to know that the school they have chosen will assist them at every turn no matter what type of situation arises. For example, what happens if you are deployed and lose your Internet connection for several days? Will the professor take your assignment late without penalizing your grade?

Always try to discuss with the professor any concerns you may have at the start of your class. Most will understand and try to make accommodations. If that pathway does not work, try talking to your academic counselor. This is why it is imperative that schools with significant military populations maintain veteran-only academic counselors. These individuals understand service members' special needs and how to help in situations such as this one. Unfortunately, many sailors tell me they cannot find their academic counselors. Some schools put people in these positions who are not trained, do not understand the special needs of the military population, or do not hold the proper level of education. In this case, these positions tend to turn over often, and students might find themselves with a new counselor so often that the individual does not understand their concerns.

Many schools have clear policies in regard to deployments and may even allow students to finish courses remotely. Institutions with academic counselors strictly for active duty and veterans may be able to provide more tailored help. At a minimum, they can give an active-duty service member a clear chain of command to contact when in need of assistance.

Often sailors do not have enough time left in service to finish an associate or bachelor's degree before separation but would like to start working toward their education. Others are interested in pursuing a degree that is difficult or impossible to find in an online format from a reputable institution. Several concerns should be considered before moving forward.

Credit transferability should be at the top of that list. Transferability is a sticky topic. Ultimately, credit acceptance is up to the final institution. Schools usually consider the accreditation of the prior institution and specific program requirements when reviewing transfer credit.

Classes do not always transfer for the credit they were originally intended to fill. You must also keep an eye on how many credits an institution will accept. For example, Arizona State University (ASU) will transfer a maximum of sixty-four lower-division semester hours (i.e., 100- and 200-level classes) from a regionally accredited community college (https://transfer.asu.edu/credits), although some exceptions apply for veterans. If you intend to transfer to ASU to complete a bachelor's degree, taking more than sixty-four lower-division credits from the school you are currently attending would be unproductive. Try your best not to find yourself in a situation where credits will not transfer or might need to be repeated.

Consider a few questions before moving forward in this situation:

- Always check the institution's accreditation. I cannot emphasize this point enough. Chapter 4 in this book reviews the different types of accreditation and concerns to be aware of prior to selecting an institution. If you make the wrong choice, you might have to backtrack later.
- Consider the state you come from or intend to move to before choosing a school to attend. Many schools have satellite locations in other states or at military installations. If you can find one from your state, in most cases it will be better for your needs.
- If you know which institution you would like to attend after separation from the military, check whether the school offers online classes. If feasible, it would be best to start while on active duty at the school where you intend to finish when you are a veteran. Many schools, including state-based two-year and four-year institutions, offer online classes and are approved for Tuition Assistance (TA). Colorado State University, Pennsylvania State University, and University of Maryland are a few of the big four-year universities with fully online bachelor's degrees that are TA approved. Many community colleges offer fully online associate degrees,

such as Central Texas Community College, which is located at several military installations. Check the Department of Defense Memorandum of Understanding website (http://www.dodmou.com) to see if your school is approved for TA. Attending a school online that you can continue to attend once separated will make your transition much easier, and you will not run the risk of losing credits during the transfer process.

- If these options are not possible, contact the school you are interested in attending upon separation and ask if it has transfer agreements with any particular schools. Most big universities are fed by local community colleges, and most community colleges offer online classes. Usually, big state universities have transfer agreements with the local state community colleges.
- Check with the local Navy College to see which schools have a presence on the base.

Veterans' educational needs have been the topic of much discussion. The Post 9/11 GI Bill has allowed today's veterans more flexibility in their educations than ever before, and schools across the country have had significant increases in their veteran student populations. Unfortunately, veterans of the current conflicts face transition issues that pose many difficult challenges. Schools that recognize these challenges and tailor services on the campus to meet the special needs of their veteran populations should be recognized for their support.

Be careful when choosing a school that claims it is veteran friendly. A study conducted by the Center for American Progress determined that the criteria for listing schools as "veteran friendly" on some websites and media outlets are unclear. Schools should offer you a proper academic pathway as well as veteran-based support. Be leery of any institution that claims it is "veteran friendly" but cannot back it up with concrete proof.[1]

Ask about campus support services for veterans. You should look for veteran-only academic counselors, VA services on the campus or nearby, nonprofit veteran assistance such as American Veterans (AMVETS) or Disabled American Veterans (DAV), student veteran organizations such as the Student Veterans of America (SVA), financial aid support, unemployment support, contact with off-campus services that specialize in veteran outreach, and a significant student veterans center that is consistently manned. The center should be prepared to handle, or refer to the appropriate agencies, any problem that comes its way.

Many institutions even offer peer-to-peer mentoring. Saddleback College in Mission Viejo, California, has a peer-mentoring program that may end in a small scholarship for the mentor. The scholarship has rigorous qualifications to be accepted. The application requires several essays be submitted for acceptance and again after completion in order to receive the award. The program enables new veteran students and those who have attended the institution for a while to intermingle. This interaction will boost the confidence of the incoming veteran and provide him with a support system, while enabling the veteran mentor to give back to his community.

Many academic institutions, including ASU, host the Veterans Upward Bound (VUB) program on their campuses (https://eoss.asu.edu/trio/vub). The VUB program is designed to encourage and assist veterans in their pursuit of higher education. The federally funded program aims to increase and improve qualified veterans' English, math, computer skills to assist with literacy, laboratory science, foreign language, and college planning skills. All of the courses are free, and ASU offers courses daily on three of the school's campuses. One campus has classes offered at three different times during the day to better meet the schedule of the veteran population. Check the national VUB program website (http://www.navub.org/) to find out if your school offers the program.

School location is important for veterans for many reasons other than the Monthly Housing Allowance (MHA) attached to Post 9/11. Try to find a school that is within a decent driving distance. Usually, in a traditional education environment, we live where we go to school. This may not be the case for many veterans. Often, veterans are older and have families they must support while they pursue higher education. Sometimes jobs dictate where we can live, and driving far distances to get to class may add unneeded stress to an already stressful transition. Check for veteran services offered around the school, because if you need help, you may not want to drive one hundred miles to get it.

The setting of the school's location is also important. If you need to be in a city for nightlife or a more fast-paced lifestyle, you should take that into consideration. If you prefer something without many distractions, consider a quieter institution in a smaller town location. You can also check to see if the veterans' center at the school has a designated veteran-only study space allocated for quiet study time.

Class availability is imperative for veterans for reasons such as MHA amounts under 9/11 and socialization. Both of these subjects are vastly different in nature but extremely important to consider when thinking about your transition to school. The MHA and degree plan requirements under Post 9/11 are addressed in the "Cost and Payment Resources" chapter.

Socialization is sometimes an issue that doesn't become a concern until several months after separation. Although I (Jillian) am not writing this book to depress my readers about some of the issues facing the veteran population, I do want to remind you of a few things to consider.

Isolation can become a concern for transitioning veterans who face an unknown civilian population that doesn't operate in the regimented fashion they are used to in the military. Sailors who isolate themselves run a great risk of facing difficulty in the transition process. Making contact and developing relationships with other veterans at the school is a good way to combat this problem.

Sailors should review the following checklist with a veterans' representative at the school they plan to attend:

- Make contact so you have a face to to put with the name.
- Explain your situation and ask for helpful hints for anything you may need.
- Ask about housing and where you can find other veterans for roommates.
- Find out what services the school has set in place for its veteran population. Maybe the school has a veteran-only student body (president, vice president, secretary, etc.) that helps plan social events or promotes veteran well-being at the institution.
- Determine where the closest VA center is located.
- Ask about student veteran organizations (such as Student Veterans of America) available on campus.
- Find out about the institution's veteran population. How many veteran students attend the school? Does the school/vet center host any veteran-only events?
- Ask whether veterans receive early admission.
- Ask whether there is a veterans' academic counselor.
- Ask whether the institution is a Servicemembers Opportunity College (SOC). Does it award the SOCNAV? (Information on the SOCNAV can be found in chapter 7, "Prior Learning Credit.")

Veteran interaction on campus is important for veteran success. Many veteran departments at schools actively participate in community events involving veterans. This is a great way to meet new friends and help your peers. Interaction is not solely for you to create a school support web and make friends. Networking with other veterans is also a great way to keep in touch with other people who have shared similar experiences. Sharing experiences with those who have "been there, done that" may help you reintegrate faster into civilian life. This network can also be an amazing tool later for job searches and entrepreneurship possibilities.

Researching the topics mentioned above may help you understand the school's overall culture and attitude toward its veteran population. If the school does not seem to have many veteran services set in place, you may want to consider other options. Schools should provide veterans a multitude of support services in case they face unforeseen issues while transitioning and need help.

The VA recognized the need for veterans to hear transition troubles and successes from peers and created a website to help. Make the Connection (http://maketheconnection.net/) helps veterans through shared experiences and support services. The site contains resources and videos from veterans who have faced issues you may be facing and offers advice based on personal experience.

Chapter Three

Research Tools

Prior to making any major decisions, learning how to use the numerous research tools available to service members for education and career research should be a top priority for sailors. Users are able to make better-informed decisions in areas such as school selection, degree choice, career planning, and résumé building. Each tool offers invaluable information in the different levels involved with planning your future, whether that is a long-term career in the Navy or a civilian-sector route. Using all of these sites and cross-referencing the information will benefit the overall organization of your profession:

- College Navigator
- O*NET OnLine
- DANTES College & Career Planning Counseling Services, powered by Kuder® Journey
- VA Chapter 36
- Navy COOL
- Navy Knowledge Online
- Counseling Services

COLLEGE NAVIGATOR

http://nces.ed.gov/collegenavigator/

College Navigator offered by the National Center for Education Statistics is a beneficial tool for both active-duty and transitioning sailors. The free site enables users to search schools based upon very detailed criteria. Searches may be saved for future reference and dropped into the favorites' box for side-by-side comparison. Comparing schools side-by-side enables users to determine which school better suits their needs. For example, I searched California State University, San Marcos (CSUSM), and University of San Diego (USD) to determine which school would be less expensive. After dropping both schools into my "Favorites" box, I selected the compare option in that section. The side-by-side comparison tool listed CSUSM's current tuition rates at $22,288 and USD's at $58,537. I still needed to go directly to both schools' websites for more information, but my initial search demonstrated to me the vast difference in yearly costs between the two institutions. Of course, I understand that the Post 9/11 GI Bill will currently only cover up to $20,235.02 per academic year for a private school, and I know further research will be required to determine whether USD is a viable fiscal option for me as a veteran student.

College Navigator allows detailed searches in fields such as distance from ZIP codes, public and private school options, distance-learning possibilities, school costs, percentage of applicants admitted, religious affiliations, specialized missions, and available athletic teams. This way, users can narrow down selections based upon specific needs. For example, if I were interested in attending a school with a Christian background as part of my learning, I could click on the "Religious Affiliations" tab at the bottom of the search section and add that criterion to my list.

Beginning each search within a certain number of miles from a ZIP code will enable users to narrow their search parameters from the start. If the selection is insufficient, try broadening the distance a bit prior to removing all of the other parameters you deem important. Many schools offer some degree of online schooling as part of the learning environment. If you are open to online learning, you may find that you can still attain all of your search parameters comfortably even if the school is a bit further in distance.

A generic initial search on College Navigator might resemble this:

1. State—California
2. ZIP code—90290, with a maximum distance parameter set at fifteen miles
3. Degree options—business
4. Level of degree awarded—associate
5. School type—public

Results demonstrate that four schools meet my (Jillian's) search criteria: Los Angeles Pierce College, Santa Monica College, Los Angeles Valley College, and West Los Angeles College. Because each of these institutions met my initial search criteria, I might want to narrow the mileage to a selection closer to my home base, or look for other, more specific areas that demonstrate the differences. These areas may include the student population, programs offered, and veterans' department structure. I may find that the veterans' department is nonexistent, which would not inspire my confidence in the institution's ability to take care of my unique needs.

O*NET ONLINE

http://www.onetonline.org/

O*Net OnLine is a career occupation website that enables users to complete detailed research on any careers they might be interested in pursuing. The career departments on the military bases use O*Net OnLine for résumé development. The site details areas such as career fields, needed skills, income possibilities, work contexts, and required education levels.

To research a potential career on O*Net OnLine, enter the name in the upper right-hand corner under the "Occupation Quick Search" tab. For example, I entered *civil engineer*. Upon clicking the link, I was taken to a page that listed civil engineering along with numerous other possibilities that are similar in nature: wind energy engineers, traffic technicians, construction and building inspectors, and civil drafters. This option enables users to research a broader base of potential career pathways prior to settling on one.

Occupations listed as "Bright Outlook" have growth rates that are faster than average in that field and are projected to have a large number of job openings during the decade from 2012 through 2022. These fields are also considered new and emerging, meaning they will see changes in areas such as technology over the upcoming years. Offering several different occupations under one overall search enables users to broaden their horizons and complete numerous searches that are similar in nature.

Clicking on one particular career pathway will allow you to find the national and state-based median wages for the chosen occupation—for example, the search I conducted under civil engineer listed the national median wages at $39.14 hourly or $79,340 annually. The projected annual growth rate is between 15 percent and 21 percent, with 120,100 job openings during this time frame. Also listed are the majority of industries where civil engineers are finding employment—in this case, professional, scientific, and technical services government.

Lastly, schools that offer the proper education pathways can be searched by state. Unfortunately, the school search cannot be narrowed down further by location, type of institution, or other minute detail. For more detailed searches, return to College Navigator.

DANTES COLLEGE & CAREER PLANNING COUNSELING SERVICES, POWERED BY KUDER® JOURNEY™

http://www.dantes.kuder.com/

DANTES College & Career Planning Counseling Services is available to service members for free, whether you are still on active duty or already separated from the service. Four main areas of education and career research and planning are available on the site—assessments section, occupations, education and financial aid, and job/job search.

Sailors can conduct inventory assessments that enable them to see their areas of strength and weakness. This gives test takers insight into career fields that match their personality types, thereby offering a broader base of potential careers to research. Background information on the careers can be researched to determine whether users are interested in pursuing the option further. Under the education section, users can match the requisite type of education to the chosen vocation as well as find schools that offer the desired degrees.

Résumé building and job searches can be conducted through the site as well. One interesting tool Kuder offers is the ability for users to build résumés and cover letters, attach other needed or pertinent information, and create a URL that hosts the information to submit to potential employers. This allows multiple pieces of information to be housed in one place in a professional manner for viewing by others.

CAREERSCOPE® AND MY NEXT MOVE FOR VETERANS

http://www.gibill.va.gov/studenttools/careerscope/index.html
http://www.mynextmove.org/vets/

CareerScope hosts an interest and aptitude assessment tool similar in style to DANTES Kuder. CareerScope is hosted by the VA on the main GI Bill Web page. The free site assists service members in finding and planning the best pathways for those transitioning off active duty and into higher education. Assessments are conducted directly through the site, and a corresponding report interpretation document demonstrates how to interpret assessment results. The easy-to-understand site is a valuable research tool both for those who have already identified which career pathway they want to take and for those who are still undecided.

VA CHAPTER 36 EDUCATIONAL
AND VOCATIONAL COUNSELING

http://www.gibill.va.gov/support/counseling_services/

Although it is not widely known, the VA offers free education and career counseling advice. The counseling services are designed to help service members choose careers, detail the required educational pathway, and assist in working through any concerns that arise that might deter success. Veterans should refer to the website for eligibility, but the main determining factors are that the veteran must:

- be eligible for VA education benefits (or dependents using transferred benefits) through one of the following chapters: chapters 30, 31, 32, 33, 35, 1606, or 1607;
- have received an honorable discharge not longer than one year earlier; or
- have no more than six months remaining on active duty.

Fill out an application that can be found at http://www.vba.va.gov/pubs/forms/VBA-28-8832-ARE.pdf and return it to get the ball rolling. Sailors who have already separated from active service and are not located near a naval base (for assistance from a Navy College office) will find this to be a solid outlet for assistance.

NAVY COOL

https://www.cool.navy.mil/

The Navy Credentialing Opportunities On-line (COOL) website is a free tool designed to help sailors find certificates and licenses related to their ratings or occupational specialties. Navy COOL can help sailors who become familiar with the site harness their military training for potential civilian-sector value. The site lists potential licensure and certification possibilities that sailors occupying certain ratings may be eligible to pursue while still on active duty, thereby enabling them to fast-track their future civilian-sector career preparation. Test preparation resources, testing locations, and payment options such as the GI Bill or Navy vouchers are also detailed under each rating. Sailors who have already passed their end of active service date may find many opportunities still relevant to them.

Becoming acclimated to the website will allow for more productive understanding and usage. First, review the "Resource Icon Overview" section that is listed under "COOL Overview." This will help you understand the meaning of the symbols used throughout the website. Then read through the rest of the tabs located under the "COOL Overview" for a better understanding of the information the site encompasses.

Second, review the four selections under the main Navy COOL home page prior to beginning the search. That will give you a better idea of the overall process of taking and paying for a credentialing exam prior to delving into detailed research of your military occupation. The four selections are:

1. Find and Select Related Credential
2. Get Exam Voucher
3. Apply for Credential and Take Exam
4. Report Results to Navy COOL

When you feel well versed in the offerings of the site, it is time to begin reviewing the various options available to you under your rating and rank. On the main page of the Navy COOL, site select either enlisted or officer search and find your specialty. For example, I selected the enlisted rating of EN-Engineman. The engineman rating encompasses three different detailed positions, including auxiliary systems maintainer, auxiliary systems manager, and auxiliary systems technician. Detailed information can be found on each pathway by clicking on the relevant links. A link to a PDF card of the engineman rating pathway can be found on the right-hand side of the page.

Under the three possible positions encompassed in the engineman rating, numerous different certification and licensing possibilities are listed. The following are the three main sections:

1. National Certifications and Federal Licenses
2. State Licensure
3. Apprenticeships

The "National Certifications" and "Federal Licenses" tab lists thirty-eight different possible options related to the occupation. The Electronic Diesel Engine Diagnosis Specialist Certification, the Collision Repair and Refinish Certification, and the Certified Maintenance and Reliability Technician are just a few of the options available to peruse.

Looking over the sections listed before researching the different offerings will help familiarize users with the available options under each column. The sections listed are: credential, agency, type, Navy $, analysis, learning and development roadmap (LADR), GI Bill, American National Standards Institute (ANSI), National Commission for Certifying Agencies (NCCA), and college credit, which details the American Council on Education's recommendations.

In this case, we will review the Electronic Diesel Engine Diagnosis Specialist Certification. The certification is conducted through the National Institute for Automotive Service Excellence (ASE). The Type column lists that the skill is related to at least one section of job duties. Credential vouchers are available for the pathway, or GI Bill dollars may be used for testing if the service member has already separated from active duty.

Scrolling down the page, the "Other Certifications" and the "Other Licenses" sections list related fields of testing; however, these areas are not covered by Navy vouchers. This section details the credentialing agency, GI Bill reimbursement options, ANSI, NCCA, and whether college credit is a possibility.

Related Occupational Opportunities details the civilian-sector occupations that are similar in nature to this Navy rating. This section allows sailors to pursue possible options that relate to their military specialty and enables them to continue along the same career pathway after the military in which they have already gained invaluable training and knowledge, giving them a competitive edge. This section also houses the continuing education pathways and collateral duty options.

Going back to the top of the section and clicking on the "State Licensure" tab reveals nine different state-based options relevant to the selected rating, including industrial machinery mechanics and ship engineers. Clicking on each link takes users to detailed explanations of the careers on the Career One Stop website.

The "Related Occupational Opportunities" section houses a wealth of information on the career possibilities that can be accomplished through further training within the engineman rating. Civilian and federal sectors pathways are listed as well as military sealift command jobs that are similar to EN-Engineman and career considerations. The "Career Considerations" tab lists the possibility of maritime industry or energy sector jobs relevant to engineman ratings.

Finally, the "Apprenticeship" tab lists the availability of career-enhancing apprenticeships under this rating. The United Services Military Apprenticeship Program (USMAP) is available to sailors holding the engineman rating. USMAP is discussed in the chapter detailing apprenticeships and on-the-job training.

Further career credentialing research can be conducted on the following websites:

- Career One Stop: http://www.careeronestop.org/EducationTraining/Keep Learning/GetCredentials.aspx
- Bureau of Labor Statistics: http://www.bls.gov/ooh/
- Navy Knowledge Online (NKO): http://www.nko.navy.mil

Navy Knowledge Online is a wonderful resource for career and education-based information for active-duty sailors. Recently NKO has gone to Common Access Card (CAC) only, which unfortunately restricts sailors who have separated from having access. The site hosts many pathways to help build upon sailors' existing knowledge base and assist with career self-promotion. NKO has five main tabs under which sailors can search for information: Career Management, Personal Development, Leadership, Learning, and Reference.

The "Career Management" tab hosts information ranging from career support to transition and retirement. Learning to navigate the site will take a significant amount of time, not because it is difficult, but because an amazing amount of knowledge is stored under each main search tab. This section hosts six main sections sailors can use for research: Career Toolbox, Sailor and Family Support, Command Career Counselor, Enlisted Learning and Development (LaDR), Navy Advancement Center, and Personnel Qualification Standards. Although this section is used mostly for career development, it also provides information for family support, including deployment assistance, spousal job search websites, voter assistance, and the Exceptional Family Member (EFM) program.

The "Personal Development" tab hosts twenty-two search sections that focus on topics in five different areas: health and wellness, personal financial management, fleet and family readiness, command fitness leader, and General Military Training (GMT). Detailed searches consist of information pertaining to prevention resources and information, Navy military training designed for junior enlisted sailors, risk management/safety, lifelong learning, and mandatory training requirements for the current fiscal cycle (GMT). This section contains information concerning sailors in an active status with the military. Current training demands, important contacts, and some specific rating-related information are housed here.

The "Leadership" section focuses on four main subsections that include the Naval Education and Training Command, Command Leadership School, Senior Enlisted Academy, and the Defense Leadership Program. Many of the nineteen subtopics listed in this section are rank and rating/billet related. Training information is shared under this section, and sailors are able to access documents designed to assist in their daily duties, such as lesson plans and reference materials.

The "Learning" tab houses the educational information designed to assist sailors who pursue higher educational or education-based self-development options. The five central areas of information located here include Navy e-Learning, college and credentialing, language resources, electronic training jacket, and the Joint Services Transcript (JST). Sailors should make a point of reviewing this section if they have decided to pursue academic learning. All links to many of the resources this book details are available in one location through this section, including the JST, Navy COOL, and the Naval Postgraduate School. Sailors can also access the Peterson's learning account from this site. Information regarding DSST exams, including quick practice tests, is located in the bottom right-hand corner of the page.

Finally, the "Reference" tab houses five main areas of information, including the Navy e-Library, new Navy doctrine, DON sites of interest, the

Defense Acquisition Library, and NKO guides and tutorials. Libraries from the Naval War College, Homeland Security, the Naval Postgraduate School, the U.S. Naval Academy, the U.S. Marine Corps, the Defense Acquisition University, and the U.S. Naval Research Library can be accessed from this section, offering readers numerous outlets for research and information gathering.

COUNSELING SERVICES

From the Navy to College offers a solid, unbiased account of higher education and available benefits for sailors. Service members will be able to make more educated decisions after reading this book and be bettered prepared to begin their educational journeys. The Navy also offers free and unbiased counseling services at the different bases that sailors can use. Counselors can offer assistance with decisions and ongoing advice for your educational needs. They are especially useful in helping you pick reputable schools prior to beginning your educational pursuits. This chapter reviews examples of when a counselor from one of the many Navy College offices might have been the best initial contact for a sailor.

Petty Officer Third Class (PO3) Chang wanted to start a degree program in criminal justice. Petty Officer Third Class Chang conducted an online search for the degree program. Many schools about which she knew nothing popped up on the list. The school websites that she browsed did not have any information on their tuition and fees, but they did have helpful links to request more information by providing an e-mail address and a phone number. She was interested in learning more about the institutions and whether they would be a good fit for her needs, so she provided the requested information on the websites and waited to see what she would learn.

Petty Officer Third Class Chang was soon bombarded with e-mails and phone calls from individuals who referred to themselves as education counselors and wanted her to enroll in their school. Some of the counselors made her feel as if she were visiting a used car lot. All of them told her that the schools were fully accredited by the best accrediting agencies. They also said she could easily afford the tuition but refused to tell her the total cost or even the cost per credit hour. Some even attempted to make her feel guilty about not enrolling right away.

Petty Officer Third Class Chang decided on ABC University and signed up for it. The school's financial aid office helped her apply for Federal

Student Aid (FSA). The financial aid office also advised her to talk to Navy College about applying for Tuition Assistance. Petty Officer Third Class Chang finally visited her base Navy College Office and talked to an education counselor.

The Navy College counselor asked some key questions and found out that Petty Officer Third Class Chang had had quite an experience before settling on a school. The ABC University counselor preached the value of education, yet did not possess a degree herself. Academic counselors at highly reputable schools are required to hold master's level degrees.

Petty Officer Third Class Chang was going to be charged $480 per semester hour and did not realize Navy Tuition Assistance can only pay up to $250 per semester hour. Petty Officer Third Class Chang qualified for a Pell Grant, but with a lower-cost school the Pell Grant dollars are able to go toward other educational expenses such as books, computers, and even extra courses. All of the colleges on Navy bases charge $250 per semester hour or less, because that is the maximum allowable rate under TA.

Many of the school's offerings that the admissions' representative discussed with Petty Officer Third Class Chang were also available through schools located right on the base where she was stationed, giving her more options to choose from prior to making a decision. Navy College counselors should always be a sailor's first stop before choosing an institution. School representatives work for the institutions that employ them; Navy counselors work for the Navy. They are an unbiased source of information that can arm sailors with the knowledge they need to make informed decisions. Navy counselors will make sure that sailors choose degrees that align with career objectives, accredited schools and programs, and reputable institutions. They will discuss numerous viable options for institutions and the pros and cons of each, while making sure sailors can find their best fit.

Educational counseling services are offered at more than thirty Navy College offices worldwide and through the Virtual Education Center in Dam Neck, Virginia. For the many sailors assigned to Marine Corps bases, counseling services are also available at Marine Corps Education Centers. Although Marine Corps Education Centers are not familiar with all Navy education programs, they can help with information about base schools (on base and off base), college degrees, college credit exams, testing programs, and so on. Their information can be supplemented by making a video counseling appointment with the Virtual Education Center (VEC), a service available to sailors at sites without a Navy College office.

Use your counseling services for anything to do with education, including traditional and nontraditional (vocational). In many military base towns, salespeople actually peddle college credit study-guide programs for CLEP and DANTES exams. Some study-guide salespeople rent booths at local shopping malls and stand around watching for service members. They will approach sailors and make extravagant claims about college credit exams, even stating that entire college degrees in any major can be completed by simply passing CLEP exams—no actual college courses need be completed!

Sailors sign up and sometimes pay thousands of dollars for study material. Navy College counselors could have advised them about similar study sources available at no cost (www.petersons.com/dod). College credit exams can speed the process of completing general education and elective credits, but they cannot be used to complete entire degrees.

Navy College offers counseling services on many education programs, such as:

- Colleges on base and off base
- Navy College Distance Learning Partnership Program
- Distance-learning degree programs, including online and CD-ROM
- Joint Service Transcript College credit recommendations for military experience and training
- United Services Military Apprenticeship Program
- Exam program for Defense Language Proficiency Test (DLPT), SAT, ACT, CLEP, DANTES, and distance-learning proctored exams
- Navy College Program for Afloat College Education (NCPACE)
- GI Bill

Make an appointment to talk with a Navy College counselor to determine your best possible pathway for college. Reading *From the Navy to College* is the first step in arming yourself with important information that will assist you in making more informed decisions regarding higher education. Following up by obtaining free, nonbiased advice that will assist you with your specific personal needs is the second step to attaining your degree.

Chapter Four

What Should I Look for in a School?

Schools are not a dime a dozen. The best possible pathway for your education will depend upon your personal needs. Within this chapter, five important factors will be discussed that should be considered prior to committing to an institution:

1. Types of schools, including NROTC
2. School accreditation
3. Admissions requirements
4. Admissions process
5. Standardized admissions tests

TYPES OF SCHOOLS

Now you know how to conduct research, but what are you looking for during your search? Understanding the differences between the types of schools will assist you in your work. Career choice dictates most educational pathways. For example, are you taking a vocational or traditional pathway? Do you need a two-year degree or a four-year degree? If two years are sufficient, then you can eliminate most four-year universities from your search. Narrowing your search by a few key factors will help in the selection process.

Understanding the options for higher education will enable you to choose the appropriate school for your educational pathway. Technical schools, community colleges, universities, and public and private not-for-profit and for-profit schools have different guiding factors and structures. This section

offers brief explanations of the types of schools and how to choose the one
that best suits your needs.

Two-Year Schools

Two-year schools are community colleges (CCs) or technical schools. Most
are state based, but not always. CCs offer the following:

- Associate degrees
- Transfer pathways to universities and colleges
- Certificate programs
- Vocational programs
- Open enrollment, which is especially good if you had trouble with your
  high school GPA
- No SAT, ACT, or essay required
- Significantly cheaper tuition and fees than universities and colleges

Students who are on a budget can start at a two-year community college
before transferring to a university and save a tremendous amount of money.
Because community colleges are usually found in numerous locations
throughout each state, they are easy to find and often near your home. The
open-enrollment policy makes for a stress-free transition from active duty
and is the fastest way to start school. Most of the sailors I assist opt for a
community college when they are on a time crunch because of deployments
or training. Sometimes it is the only pathway, especially if university admission deadlines have passed. This often happens to sailors deployed to Afghanistan or a Marine Expeditionary Unit (MEU) and to sailors stationed
overseas.

Most CCs offer vocational programs that require an associate degree or a
certification process. Many of the vocational pathways also have available
significant hands-on learning options. Attending a vocational program at a
state CC gives you safe, regionally accredited transfer credit if you decide
later to pursue a bachelor's degree at another regionally accredited school.

Always check with the specific school about the program you would like
to attend. Oftentimes programs such as nursing are impacted. This means
there are more students than spots available, so acceptance may be delayed.

Community colleges frequently offer internships and apprenticeships
within the surrounding community. These programs may help you gain em-

ployment at a faster rate, generate work experience for a résumé, or credential you for a specific career.

Four-Year Schools

Four-year schools are colleges or universities. Each state has a state university system, but not all colleges and universities are state based, as you will read about in the next few paragraphs. Four-year schools can offer the following:

- Bachelor's degrees
- Research institutions, centers, and programs
- Financial aid—four-year colleges can be very expensive
- On- and off-campus enrichment opportunities, such as study abroad and guest lecture series
- Various fields of study that offer a wide range of job opportunities
- Broader range of course selection than community colleges
- Large, diverse campuses and populations at some of the bigger universities and state schools; smaller campuses and smaller, more familiar class sizes at smaller liberal arts colleges
- Competitive admissions process

Many universities also have graduate schools, where students can continue their studies to obtain advances degrees such as an MA, PhD, MD, JD, and others. Before going to graduate school, however, students must finish their undergraduate coursework, and another admissions process is necessary for acceptance.

Attending a university can sometimes be overwhelming. Classes can be so large that you never have a one-on-one conversation with your professor, which sometimes makes students feel anonymous. Finding your niche might take some time in a large population, but it will afford you more opportunities to interact. Large institutions usually offer numerous degrees and classes to choose from; smaller liberal arts colleges may be a bit more specialized.

Many students start at their local community college, then finish their junior and senior years at a university or college. This is an easy pathway to pursue if you are running short on time to prepare, feel like you need more individualized attention at the start of your education, do not want to take the SAT or ACT, or simply have not been to school in a long time and feel safer in a smaller, less competitive environment. Whatever the case, arm yourself with information before making a decision. Sometimes, a visit to the campus will settle the issue. The school should be a comfortable fit because you will be spending so much time there.

Study abroad can be a fun option. Many Marines and sailors opt for school overseas. I met a sailor who went to medical school in the Netherlands, a Marine Corps sergeant who was attending university in Australia, and a corporal who was attending an institution in Canada.

Preparing correctly for study abroad takes some time. Most foreign schools do not abide by the regional accreditation that is preferred for traditional education in the United States. This can cause future problems. Make sure to find out if the degree can be translated in the United States prior to committing to attending a foreign institution. Information on foreign degree or credit evaluation can be found on the National Association of Credential Evaluation Services (NACES®) website (http://www.naces.org/). If the degree from the foreign institution you are considering attending cannot be evaluated by our standards, you may have difficulty later. You run the risk that a potential employer may not value your degree or that a master's degree program may not recognize the level of education you have achieved.

Public Schools (Universities and Community Colleges)

Public schools, often referred to as "state schools," are typically funded by state and local governments. In-state residents pay lower tuition charges than out-of-state students. Some schools' out-of-state tuition charges can total an extra $10,000 or more per academic year. Sometimes state schools have reciprocal agreements with schools in other states that allow for reduced out-of-state tuition charges—for example, the Midwest Student Exchange Program (MSEP; http://msep.mhec.org/). MSEP, based in the Midwest, has nine participating states with public schools that charge undergraduate students a maximum of 150 percent of the in-state tuition charges and private schools that offer a 10 percent reduction in tuition.

State schools offer a wide range of classes, degree options, and degree levels, and state residents get priority admissions. Class size at state schools can be a concern. Sometimes, upward of 250 students may be enrolled in a lecture class. This can make it difficult to interact with professors or staff.

Most states have a flagship university with smaller locations available throughout the state for easier access. In some instances, students attending state universities cannot graduate in the standard four-year time frame because mandatory classes are often full, although many institutions now offer priority registration to veterans and active-duty service members. This enables veterans to maintain full-time status while using their GI Bills so that they also rate full-time benefits.

Private Schools

Private schools do not receive funding from state or local government. They are financially supported by tuition costs, donations, and endowments. They may be nonprofit or for-profit in nature, traditional or nontraditional. Private schools usually charge students the same price whether they are in-state or out-of-state residents. The cost of private school tuition is often more than resident tuition at a state school, but not always. Many private schools offer scholarships and grants to greatly reduce the tuition costs. Usually, private schools have smaller class sizes than public schools, which can mean greater access to your professor. Private-school acceptance may be less competitive than state acceptance, but not in top-tier or Ivy League institutions. Some private schools have religious affiliations, are historically black or Hispanic-serving institutions, or are single-sex institutions.

For-Profit Institutions

The difference between for-profit and not-for-profit basically is in the title. For-profit schools are operated by businesses, are revenue-based, and have to account for profits and losses. According to a recent government report on for-profit schools, the "financial performance of these companies is closely tracked by analysts and by investors"; this means that the bottom line is always revenue.[1] For-profit schools typically have open enrollment. Open enrollment can be helpful when you are transitioning from the military and have many other urgent needs at the same time. Open enrollment means that everyone gains entry to the school. That may prove disastrous for an individual who is not ready for the demands of higher education, but if the student is well prepared, it might provide a good pathway.

If you are looking for ease in the transition process and flexible class start dates, for-profit schools can offer you that benefit. Usually, they have classes starting every eight weeks, or the first Monday of every month, with rolling start dates.

Be informed when choosing your school. The College Board reported average costs of published state-school tuition and fees for 2012 at $8,660, and average private-school tuition and fees at $29,060.[2]

For-profit institutions have come under fire recently by Congress for several different concerns, including their intake of Federal Student Aid (FSA) and GI Bill money. If you would like more information on these concerns, see these two websites:

1. http://www.harkin.senate.gov/help/forprofitcolleges.cfm
2. http://www.sandiego.edu/veteransclinic/news_research.php

Veterans should be concerned about private-school cost because the average cost of private school listed for 2012 was significantly higher than the current Post 9/11 payout of $20,235.02 the for academic year 2014–2015. If you decide on a private school that charges tuition and fees above and beyond the Post 9/11 payout amount, check to see if the school is participating in the Yellow Ribbon Program (YRP). The YRP, which is explained in-depth in the "Cost and Payment Resources" chapter (chapter 6), may help you close the tuition gap.

Not-for-Profit Institutions

According to the National Association of Independent Colleges and Universities, "private, not-for-profit higher education institutions' purposes are to offer diverse, affordable, personal, involved, flexible, and successful educations to their students."[3]

Not-for-profit private schools sometimes offer flexible admissions for veterans that many state institutions cannot. Offering flexible admissions to veterans is a school-specific benefit, and veterans should address that option with their preferred institution.

Private, not-for-profit schools can have tremendous name recognition, such as Harvard and Yale University. On a smaller scale, many private, not-for-profit colleges and universities are well known in our own communities. For example, in my (Jillian's) hometown of Chicago, three well-known private, not-for-profit schools are DePaul University, Loyola University, and Columbia College. Each of these schools enjoys an excellent reputation, has a comprehensive veterans' department, and is well known throughout the Midwest.

Attending this type of school is typically a safe pathway, especially when listing your school on a résumé. Be aware that private schools can be very expensive, and the cost can sometimes be prohibitive. For example, DePaul is roughly $34,000 per academic year.

The good news is that many private schools also participate in the YRP. For example, DePaul participates with unlimited spots and $12,500. As you will read in chapter 6, which addresses the YRP, this means the VA matches that amount, and you end up with an extra $25,000 on top of your private school maximum of $20,235.02. Basically, your tuition is covered. Make sure to determine whether the school is participating in the YRP and in what manner before committing to attend.

Vocational-Technical and Career Colleges

Vocational-technical (votech) schools and career colleges prepare students for skill-based careers in technical fields. Many technical schools are state-run, subsidized, and regionally accredited. Credits from these schools are generally accepted elsewhere. Career colleges are private, usually for-profit institutions, and they mostly hold national accreditation. Credits from these schools may not be widely transferable.

Programs at these schools can run anywhere from ten months to four years, depending on the skills required to finish training. Many have rolling admissions. Programs often run year-round, including the summers, in order to get students into the workforce faster.

Typically, in a votech-based program, general education classes such as English and math are not necessary. Program completion results in a certificate of completion or an associate degree in applied science. The associate in applied science will require entry-level math and English classes. Votech schools focus directly on the task at hand, meaning training in a need-based skill and preparing students for a career.

If you have decided to take a votech pathway, research the school's cost, credentials, faculty, program requirements, and student body prior to committing to a specific institution. Cost is important: the GI Bill has a set maximum amount it will pay for private school. Find out whether you will also be eligible to apply for FSA, but remember: you are mainly interested in the Pell Grant. You can find more information regarding student aid in the "Cost and Payment Resources" chapter (chapter 6).

Determine whether the school is licensed by the state and which accreditation it holds. Ask about the professors' backgrounds and qualifications.

Find out if you will be able to apply any military credit toward the program and if the program includes on-the-job training or internship possibilities.

Visit the campus to determine what type of equipment you will be trained on and review the faculty setting. Check the school's completion rates, meaning how many students graduate and whether they graduate on time. Last, verify that the school offers job placement services. Find out the following:

- What is its rate of placement?
- Where are students being placed?
- What positions are they getting right out of school?
- How much money are they earning?

Usually, a phone call and follow-up school visit are required to fully understand the program benefits. Remember that vocational fields prepare students for specific career pathways, so transitioning later to a different pathway will require retraining.

Votech schools usually hold national accreditation. In the accreditation portion of this chapter, I (Jillian) explained the difference between regional and national accreditation. Nationally accredited programs' credits frequently cannot transfer into a regionally accredited school, although some exceptions exist at schools that hold dual accreditation. For this reason, always check the local community college for similar programs. Many community colleges offer vocational programs that can be converted later to transferable college credit.

Naval Reserve Officers Training Corps (NROTC) Program

The Naval Reserve Officers Training Corps (NROTC; http://www.nrotc. navy.mil/) is a program that potential or current sailors and Marines might be able to attend concurrently with school in order to receive scholarships toward tuition, fees, and books. The NROTC program helps to train eligible students to become unrestricted officers in the Naval Reserve and Marine Corps Reserve. According to the Navy's NROTC Web page, "As the largest single source of Navy and Marine Corps officers, the NROTC Scholarship Program plays an important role in preparing mature young men and women for leadership and management positions in an increasingly technical Navy and Marine Corps."[4]

The Navy's NROTC website hosts a link that lists every participating school, including their cross-town affiliates, which you may attend (http://www.nrotc.navy.mil/colleges_nrotc_unitsXP3.aspx). Several types of institutions are available to choose from, but all are traditional in nature. Many NROTC schools are large state universities; some are highly reputable private institutions such as Yale University, Massachusetts Institute of Technology, and Northwestern University; others are historically black universities such as Howard and Tuskegee. Depending upon the institution you attend, you may find that you have a greater degree of academic competitiveness, more organizations to join that are relevant to your interests, or are in a rigid military-based environment if you choose one of the military schools—for example, The Citadel, Maine Maritime Academy, or Virginia Military Institute.

Prior to applying, consider your life as an NROTC student and whether it is your ideal college experience. The program can help you alleviate a tremendous amount of potential student debt, but it comes with a strict lifestyle that is not within the parameters of what most people expect of their university experience. You will not have the same level of flexibility as civilian students and will have demands such as weekly drills and wearing your military uniform. These demands are designed to help integrate you into the military lifestyle. NROTC scholarship students will need to maintain satisfactory academic progress as well as excel in their military-based pursuits. University life holds many distractions, making this a difficult challenge.

If you are considering the program, you may find it to be very rewarding. NROTC students might have a more regimented structure, but think about the opportunities afforded to participants as well, such as summers spent traveling, training, and learning leadership skills that put NROTC students years ahead of their civilian counterparts. While civilian students are searching for a job, NROTC students become commissioned officers in the Navy or Marine Corps, immediately embarking on a career.

If accepted into the program, students are referred to as midshipmen. During the time that midshipmen attend school, they also drill with the unit, complete physical fitness training, and take classes in naval science while they learn to become military officers. Summertime is not downtime. Midshipmen pursuing the naval pathway will have summer programs such as the following:

- Career Orientation and Training for Midshipmen (CORTRAMID) for midshipmen third class and Atlantic/Pacific Training of Midshipmen (LANTRAMID/PACTRAMID) for midshipmen second and first class.
- Nuclear submarines or surface vessels
- Marine Corps six-week course for midshipman on Marine options (usually in Quantico, Virginia)
- Afloat aviation
- Ashore aviation
- Foreign exchange training

To be eligible for the NROTC program, potential candidates must:

- Be a U.S. or naturalized citizen
- Be at least seventeen years old by September 1 and no more than twenty-three years old by December 31 of the year you are starting college
- Be no more than twenty-seven years old by December 31 of your graduating and commissioning year (age waivers for prior military members might be possible)
- Have a high school diploma or GED by August 1 of the year you enter school
- Be medically qualified
- Not have piercings or tattoos that violate military branch policies
- Be willing to support and defend the Constitution of the United States
- Have no more than thirty semester college credit hours
- Be within the branches' height and weight standards
- Receive acceptance to an approved NROTC school
- Apply for the Navy, Marine Corps, or Navy Nurse option
- Apply through a Navy recruiting office for a Navy or Nurse option; Marines, through a Marine Corps recruiting office
- Be responsible for your own college enrollment and room and board fees
- Maintain a normal course load as required by the college for degree completion

NROTC scholarships vary in length from two to four years. The scholarships share some of the basic requirements; however, the two- and three-year scholarships place a few extra demands on the applicant. An individual applying for the shorter scholarships must have completed at least thirty semester hours of higher education but not have accrued more than ninety in total. An applicant's GPA must be a minimum of a 2.5 on a 4.0 scale. Students applying for this scholarship must already be admitted to the NROTC institution they plan to attend. Unfortunately, this option is not available for Marine option candidates. Potential two- or three-year NROTC scholarship applicants may apply only for the Navy or Nurse (Navy) option. Four-year scholarships are for four-year students just entering a university. Two- or three-year scholarships are for those who already have college credit (and maybe are even attending an NROTC institution). Be aware that either scholarship length incurs the same length of commitment to the service.

Two-year scholarship applicants will attend a summer program between their sophomore and junior years of college. The program runs at the Naval Science Institute in Newport, Rhode Island, and lasts six and a half weeks. Participants in the two-year scholarship program will also be required to attend one summer cruise. Participants in the three-year program will attend two cruises. As stated earlier in this chapter, your summers are not downtime. They are considered leadership and skills training opportunities.

If you are following along, you realize that this program can potentially cover most of your college costs, and you might be able to become a Navy or Marine Corps officer. Be aware, however, that even if you complete the program, you are not automatically augmented into the service. You are a reserve officer on active duty for a specific amount of time; typically, it is an eight-year commitment with at least three years on active duty. Commitment times may vary depending upon the career pathway you undertake—for example, three years for USMC ground and six years for naval flight officers. The augmentation board convenes at that time and determines who gets to stay and who gets to go.

Room and board are not covered within an NROTC scholarship program. Scholarships and Federal Student Aid (Pell Grant) money might help you make up the difference. Consider planning for this expense prior to submitting by checking with the institutions you are interested in attending and researching any scholarship options available through the institution. For example, Fordham University, which is a cross-town affiliate of the State University of New York Maritime College and an NROTC school, has a grant it might award to cover full or partial costs of room. This grant is only available to NROTC scholarship students.

The NROTC scholarship covers:

- Full tuition at participating NROTC schools

- Mandatory fees, but some exceptions apply (e.g., failed or repeated courses, refundable fees, fees incurred from withdrawing, medical insurance); more information on fees that are not covered is available at http://www.nrotc.navy.mil/scholarships.aspx
- A textbook stipend of $750 per academic school year
- Uniforms
- Required summer training
- Monthly subsistence allowance (freshmen year, $250; sophomore year, $300; junior year, $350; senior year, $400)

If you are an active-duty Marine who applies for an NROTC scholarship, the day before classes begin you are released to the Individual Ready Reserve (IRR). This means that all pay and allowances are stopped. Marines in this category may consider using their GI Bills at the same time as the NROTC scholarship to help augment their income. Marines can find more information on the NROTC scholarship at http://www.mcrc.marines.mil/UnitHome/OfficerPrograms.aspx; also check the most recent MARADMIN for relevant information.

Planning for an NROTC application takes some time. Submissions run cyclically within an eighteen-month time frame. Cycles start in the springtime, and deadlines fall at the end of January for the school year in which applications are being solicited. Early submittal may help your application, but it does not guarantee placement for your choice of school.

SAT/ACT test scores are required for the application process to be complete. The Navy and Nurse option require SAT minimum scores of 520 in math and 530 in critical reading, or ACT minimum scores of 21 in math and 22 in English. The Marine Corps application requires an SAT combined score of 1000 or an ACT combined score of 22. In addition, the Marine Corps option requires a minimum score of 77 on the Armed Forces Qualification Test (AFQT).

Applicants interested in the Navy Nurse option might want to consider completing some research on life as a nurse in the Navy prior to submission. For more information on this pathway, review the Navy's website on nursing careers at http://www.navy.com/careers/healthcare/nurse/. Schools must be chosen carefully for the nurse program. The institution must be NROTC and offer a bachelor of science in nursing program that is state approved or National League of Nursing (NLN) approved.

Conduct research on the following websites to determine application deadlines and procedures:

- http://www.navy.com/joining/education-opportunities/nrotc.html
- http://www.nrotc.navy.mil/
- https://www.facebook.com/nrotc
- http://www.mcrc.marines.mil/UnitHome/OfficerPrograms.aspx
- http://www.nrotc.navy.mil/pdfs/Application_Instructions_and_ Information_Checklist.pdf

ACCREDITATION

At this point, you have conducted research and might now have a better idea of a possible future career. You are also armed with the tools you will need in order to search for a school and understand the differences between the types of schools. Besides veteran support and degree type, what should you be looking for in an institution? Accreditation should be number one on your list of important factors. Attending a school that is not accredited, or does not have the proper accreditation for your career pathway, could cause significant problems later.

The United States does not have a formal, federal authority that oversees higher education. Each state exercises some level of regulation, but, generally, colleges and universities have the ability to self-govern. Accreditation was born to supervise and guide institutions of higher learning in order to assure students that they are receiving valuable educations.

Institutional accreditation means that the college or university as a whole is accredited. This enables the entire school to maintain credibility as a higher-learning institution. Only regional or national accrediting agencies can give institutional accreditation.

Accredited schools adhere to the accrediting bodies' standards. Having accreditation is like having quality control for higher education. When searching for schools, accreditation should be an important factor to consider. Students who attend accredited universities and colleges have a greater chance of receiving a quality education and recognition for their degrees.

If a school does not hold an accreditation, you will most likely not be able to apply for federal or state-based financial aid. Credit hours earned from nonaccredited schools usually will not transfer to accredited institutions or be recognized for entrance into most master's degree programs.

Always look for regional or national accreditation. Before deciding which type is best for you, think about the type of education you are pursuing. If you are pursuing education that is traditional in nature, look for regional accreditation. Traditional education typically prepares students to complete a bachelor's degree and to pursue advanced degrees. Examples of degrees that are considered traditional encompass such subjects as criminal justice, education, engineering, and business. Regional accreditation is the most widely recognized and transferable (credit hours) accreditation in this country. All state (public) schools hold regional accreditation.

There are six regional accrediting bodies in the United States. The accrediting bodies are based on the region of the country.

1. Middle States Association of Colleges and Schools: http://www. msche.org/
2. New England Association of School and Colleges: http://cihe.neasc. org/
3. North Central Association of Colleges and Schools: http://www. ncahlc.org/
4. Northwest Commission on Colleges and Universities: http://www. nwccu.org/
5. Southern Association of Colleges and Schools: http://www.sacscoc. org/
6. WASC Senior College and University Commission: http://www. wascweb.org/

The regional accrediting organizations review schools in their entirety. Two- and four-year schools (both public and private) can be reviewed. Holding regional accreditation should allow credits to transfer smoothly between member schools, depending upon the established transfer criteria at the receiving institution. Remember, ultimately the college or university you are transferring into has final say on credit transferability.

Nontraditional education usually requires national accreditation, but not necessarily. Nontraditional education is vocational training through a vocational school or career-technical school that leads to a completed apprenticeship or certification. Vocational education is a means of training future workers with skills more directly relevant to the evolving needs of the workforce. Vocational education encompasses such fields as electrician, welding, and phlebotomy. (Did I catch you? Are you wondering what that word means?

Phlebotomists are the individuals who draw your blood at the hospital. Phlebotomy is a common pathway for many hospital corpsmen.) These types of career fields are more hands-on and technical in nature.

Many nationally accredited schools can offer students successful pathways to promising careers. The programs are designed to get students into the workforce as soon as possible, and they usually can be completed in two years or less, significantly faster than a four-year bachelor's degree.

According to the president of the Council for Higher Education Accreditation (CHEA), of the four main accrediting agencies, two award national accreditation, both national faith-related and national career-related. The national faith-related accreditors work with institutions that have religious affiliation and are mostly nonprofit, degree-awarding. The national career-related accreditors work with mostly for-profit degree- and non-degree-awarding institutions.[5]

To search for a specific school's accreditation or a particular program of interest, go to http://www.chea.org/search/default.asp and agree to the search terms. You can also complete a search of the national accrediting agencies that the U.S. Department of Education considers reliable at http://ope.ed.gov/accreditation/.

You do not necessarily need to attend a nationally accredited college for vocational education. Credits from nationally accredited schools will not transfer into regionally accredited schools. This may cause significant issues down the road if a student ever decides to pursue more credits in higher education. Many state community and technical colleges offer vocational training programs that award associate degrees or certificates. There are positives to attending a community college. For example, if you complete a certificate program in welding at a state community college that also offers an associate degree in welding, you should be able to transfer those credits later toward the associate degree if you decide to pursue higher education.

Last, and not to confuse you even more, programmatic accreditation is needed for certain degrees above and beyond the institutional accreditation. Programmatic accreditation organizations focus on specific courses of study offered at a college or university. Degree pathways such as law, engineering, and nursing require that the course of study receive special accreditation; the institutional accreditation of the school is not sufficient. Attending a program that maintains programmatic accreditation can help your degree be more effective (as in getting you a job!) or make earned credit hours more transferable.

If you are not sure whether your degree requires programmatic accreditation, search CHEA's website at http://www.chea.org/Directories/special.asp for further information.

To search for a particular institution's accreditation use the following websites:

http://www.ope.ed.gov/accreditation/
http://www.chea.org/search/default.asp
http://nces.ed.gov/collegenavigator/

ADMISSIONS REQUIREMENTS

Every institution has its own set of admissions requirements. Some, such as community colleges and many vocational schools, maintain open admissions. Others, mainly four-year institutions of higher learning (universities), have a predetermined set of admissions qualifications that can be quite rigorous. Many institutions are starting to offer flexible admissions to veterans. This section will discuss the possible requirements for admission into colleges and vocational schools.

State-based Community and Technical Schools

Entrance into the local community or technical college is typically much less stressful than entrance into the four-year universities. Attending community college is a great way to get started with school for sailors who have little or no time to prepare the required documents or manage application deadlines. Many sailors return from deployment and separate from the military in less than a month. With deadlines for university admissions as early as ten months prior to class start dates, community college is sometimes the only option available.

State-based community and technical colleges may offer or require the following:

- Open admissions
- Acceptance, in most cases with or without a high school diploma or GED
- Early registration for active duty and veterans
- An application fee
- Registration deadlines

- Special entrance criteria (prerequisite classes), and a waiting list for start times in specific, high-demand impacted programs (too many applicants and not enough available open spots)
- English and math placement tests, typically, to determine proper level placement
- Admissions application, typically online, that only takes a few minutes
- Supporting documents—for example, high school transcripts, military transcripts, and proof of residency
- Proof of immunizations

Four-Year Colleges and Universities

Four-year institutions of higher learning usually have selective admissions with application requirements and deadlines. Some may offer veterans flexible admissions, but, in most cases, veterans will follow the same pathway as civilians. A written timetable of deadlines for all materials can be obtained by contacting the school and checking the admissions sections of the website. Be prepared to spend a fair amount of time preparing.

College and university admissions may require the following:

- An application (in most cases, this can be done online)
- Application fees
- ACT and SAT test scores (see the "SAT/ACT" section)
- Essays
- Letters of recommendation
- A college pathway in high school, meeting minimum subject requirements
- High school and college transcripts
- Minimum high school GPA
- Minimum high school class rank
- Demonstration of community service (military service may fulfill this requirement)
- Proof of immunizations

Vocational-Technical and Career Colleges

Depending upon the program to which a student is applying within the school, admission requirements may vary. In certain fields, such as nursing, entrance exams may be mandatory. Exams can include physical fitness tests, basic skills exams, and Health Education Systems, Inc. (HESI) entrance exams.

Always research carefully the career you are choosing to determine whether your certification or license from a career college is valid. Oftentimes states have mandatory requirements pertaining to the fields of education taught at a technical school, and students need to verify that the school meets these standards. Always check the state government website; many list the state-approved programs right on the site.

Typically, admissions are open with a few minimum requirements, such as the following:

- High school transcript and diploma or GED
- Completed admissions forms
- An interview
- Statement of general health
- Any mandatory subject-specific exams

THE ADMISSIONS PROCESS

Most schools generally follow the same admissions process even though the requirements can change drastically from school to school. Whether a student is an incoming freshman, a transfer student, or an applicant to a vocational school, the pathway to gain admittance will follow the same route, but it may vary in difficulty. Prospective students at schools with an open-enrollment policy will normally have a less intensive pathway to admittance. Students pursuing schools with selective admissions will spend more time preparing.

On a typical pathway, you:

1. pick a school or schools, call the veterans' representatives, discuss admissions requirements, and decide on an institution;
2. apply (usually online);
3. receive acceptance;
4. apply for Tuition Assistance (TA), the GI Bill, or Federal Student Aid (FSA); and
5. register for classes (choose classes based on a degree plan).

Pick a School

Contacting the veterans' representatives should initially give you a good feel of a school's perspective toward its veteran students. The vet reps have been there, done that already. If there are any tricks to gaining admission, they will know. Also, it enables you to identify yourself as a veteran, active duty, or military spouse. The admission's pathway, cost, and required documents may be different from those for the civilian population, and the vet reps will be able to guide you in your quest for the appropriate resources.

Request pertinent information, either paper-based or through online resources. You will need to know all relevant information, including application and registration deadlines, financial aid time lines, class start dates, dorm-based information (if applicable) or in-town housing options, and who will be your point-of-contact for GI Bill concerns and Certificate of Eligibility (COE). This topic is covered in depth in the "Cost and Payment Resources" chapter (chapter 6).

Contacting the veterans' department of your school of choice should be a top priority. Difficulty in reaching representatives at your chosen location it is not a good sign. The veterans' department at the school is your support system. If you cannot find anyone prior to attending the institution, how hard will it be to find a rep when you are in residence?

Apply

You have finished your research and settled on a particular school or schools. Now it is time to apply. Make sure you verify with the vet reps whether you need to pay the application fee; many schools waive the fee for active duty and veterans.

Check the school's website prior to applying. In most cases, schools have an application checklist on their admissions page. This should help you prepare all relevant documents such as your Joint Services Transcript (JST), DD214, personal statement, SAT scores, or immunization records in advance.

Oftentimes the application checklist for a four-year college or university does not list a personal statement, but after you begin, the process will surprise you by requiring it. Personal statement length requirements range from 350 to 3,000 words. Some institutions list very specific essay prompts they want you to follow instead of writing a generic personal statement.

Writing a personal statement should not be nerve racking, although many sailors feel tremendous stress during the experience. Most are just finding a starting point. Once you get going, you will find the experience to be a good precursor to your new college life. College does require a fair amount of writing. Here are a few steps to guide you through your personal essay.

Step 1

If you are having trouble starting, try brainstorming. I recommend sticking to topics around your military experience. Usually, I can glean a lot of good topics from just asking a sailor about his or her time in the service. Here are some of the questions I ask:

- Why did you join the Navy?
- What do you do in the Navy?
- Does it require specialized training, such as "A" school or "C" school, or even something like BUD/S training or Recruiter School?
- Were you assigned anywhere to put that training to use? Anywhere interesting to conduct that training (local ops or overseas deployment to Asia? Europe? Africa? Middle East?)?
- Have you visited interesting ports? Where? What did you do while deployed?
- Did you deploy to a war zone? How did it make you feel?
- Did you meet people from other countries on deployment or overseas assignment? What were the cultural differences?
- Did you deploy with Marines on your ship or even as part of a Marine Corps unit? What was that experience like?
- Did your deployments or combat experiences help shape the decisions you are making now? Is that why you are pursuing higher education?

Step 2

Next, typically you can pick a subject and narrow the talking points. Sometimes it helps to brainstorm topics on paper that interest you to see if subjects overlap. Many sailors feel that they do not do anything exciting in the military, which is definitely not true. Everything service members do is exciting to civilians. Watching civilians visit ships and military bases proves that fact to me. They are always impressed with sailors standing watch on the quarterdeck, working on huge turbines or engines, repairing aircraft, or just conducting tours of ships demonstrating knowledge about equipment and operations.

Where else can you see these types of activities? Maybe it is all in a day's work for a sailor, but civilians find it fascinating.

Step 3

Once you settle on a topic, write it down on a piece of paper. Think about the topic, and write brief statements about everything that comes to your mind surrounding it. For example:

> *I joined the military after I graduated high school because I come from a military family.*

- Work
- Training
- Adventure
- Education
- Patriotism
- Security
- The War

Once you have drawn up a list, you need to add more layers to discuss. Here is an example:

- Work: productive suffering, meaningful work equals personal satisfaction, physical work, community environment
- Timing: graduated high school or college, came of age, rite of passage
- Patriotism: American flags, Pledge of Allegiance, 9/11 firefighters, serve my country, family military history, higher calling
- Security: airports, military bases, national events, worldwide, job security, pay, career
- The War: participate, serve my country, combat veteran, benefits, test of strength and willpower, face the unknown, perseverance

Step 4

Think about the notes you have written. Narrow your subject or topic by eliminating areas that don't seem to fit. For example, I (Jillian) don't think the section on security follows the theme of the other topics. When I review each section, it seems that I joined the military after high school graduation because it is a rite of passage that occurs in my family. The military taught me good work values and community involvement. I was able to participate in the defense of my country, which bolstered my perseverance to succeed. Somehow, the security section does not seem to fit with the rest, so I am eliminating it.

Step 5

Organize your thoughts in a good writing order, and start to think about expanding the topics into a paper format.

- Patriotism: American flags, Pledge of Allegiance, 9/11 firefighters, serve my country, family military history, higher calling
- Timing: graduated high school or college, came of age, rite of passage
- Work: productive suffering, meaningful work equals personal satisfaction, physical work, community environment for the greater good
- The War: participate, serve my country, benefits, test of strength and willpower, face the unknown, perseverance

Now you need to determine why this experience shaped your current perspectives on education and organize the thoughts you listed in a logical written order. You should also start thinking about your career goals, your character strengths, and why you have chosen this particular institution. Below, I have labeled each group in the order I feel it belongs to be able to write an effective personal statement.

- Patriotism: American flags, Pledge of Allegiance, 9/11 firefighters, serve my country, family military history, higher calling (2)
- Timing: graduated high school or college, came of age, rite of passage (1)
- Work: productive suffering, meaningful work equals personal satisfaction, physical work, community environment for the greater good (3)
- The War: participate, serve my country, benefits, test of strength and willpower, face the unknown, perseverance (4)

Before you begin to write your essay, you need to consider your audience. Here are a few questions to consider while writing:

- Who will read this essay?
- What does the reader already know about this subject, and why is it important?
- What do I want the reader to know about this subject?
- What part of my topic is the most interesting?

Your reader could be a dean at the school, an academic counselor, a professor, or the like. Most likely, this individual has no knowledge of your topic if you write about a particular military experience, but do not discount the fact that she could also be a veteran. You need to explain why this experience shaped your decisions moving forward. You want her to see you in a different light than other applicants. You want your essay to stand apart and be more memorable than all of the others. Make sure to pick a topic that you can write about easily and that will attract interest.

Here are two sample essays we (Jillian and Robert) wrote to demonstrate the process:

> After graduating high school in June of 2004, I enlisted in the United States Navy. My family was worried, but after watching the September 11, 2001, terrorist attacks on television during my freshman year, I knew I could not pledge allegiance to the flag every morning without following the call I felt to serve. I come from a long line of service members, and I wanted to follow in the family tradition. I chose to become a corpsman, because ultimately I am interested in a civilian career as a nurse.
>
> After training and serving on a ship, I was sent to serve with a Marine Corps infantry battalion. Both Iraq and Afghanistan were combat-laden hotspots at this time. Not long after, I found myself patrolling the streets of Ramadi, Iraq, coming under constant fire. The Navy trained me how to respond during high-stress situations, and these experiences taught me the value of community involvement. Our cooperative teamwork saved us on numerous occasions. The preparation and training we went through as a group prior to deploying paid off when we needed it most.
>
> Iraq was a meaningful experience for me. It shaped my perspective on hard work and productive suffering. Although I love the Navy, getting shot at repeatedly changed my outlook on life. I am ready for the next chapter: my education. Compared to most, I know what it takes to succeed. I learned that skill in the Navy. I know that success takes teamwork and willpower.
>
> I chose to attend XYZ University because of its reputation as a leader in the field of community involvement and its excellent nursing program. The university offers a holistic approach to the education of its students, and I feel my background will be respected and put to use to enhance the effort and learning of my peers. The university's Veterans' Center offers numerous services to assist me should I need anything and offers many opportunities for veteran interaction. I hope that XYZ University will take the time to consider me as a prospective freshman student. If selected for admission, I will enhance the professors' learning environment, and I know that working together we can make the classroom more productive and challenging.

I was assigned as an Aviation Machinist's Mate in an F/A-18 Hornet squadron and deployed with my unit for ten months on an aircraft carrier. During our deployment, we provided support to typhoon victims in Japan, deployed to the Middle East in support of a NATO mission to support freedom fighters in Libya, conducted maritime operations with the Royal Australian Navy, and participated in a Project Handclasp program in the Philippines to help rebuild an orphanage. I learned to work with people of many diverse backgrounds, which will help me in my chosen major of business management (or social work, teaching, psychology, human resources, political science, etc.). My perspective on international affairs is based on firsthand knowledge and direct interaction overseas.

Part of receiving a university education is learning to contribute to society. To me, this is one of the most important factors in putting a great education to use for the greater good. I have seen how American foreign policy can affect people of other nations, how people-to-people interactions can change the world one small part at a time, and how witnessing people campaigning for political office in a nation that had been freed from dictatorship can be an inspiration for those who so often take democracy for granted.

During one overseas deployment, I participated in rebuilding an orphanage as part of the Navy's Project Handclasp. Project Handclasp uses tools and equipment donated by American companies. The Red Crescent representative heading the orphanage teared up as we put that equipment to good use on the construction project.

I truly feel like a citizen of the world who can bring a unique global perspective to the classroom. XYZ University's holistic approach to the education of its students enables the institution to value my experiences and put them to use to enhance the effort and learning of my peers. The university's Veterans' Center offers numerous services to assist me should I need anything and offers many opportunities for veteran interaction. I hope that XYZ University will take the time to consider me as a prospective freshman student. If selected for admission, I will enhance the professors' learning environments, and I know that working together we can make the classroom more productive and challenging.

Now you need to create your JST account (chapter 7) and be prepared to send your official transcripts to the school immediately. Although many schools will take these at a later date, the earlier you submit them, the faster your application process can be completed.

You will also need to apply for your Federal Student Aid (FSA) (see chapter 6, "Cost and Payment Resources"). If you are applying to multiple schools, you can list up to ten on the federal aid application. This might lead to federal money for education expenses that does not need to be paid back!

Receive Acceptance

Most open enrollment schools quickly offer official acceptance. Schools with selective admissions often send official acceptance after many months. Check the school's website for reporting dates, or ask the vet reps. I have found a few schools with selective admissions that are able to give almost immediate acceptance or denial to veterans—for example, DePaul University in Chicago and Robert Morris University in Pittsburgh.

In most cases, your acceptance letter or your student account website will tell you the next steps you must take. These steps may include payment of fees to hold your spot in the school or for on-campus housing. This is typical for face-to-face schooling. Most active-duty service members pursuing school will not face these extra fees. Determine the final date for reimbursement of these fees in case you decide to attend another school at the last minute. That way you will not lose that money!

Apply for Tuition Assistance, GI Bill, or Federal Student Aid

You have received your school acceptance letters and decided upon an institution. Now it is time to activate your GI Bill or apply for Tuition Assistance to pay for your schooling. If you are still on active duty, you should contact the local Navy College to inquire about TA.

If you are separated already, or soon will be, it is time to activate your GI Bill. If you rate both MGIB and Post 9/11, the "Cost and Payment Resources" chapter will help you decipher which one to choose. The veterans' representatives at your school of choice should be able to help as well. The section in chapter 6 titled "GI Bill Application/Conversion Process" will explain how to get your benefit started.

If you have a state-based benefit that pertains to your situation, you may need a bit more one-on-one help to determine your best pathway. Review carefully the explanation in chapter 6 of the benefits available to you before committing to either federal GI Bill. In some states, veterans can bring in more money by double-dipping on state-based educational benefits and MGIB than those strictly under Post 9/11. Again, if you cannot determine the best pathway on your own, contact the vet reps at your school for advice on what other veterans have chosen. Never guess about the benefits—you could miss out on hundreds of dollars every month.

Now is also the time to apply for your FSA. Remember, TA and the GI Bills only go so far. TA does not cover books, computers, or tools, and it is capped at $250 per semester credit hour. FSA money can help bridge any gaps.

Register for Classes

You will need to meet with an academic counselor in order to choose the appropriate classes for your degree. If attending school online, oftentimes your academic counselor will e-mail you a degree plan. The degree plan lists every class you need to take to attain your declared degree or certification.

Typically, degree plans will also reflect any free military credits the school awards you based on the information provided in your JST. Most schools will not inform you of the evaluation outcome until the end of your second class, so more guidance may be needed from an academic counselor prior to class selection for the first term. Starting with general education subjects is a safe route. Most of the time military credits only knock out elective credits, and general education subjects in a traditional degree pathway are always necessary.

If you need help registering for classes, you may want to visit the registrar's office of your school. In most cases, face-to-face registration will still be possible. You may also need to check to determine if a "hold" has been placed on your account. Sometimes, if the TA voucher has not arrived on time, for example, or documents are missing, your account may be on hold. The registrar can tell you why.

Always be aware of the registration deadlines. Check with your school to see if the institution offers early registration for active duty or veterans. This is an especially crucial step for veterans using their GI Bills. The VA will only cover classes listed on your degree plan (just like TA). Early registration allows veterans to pick classes before the civilian population. Basically, every class you want should be open. If you miss these deadlines, you may have trouble getting into the classes you need to maintain full-time status according to the VA (full-time status = full-time housing allowance on Post 9/11). If you miss the final deadline, you also may lose your spot at the school.

Veterans will most likely need to produce a copy of their DD214 to the veterans' department at the school to prove benefit eligibility. It is a good idea always to keep a copy on hand along with your student identification number. Active duty may need a copy of their orders to be on the base where they are currently stationed. Oftentimes, the local community college will want to see a copy of these orders in order to grant the service member in-state tuition. Spouses may need a copy of the orders as well as their dependent identification card in order to receive the in-state tuition rate. Make sure your spouse has access to a copy of your orders just in case you deploy. Spouses using transferred Post 9/11 benefits should keep a copy of their service member's DD214 if he or she has already separated.

If you previously attended other schools, you will need to have those transcripts sent to the new institution for evaluation. In most cases, the transcripts will need to go from the old school directly to the new one in order to remain official. It is usually a smart idea to have a couple of spare sets of transcripts on hand. Once a transcript is opened, it is no longer considered official, so order an extra one for yourself. You should take a copy of the transcript with you to meet with your academic counselor to help guide your class selections prior to evaluation of your official transcripts. No point in taking a class you have already taken!

You are most likely ready to matriculate at this point. At a community college, you will need to take the math and English placement tests to determine your starting point for these two classes. If you test below college freshman level, the school will place you in remedial classes. This is not a big deal, but it can slow your progress. These classes will help boost your baseline skill level and make you more successful in your future classes. If you would like to boost your math and English skills prior to taking the placement test, see http://www.petersons.com/DOD and click on the "Online Academic Skills Course (OASC)" link. OASC is like an online self-paced Military Academic Skills Program (MASP) class that is offered on Marine Corps bases. The class is designed to boost students' math and English skills. The same Peterson's website has recently posted another course, College Placement Skills Testing (CPST), which was designed to help students score better on college placement tests. Testing into freshman level math and English helps you avoid remedial coursework. Matriculation usually requires an orientation session. Some schools offer the orientation in an online format; others require you physically to attend. Your academic counselor should inform you when your paperwork has been processed and your official degree plan is on file. Then you have matriculated!

All of the initial hard work to start school is done at this point. Now you need to prepare for everything else. If you are a veteran, you may need housing. Again, check with the vet reps for recommendations. Some service members find roommates through the vet reps, the Facebook page for veterans attending the school, or the student veterans' associations.

Start checking out all of the veteran services offered on the school campus or in the surrounding areas. Knowing where the services are located may save you heartache and time later on. Some of the services offer outreach; some might be strictly for socialization or networking. Take advantage of both.

If you have served in a combat zone, find your closest VA Vet Center at http://www.va.gov/directory/guide/vetcenter_flsh.asp. The Vet Centers may offer eligible veterans counseling, outreach, and referral services to help with postwar readjustment to civilian life. Research the VA service at http://www.vetcenter.va.gov/index.asp.

Student veteran organizations that are school specific operate on many campuses. Usually, you can find their information on the school's website. Student Veterans of America (http://www.studentveterans.org/) connects veterans through social media outlets to offer support and promote student vet success. Participating in an organization can help veterans integrate into their local veteran community. Veterans who seek out other veterans typically have higher success rates. Veterans who isolate themselves may have difficulty transitioning.

SAT/ACT

Depending upon the school you select to attend, an ACT (www.act.org) or SAT (www.collegeboard.org) score may be necessary for acceptance. Many schools offer veterans flexible admissions by bypassing these exams and accepting writing samples and/or placement tests instead. To determine individual requirements, call the veterans' representatives at the school. Typically, a quick call can supply you with all the required application materials.

If the school requires an ACT or SAT score, you need to develop a plan of attack. Application deadline dates, test dates, and study resources need to be located. To find the required application dates, check the school's website and contact the vet reps. In some cases, schools can accept scores for veterans at a later date. Many institutions are aware that oftentimes sailors return from deployment and transition shortly thereafter, leaving little time for test preparation and test taking.

Test dates can be tricky. ACT and SAT tests are only offered on specific dates on naval bases. Sailors need to book an appointment through their education centers and clear the time with command. Make sure to leave plenty of time to prepare appropriately. If possible, SAT and ACT exams should not be taken at a moment's notice.

Always check with a school to determine which test the institution accepts, then focus on that particular test for preparation. Some schools will take either; in that case, students may want to take both and submit their best score.

When testing at a base, you can list your school's name or leave it blank. If you decide to take both the SAT and the ACT and submit your top score, do not list the school's name on the test application. If you list the school's name, your scores will go directly to the institution. If you *do not* list the school's name, later you can request that your scores be sent from either organization. Scores take much longer to come back to the base Navy College offices than they do to the school or to be posted on the websites.

If you opt to send your scores to a school or schools during test registration either on the base or off, you will receive four free score reports for ACT and SAT. If you decide to wait and send your scores after determining the results, each SAT request will cost $11.25 (http://sat.collegeboard.org/register/us-services-fees#), and each ACT request will cost $12 (http://www.actstudent.org/scores/send/costs.html). To put your best foot forward, I recommend that you take both tests, wait until your scores are posted, and then pay to send whichever test produces the most competitive results.

If sailors are not satisfied with their score, they may retest the ACT and SAT off-base during the next test date with no waiting period. On base, a six-month waiting period applies. Sailors receive one free test on the base. Currently, the SAT runs $49 and the ACT $39 on base.

SAT and ACT scores are not returned immediately. Typically, when testing on a base, test scores take approximately ten weeks to be delivered. However, scores can be viewed earlier on the SAT and ACT websites. ACT multiple-choice scores are typically reported within eight weeks (http://www.actstudent.org/scores/viewing-scores.html); essay scores come roughly two weeks later. SAT scores (http://sat.collegeboard.org/scores/availability) take approximately three weeks to be posted online.

SAT and ACT are not exactly the same test. The chart on the next page demonstrates some of the differences. For more detailed explanations of the tests, visit the SAT and ACT websites.

You will notice when looking at table 4.1 that the SAT does not test science, but the ACT does. You will not need to know incredibly specific science information for the ACT; rather, it tests your reading and reasoning

Table 4.1. SAT and ACT Comparison Chart

SAT	ACT
Test covers reading, vocabulary, grammar and usage, writing, and math (includes essay) Three main components: critical reasoning, mathematics, and an essay	Test covers grammar and usage, math, reading, science reasoning, and an optional writing section Five main components: English, mathematics, reading, science, and an optional essay (check whether school demands essay)
Test time frame: 3 hours, 45 minutes	Test time frame: 3 hours, 30 minutes (4 hours with essay)
Format: multiple choice and grid-in	Format: all multiple choice
Guessing penalty of a quarter point	No guessing penalty
Measures student's ability to draw inferences, synthesize information, understand the difference between main and supporting ideas, know vocabulary in context, apply mathematical concepts, problem solve, interpret charts, communicate ideas, revise and edit, and understand grammatical structure	Measures student's written and rhetorical English, mathematical skills, reading comprehension, interpretation, analysis, reasoning, problem solving, and writing skills stressed in high school and entry-level college classes
Scoring: Penalty for guessing. Maximum score 2400; each section is worth 800. Average score in 2012 was 1498 (critical reading, 496; mathematics, 514; writing, 488).	Scoring: ACT assessment only counts correct answers. Composite scores range from 1 to 36, and sub-scores from 1 to 18. The composite score is an average of the four sub-scores. National average in 2012 was 21.1.

skills. The SAT has a stronger emphasis on vocabulary, and the ACT tests higher-level math concepts than the SAT (trigonometry).

The optional essay on the ACT is not factored into your composite score. If you take it, the essay is scored separately. The SAT essay is required and factored into the writing score.

The ACT keeps each subject area separate, whereas the SAT subject areas move back and forth. This may be difficult for some test takers.

Remember that free test preparation for military and dependents for both SAT and ACT can be found at http://www.petersons.com/dod. Khan Academy (http://www.khanacademy.org) has free test preparation help for the SAT math section. Check YouTube as well for more SAT and ACT videos.

Numerous test preparation companies offer classes, but no reimbursement is available for this pathway. These programs offer structured classroom environments and curriculum that may help some service members, but classes do not emphasize an individual's strengths and weaknesses as a self-paced program would. Just remember that "self-paced" means "self-motivated." You have to organize your time and effort on your own.

GRADUATE RECORD EXAMINATION (GRE)/ GRADUATE MANAGEMENT ADMISSION TEST (GMAT)

If you are planning to attend graduate school, you may find that your institution of choice requires a GRE or GMAT score. Always check with the school to determine which standardized admissions test is required for your graduate school program. Traditionally, the GRE is taken for most graduate degrees outside of business, and the GMAT is taken for business school. Only the university and college can tell you exactly which test the institution will demand, but taking the GRE might open more options.

Currently, the GRE costs $160 and the GMAT $250. Considering that active duty can only receive reimbursement for one test through DANTES, thorough research might determine which test might be more beneficial. If taking the GRE will enable you to apply to different types of programs and you would like that flexibility, the GRE might be a better option. You can receive reimbursement through your GI Bill, but it will reduce your remaining benefits. If you are still on active duty, it is best to go through DANTES and save all of your education benefits.

In the past few years, the GRE has become more widely accepted for admissions to business schools, and many top-tier universities, including Yale, Harvard, and Georgetown, have jumped onboard. Princeton Review has a link that lists more than seven hundred schools currently accepting the GRE for business school (http://www.princetonreview.com/uploadedFiles/Sitemap/Home_Page/Business_Hub/Opinions_and_Advice/MBAAccepting GRE.pdf). Try an initial search, and then cross-reference with the institutions that interest you. If your institution of choice accepts either, try taking a practice exam for each test first (check both websites). You might find that you have an aptitude for one more than the other.

Free Test Preparation

- GRE: http://www.ets.org/gre/revised_general/prepare?WT.ac=grehome_greprepare_b_130807

- GMAT: http://www.mba.com/us/the-gmat-exam/prepare-for-the-gmat-exam.aspx
- Georgetown University: http://www.youtube.com/watch?v=xFyqJSucqSo
- Others: http://www.nelnetsolutions.com/dod/, http://www.khanacademy.org/ (GMAT math)

Reimbursement while on Active Duty

To receive reimbursement through DANTES for either the GRE or the GMAT, visit your local education center for the correct forms, or follow these steps.

1. Visit the following links to download the appropriate reimbursement forms:

   - GMAT: www.dantes.doded.mil/Programs/Exams_GMAT.html
   - GRE: www.dantes.doded.mil/Programs/Exams_GRE.html

2. Sign up to take the GRE or GMAT. The applicant is responsible for all testing fees upfront.
3. Receive official GRE or GMAT scores (about two weeks).
4. Fill out the appropriate forms, and return them to the Education Center's Test Control Officer within ninety days of testing.

Veterans' Reimbursement

Through the GI Bill, www.gibill.va.gov or 1-888-GIBILL-1.

Chapter Five

Unique Navy-Based Programs

The Navy has many special programs available for sailors. The programs vary depending upon a sailors' rank, rating, and desired educational pathway. The following programs will be discussed in this chapter:

- STEM and the Navy
- Rating-Related Degrees
- NCPACE
- Naval Medical Commissioning Programs
- STA-21
- Graduate Education Voucher
- Advanced Education Voucher
- Naval Academy
- Naval Postgraduate School
- Uniformed Services University of the Health Sciences

SCIENCE TECHNOLOGY ENGINEERING MATHEMATICS (STEM) IN THE NAVY

According to a recent report by the U.S. Department of Commerce's Economics and Statistics Administration (ESA), "growth in STEM jobs was three times greater than that of non-STEM jobs, and STEM jobs are expected to continue to grow at a faster rate than other jobs in the coming decade." In addition, "STEM workers command higher wages, earning 26 percent more than their non-STEM counterparts."[1]

The report also found that STEM-based employees are less likely to find themselves without a job. What does this mean? It means that STEM-based fields are growing and that pursuing an education and career track related to science, technology, engineering, or mathematics could be a wise move on your part by helping you make more money and giving you more job stability. See www.esa.doc.gov/sites/default/files/reports/documents/stemfinaly july14_1.pdf.

The government has recognized the need for more STEM-educated students to produce a more competitive career force in the United States and is actively promoting initiatives such as Race to the Top and Educate to Innovate in order to assist and challenge students in STEM-related learning. The hope is to create more innovation and competition to drive technology development in this country, keeping us relevant on a global scale and striving to make our nation the global leader in STEM fields.

The Navy is also demonstrating its commitment to helping our nation with its own STEM initiative programs and career pathways. Many highly technical career pathways with advanced levels of training exist in the Navy. Fields such as aviation, health care, and information technology are open to sailors for career pathways. If you are looking to enter the Navy or to make a lateral move within the Navy, and you are interested in a STEM field, information is available at http://www.navy.com/stem/career-tool.html. The Navy STEM career search website has broken down each subject area, demonstrated which naval careers can be pursued within the subject, and provided videos to give users a better understanding of the different options available to pursue and how they can convert to the civilian sector.

If you are a sailor already holding a rating in a STEM-related field, consider pursuing an educational pathway that complements the career skills you are already learning. For example, if you work as an aviation electrician's mate in the Navy, consider the bachelor of science in engineering technology (BSET) program in general engineering technology (electromechanical systems) offered through Old Dominion University. The degree is designed for military personnel who have worked within a mechanical or electrical engineering field. The degree path is good for those who are interested in pursuing a career related to operation and repair of systems in these two fields.

How did I (Jillian) find this amazing information? Well, I looked up the Navy rating of aviation electrician's mate on the Navy College Program link (see https://www.navycollege.navy.mil/rates/rates.aspx?rate=AE) and referenced the list of possibilities under the selected rate. I cross-referenced on the following O*NET OnLine link, http://www.onetonline.org/find/stem?t=0, to verify that the degree was STEM-related. Now you can begin to prepare for your STEM-related educational pathway to enhance your military service training.

More information on STEM-related fields can be found on these web-sites:

> www.commerce.gov/news/press-releases/2011/07/14/new-commerce-
>   department-report-shows-fast-growing-stem-jobs-offer-hig
> www.greatmindsinstem.org/college/u-s-navy-stem-scholarship

RATING-RELATED DEGREES

Rating-related degrees are degrees that have been built by schools specifical-ly for service members who hold specific occupational specialties. Schools that offer rating-related degrees use sailors' jobs and training to knock out core class requirements. Pursuing this type of education can help sailors fast-track their educations, but it limits the subjects they are able to study. Sailors are only eligible to complete rating-related degrees for the ratings they hold, not for an entirely different discipline.

The Navy College program has partnered with numerous colleges and universities to offer rating-related degrees. Ratings in the Navy have differ-ent degree options at both associate and bachelor's degree levels. Courses offered through this program fall within Navy Tuition Assistance limits. The complete listing of available college programs by rating can be found on the Navy College website, https://www.navycollege.navy.mil/ratings.aspx.

Degree completion can be done entirely online. Participating institutions accept nontraditional credits, including the Joint Service Transcript (JST), CLEP, and DSST exams. Some degree programs can accept forty semester hours or more from the JST. Veterans can continue the degrees after leaving active duty while using either the Montgomery or the Post 9/11 GI Bill.

Here are the available options for just one Navy rating, yeoman, but the numerous available options are typical for every Navy rating.

- American Military University: BA in homeland security
- Berkeley College: AAS in business administration; BBA in business ad-ministration (with various specialization options—general business, man-agement, or marketing)

- Brandman University: BA in sociology
- Central Texas College: AAS in office management
- City University of Seattle: BS in business administration (project management)
- Coastline Community College: AAS in office support specialist (administrative management)
- Columbia College of Missouri: AS in general studies, business administration; BA/BS options in business administration, general studies, management
- Dallas Telecollege: AAS in science, business administration, child development
- DeVry University: BS in technical management
- Empire State College: BS options in business, management, economics, human resources
- Excelsior College: AA/AS options in administrative management studies, liberal arts; BA/BS options in liberal arts, business, accounting, human resources
- Florida National University: AS in business administration
- Florida State College at Jacksonville: AS options in business administration, industrial management technology
- Fort Hays State University: BA/BS options in sociology, general studies, business, organizational leadership
- Governors State University: BA in interdisciplinary studies
- Hawaii Pacific University: AS options in accounting, management, marketing, military studies, supervisory leadership; BA/BS options in business administration, finance, management, diplomacy, military studies
- Jones International University: BA options in communications management, sales and marketing management
- Liberty University: BS options in interdisciplinary studies, psychology, religion
- Norfolk State University: BS in interdisciplinary studies
- Olympic College: AA in business and economics
- Rio Salado College: AA in military leadership
- Roger Williams University: BS in public administration
- Saint Joseph's College of Maine: AS options in public administration and human services; BS options in human services, psychology
- Saint Leo University: BA in business administration
- San Diego City College: AS in business studies

- Southern New Hampshire University: AS in business administration; BS options in business administration, computer information technology
- Strayer University: AA in information systems
- Thomas Edison State College: AA/AS options in administrative studies, logistics support, business administration; BA/BS options in liberal studies, business administration
- Tidewater Community College: AS in management
- Trident Technical College: AAS options in office administration, general business (specializations in customer service, e-commerce, international business, and information systems)
- Trident University International: BS in business administration
- Troy University: AS in general business; BA in resources and technology management
- University of Maryland University College: AA in computer studies; BS in digital media and Web techniques
- University of the Incarnate Word: AA options in business, information systems, liberal arts; BA options in human resources, organizational development, applied arts
- Upper Iowa University: AA in liberal arts; BS options in human services, psychology, public administration, social science
- Vincennes University: AAS in general studies—business

The average sailor participating in this program can complete the equivalent of two or more years of college within a four-year enlistment. Sailors taking full advantage of one of the degree options will have a head start on a college degree program and might potentially save GI Bill benefits to use after separating from active duty. Remaining benefits could be used to fund a master's degree program or a certificate pathway.

NAVY COLLEGE PROGRAM FOR AFLOAT COLLEGE EDUCATION (NCPACE)

https://www.navycollege.navy.mil/ncp/ncpace.aspx#o

Seaman (SN) Wysoski completed a twelve-month overseas duty on the island of Diego Garcia, an assignment he received after graduating from boot camp. Because a sailor on a first enlistment must finish twelve months at the first permanent duty station to qualify for Tuition Assistance (at that time before the rules to be eligible to access TA changed), Seaman Wysoski decided not to take any college courses offered on the island of Diego Garcia. At the end of his twelve months, Seaman Wysoski received orders to Yeoman (YN) "A" School at Naval Technical Training Center Meridian MS— finally his chance to get designated for a rating. Eight weeks later Seaman Wysoski was Yeoman Seaman (YNSN) Wysoski and waiting for his new permanent change of station (PCS) orders.

Yeoman Seaman Wysoski's orders came, and a personnel specialist at Personnel Support Detachment Meridian called to give him his new assignment. He was hoping for a Continental United States (CONUS) shore assignment so he could use his TA benefit at an on-base college, but he was assigned ship duty instead. After he stated his dilemma, his personnel specialist explained the NCPACE option for pursuing college credit while on ship. Even though he would be floating at sea, he could still begin college.

While on sea duty, sailors are able to take college courses through the Navy College Program for Afloat College Education (NCPACE) without having to use TA. The program is completed with the use of textbooks and materials such as CD-ROMs, which have associated costs, but it can be facilitated on ship. Because Internet connectivity while afloat is sometimes sporadic, NCPACE offers sailors a way to gain college credit without the added stress of potentially being dropped from their classes because connectivity is unreliable.

The NCPACE program offers sea-duty sailors the opportunity to take college courses at the undergraduate and graduate level. Ten different colleges offer a number of associate's, bachelor's, and even master's degree programs, or you can simply take college courses to transfer into a degree plan when you enroll in a college of your choice after your sea tour or as an honorably separated veteran.

If command requests, a distance-learning option for college courses is available using CD-ROMs and proctored exams. Ships are able to request both classroom and distance-learning options, and big aircraft carriers often request a variety of college courses for sailors to complete during their time on ship.

NCPACE courses do not count toward the TA limit of sixteen semester hours or twenty-four quarter hours under the TA benefit. Schools that offer NCPACE courses are generous about accepting ACE recommend credit from the military and college credit exams (CLEP).

Degrees may be completed while on active duty or even after the service using GI Bill benefits. Many sailors who opt for only one enlistment simply take as many courses as possible in order to try to complete their general education requirements for their future degree plans.

All of the schools are part of the Servicemembers Opportunity College Navy (SOCNAV) program, which requires only 25 percent of course work to be completed through the school. That 25 percent does not have to be the last year of the degree program, unlike most residency requirements, but can even be part of the first 25 percent. So a sailor might attend school A first, follow at school B after separating from the service, complete his final requirements at school B, but actually graduate from school A.

The degree programs offered through the NCPACE program can accept many nontraditional credits from the JST and DANTES college credit testing program (CLEP and DSST). Some associates degree programs can accept more than half of the degree requirements from only the JST; many bachelor's degree programs can take 25 percent or more of degree requirements from the JST. Additionally, CLEP and DSST exams can be used to fulfill many general education requirements.

After completion of two courses with an NCPACE institution, a Servicemembers Opportunity College (SOC) agreement may be requested. Under the rules of SOC, the school must evaluate the JST, testing credits, and any other college credits earned, and then provide a degree plan that includes the accepted credits counted toward degree fulfillment and remaining credits that must be completed.

These schools are currently contracted to provide degrees and courses under the NCPACE program:

- Central Texas College: Associate of applied science, associate of arts in general studies
- Coastline Community College: Multiple associate degree programs
- Dallas Colleges Online: Associate in arts, associate in science
- ECPI University: Associate of science in computer and information science
- Governors State University: Bachelor of arts in interdisciplinary studies
- Old Dominion University: Bachelor of science in engineering technology; master of engineering management
- Saint Leo University: Bachelor of arts in criminal justice; master of business administration, master of science criminal justice, master of science critical incident management

- Thomas Edison State College: Bachelor of arts, bachelor of science in applied science and technology, bachelor of science in business administration
- University of Oklahoma: Bachelor of arts administrative leadership; master of arts administrative leadership
- Vincennes University: Associate of science

The NCPACE Program websites have complete degree and course information:

http://www.dlncpace.com/partnerslist.cfm
http://www.dlncpace.com/catalog.cfm

You can also contact a ship's Educational Services Officer (ESO) to request more information about its NCPACE program.

MEDICAL COMMISSIONING PROGRAMS
FOR THE NAVY AND MARINE CORPS

The Navy has many opportunities available for enlisted sailors and Marines to become officers in several different medical fields. These opportunities can lead to a bachelor's, master's, or doctoral degree. Walk around any naval hospital or medical facility and you will see many officers who were formerly enlisted personnel. The military has a term for former enlisted personnel who are now officers: Mustangs.

The first step to successfully navigating a Navy enlisted-to-officer program is to become your own subject matter expert on medical commissioning programs. Read the current Navy instructions and NAVADMINs, and learn the paperwork. Contact the POCs if you need help determining the listed criteria and seek assistance through your command.

Any enlisted person considering commissioning opportunities would also be well advised to seek out a former enlisted person for advice. This is the first topic I discuss when counseling sailors interested in pursuing an officer commission in any field. The real expert on moving from enlisted to officer is someone who has successfully navigated the transition through this competitive process. This individual can typically offer sound advice and guide you through the difficult process of acquiring the needed documentation and submitting it appropriately.

Next, you must learn how to present yourself before an interview board made up of commissioned officers, which is a part of every Navy commissioning program. One bad review from one interview board member can ruin your chances for selection. The make-or-break item is your commanding officer's recommendation. As the saying goes, the commanding officer's recommendation cannot say you walk on water; it must say you walk at least five feet above the water! A lukewarm recommendation has the same effect as a negative recommendation—your application will go nowhere.

Usually, a commanding officer will not give a strong recommendation unless the candidate is a superior performer. If you are not a superior performer, work on it! Work extra hours, go for warfare qualifications, work on your education and maintain a good GPA, and volunteer for various opportunities such as the Morale Welfare and Recreation (MWR) committee. Look for all possible opportunities to make yourself stand out from your peers. Only a limited number of enlisted personnel are selected, and heavy competition is commonplace.

Do not assume you can get everything organized by simply discussing your options with the career counselor, yeoman, or personnel specialist. These individuals can provide you with the necessary initial information, administrative guidance, and professional support, but no one can do it for you. Part of the process of receiving a selection for a commissioning program is your ability to navigate through the paperwork and process the application. If you cannot complete your application for commissioning, how will you deal with the many challenges you will face as an officer who must lead other sailors in a highly technical occupation?

The following pages discuss the enlisted-to-officer programs available to sailors. Review the information and determine which pathway is your best fit. Then start planning your future.

Nursing Option for Naval Reserve Officer Training Corps (NROTC)

Applicants must not have reached their twenty-seventh birthday by December 31 of the year in which graduation and commissioning are anticipated. Enlisted applicants may receive a month-by-month waiver for each month of service on active duty (maximum credit for thirty-six months of completed active service).

The NROTC program is a college pathway for commissioning naval and Marine Corps officers. NROTC has a nursing option, which only leads to naval commissions because the Marine Corps relies on the Navy for all medical support. The NROTC scholarship program is available mostly to candidates pursuing STEM degrees. It is available to outstanding enlisted personnel who apply and are accepted. The non-scholarship version of NROTC is the College Program. Enlisted Marines are selected for NROTC through a program called Marine Enlisted Commissioning Education Program (MECEP) and do not receive scholarships. NROTC offers three commissioning programs: Navy Option, Marine Corps Option, and Nurse Option. The NROTC scholarship section in chapter 4 discusses all three of these options in depth.

Medical Enlisted Commissioning Program (MECP)

The Medical Enlisted Commissioning Program (MECP) is a Navy Nurse Corps commissioning pathway for superior performing active-duty enlisted sailors and Marines who have completed some college. All Navy ratings and Marine Corps military occupational specialties are eligible to apply. Those selected for the program will participate in an accredited academic program leading to a baccalaureate degree in nursing. Distance-learning programs are not acceptable. When possible, the college or university must be within a fifty-mile radius of naval activity for PCS requirements.

MECP students receive full pay and allowances for their enlisted pay grade and remain eligible for promotion. Students are required to pay tuition, fees, books, and expenses while participating in MECP. Military TA may not be used, but other financial programs including the GI Bills may be used as sources of funding (if eligible).

All commissioning programs require U.S. citizenship. Candidates must be able to complete baccalaureate degree nursing requirements prior to their forty-second birthday. Those selected are required to complete degree requirements within thirty-six consecutive months and must attend school on a full-time, year-round basis.

Certified copies of SAT or ACT scores no older than three years from the application date are required. Candidates must have, at a minimum, a cumulative grade point average of 2.5 on a 4.0 scale. Forty-five quarter hours or thirty semester credit hours must have been completed in undergraduate courses such as English, math, psychology, sociology, chemistry, biology, anatomy, physiology, and nutrition. Credit hours may be a combination of traditional classroom courses, College Level Entry Program (CLEP) credit, distance learning, and military training credits, provided the nontraditional credits are accepted by the school to which the candidate has applied.

Prospective candidates should refer to OPNAVINST 1420.1B and discuss options with their command career counselor (Navy) or career planner (Marine Corps).

Medical Service Corps In-Service Procurement Program (MSC-IPP)

The Medical Service Corps In-Service Procurement Program is a commissioning pathway for motivated enlisted personnel of the Navy and Marine Corps to serve in a variety of medical occupations. It is open to pay grades E-5 to E-9 only. The pay-grade requirement cannot be waived. MSC-IPP options lead to bachelor's, master's, or doctoral-level degrees.

Available options are listed below.

IPP Health Care Administrator Program

This option requires a bachelor's degree for selection consideration, but it offers an option to complete a master's degree prior to commissioning. Acceptable bachelor's degrees include health care administration, business disciplines, or management. The program provides the option of pursuing a graduate-level degree prior to commissioning.

IPP Physician's Assistant (PA) Program

The PA program includes a year of formal classroom instruction at Fort Sam Houston's Inter-service Physician Assistant Program and additional practicum at Naval Hospital Camp Pendleton and Naval Medical Center San Diego. Graduates receive a bachelor's degree upon completion of Phase 1 and a master of science degree upon completion of Phase II.

Candidates must have completed sixty semester hours of transferable college credit. Thirty of the sixty semester hours must be in residence training (classroom) at the acceptable course level. CLEP is not accepted for any of the prerequisite requirements. Only baccalaureate credit on the Joint Service Transcript (JST) will be accepted and will be considered in-residence hours.

The prerequisite courses for the program must include six semester hours each of English composition, chemistry, anatomy and physiology, and psychology, and three semester hours of algebra. Successful completion of Advanced Hospital Corps-Independent Duty Tech (IDT) School satisfies the six semester hours for anatomy and physiology but does not satisfy the six semester hours for chemistry.

In addition to the prerequisite courses, an additional thirty semester hours must be completed, of which eighteen semester hours must be in the biological/chemistry sciences. The additional twelve semester hours may be in general-classroom or distance-learning coursework. Successful completion of IDT School satisfies the additional thirty semester hours; it does satisfy the six semester hours of anatomy and physiology, but it does not satisfy the six semester hours for chemistry.

IPP Radiation Health Officer Program

The Radiation Health Officer Program leads to completion of a baccalaureate degree. Applicants must have sixty semester hours of fully transferable credit that can be applied toward completion of a qualifying science degree in math, physics, biology, chemistry, or engineering and have a letter of acceptance with a degree-completion plan to a qualified school. For those with completed bachelor's degrees, qualifying majors are math, physics, biology, chemistry, engineering, radiological health science, or engineering.

Applicants must have completed one year of calculus and a general physics course. Applicants must have a GPA of 3.0 or better on a 4.0 scale. For those interested in pursuing a qualifying graduate-level degree prior to commissioning, the following graduate degree fields are authorized: medical physics, radiation health physics radiological science, or nuclear engineering.

IPP Environmental Health Officer Program

The Environmental Health Officer program allows candidates to complete a bachelor's degree in environmental health. Candidates for the program must have completed sixty semester hours of fully transferable credit with a GPA of 3.0. Applicants will be commissioned and may be enrolled in a one-year master or public health degree program. For those who already hold a bachelor's degree and will be going directly to the master of public health program, other qualifying majors include life sciences or physical sciences such as biology, chemistry, and physics.

IPP Industrial Health Officer Program

Candidates will be allowed to complete a bachelor's degree and must have sixty semester hours of fully transferable credit that can be applied toward a qualifying degree in chemistry, biology, physical sciences, physics, or engineering with chemistry minor. Specific degree requirements for applicants with completed baccalaureate degrees are physical sciences, physics, or engineering with a chemistry minor. Candidates interested in pursuing a qualifying graduate-level degree prior to commissioning must have an acceptance letter or tentative letter of acceptance to a full-time graduate degree program from a university accredited by the ABET in industrial hygiene.

IPP Entomology Program

Applicants are required to have completed a baccalaureate degree. Applicants must provide an acceptance letter or tentative acceptance letter with a degree-completion plan to a full-time accredited graduate degree program in entomology.

IPP Pharmacy Officer

Applicants must provide an acceptance letter or tentative acceptance letter with a degree-completion plan to a full-time accredited doctor of pharmacy degree program. Program course work must not commence until the fall semester of the year following selection and must be completed within forty-eight months. Applicants must be able to be commissioned prior to their forty-second birthday.

For those who seek out these programs, many commissioning opportunities are available in the medical field. Many of the programs are not well known or publicized. Oftentimes, Navy career counselors are not even aware of the available options for degree completion and commissioning as a naval officer (for complete details, refer to OPNAVINST 1420.1B). Additionally, annual NAVADMINs are released providing the most up-to-date information and points of contact for coordinators of the programs.

As I (Robert) mentioned in the beginning of the chapter, the enlisted personnel selected for the medical programs are the subject matter experts. Tracking down one who is willing to help will be worth the time. My final tip: If you examine OPNAVINST 1420.1B and the NAVADMINs but need more information or clarification, call the point of contact listed at the end of every NAVADMIN announcing the annual selection boards. This will usually provide you with the opportunity to complete a more impressive application package.

STA-21

The STA-21 program, http://www.sta-21.navy.mil/index.asp, is designed for active-duty sailors who are interested in pursuing higher education and commissioning options. Participants remain on active duty and maintain pay, benefits, and privileges while receiving a scholarship to attend university; upon completion, they become naval officers. Time spent in school counts for pay purposes, but it will not count toward a sailor's retirement.

The Navy created the STA-21 program to streamline the enlisted-to-officer program options available to active-duty personnel. Consolidating many of the old programs into a new, all-encompassing pathway enables management of the applicants to be more effective.

The program also assists sailors with school costs. STA-21 offers up to $10,000 per year to cover tuition, books, and fees. All costs above this amount are the responsibility of the participant. So, eligible participants might be able to get school paid for without tapping into the GI Bill or relying on TA, get pay and benefits while on active duty, and become officers. Not too shabby!

STA-21 is a great opportunity for enlisted sailors interested in pursuing commissions, but it does not encompass every rating. Available programs include but are not limited to pilot, surface warfare officer, human resources, oceanography, explosive ordnance disposal, and civil engineering. For more information on available programs, see http://www.sta-21.navy.mil/program_options.asp.

The program has two sets of eligibility requirements, entry into STA-21 and program-specific demands. Both sets of requirements can be viewed at http://www.sta-21.navy.mil/eligibility.asp.

After selection, sailors report on a given date to the Naval Science Institute (NSI) in Newport, Rhode Island. The NSI portion of the process is eight weeks. Fundamentals of being a naval officer are taught, including areas such as navigation, weapons, and military history. After completion of NSI, sailors follow with schooling at an NROTC-affiliated college or university.

Eligible candidates can list on their application up to three NROTC schools they are willing to attend. Many programs have specific requirements and limit the institutions that sailors may select for schooling. Students attend school on a full-time, year-round program and must be able to finish their program within thirty-six months.

If this option sounds viable for you, contact your command career counselor for more guidance.

GRADUATE EDUCATION VOUCHER

The Graduate Education Voucher (GEV) program was established in order to provide increased opportunity and incentive for selected unrestricted line (URL) officers to obtain a graduate degree during off-duty hours. GEV enables selected officers with demonstrated superior performance and potential for future contributions to the Navy to earn a Navy-relevant master's degree leading to an approved subspecialty. The program is strictly off-duty.

Only active-duty URL officers in pay grades O-3 to O-5 are eligible. It is available to the 111X, 112X, 113X, 114X, and 13XX communities and is limited to on-shore duty officers or to officers who are transferring to shore duty.

Once approved, GEV will cover graduate costs including tuition, books, registration, and application fees. It can pay a maximum of $20,000 per fiscal year, up to $40,000 total. The degree must be completed with twenty-four months.

OPNAV Instruction 1520.37B provides GEV application procedures. Program applicants should review the current annual NAVADMIN for the fiscal year in which selection is desired. The officer applying must choose a desired area of study corresponding to a Navy subspecialty listed on the annual GEV NAVADMIN. A graduate-degree program must be selected from an educational institute that is accredited by a Department of Education (DOE) recognized accrediting body. Association to Advance College Schools of Business (AACSB) accreditation is also required for the financial management subspecialty.

The applicant must develop an education plan for the graduate-degree program being pursued. The educational plan must match requirements for the respective subspecialty code. Blank education plans may be downloaded from https://www.navycollege.navy.mil/gev/gev_apps.aspx. Requests for curricula approval forms can be found on the same website and must be submitted to CENPERSPRODEV VOLED Detachment Pensacola for approval. The GEV funding application is also found at the same website. The form is used to receive a payment voucher from the local Navy College office.

Any changes to the approved education plan must be provided to the CENPERSPRODEV VOLED Detachment Pensacola for review and approval. Officers with a previously earned Navy-sponsored graduate degree that can be correlated to a Navy subspecialty are not authorized to participate in the GEV program.

Officers may request GEV quotas by submitting a formal letter to their commanding officer. COMNAVPERSCOM will notify the officers who are selected. As a condition of using GEV benefits, an officer shall agree to remain on active duty a minimum of two years or a period equal to three times the number of months of education, up to a maximum of three years. This obligation runs concurrently with any other service obligation. A minimum GPA of 3.0 on a 4.0 scale is required to continue receiving funding under the GEV program.

The sample request letter can be found in OPNAVINST 1520.37B. All required forms and documents are available at https://www.navycollege.navy.mil/gev/gev_home.aspx.

ADVANCED EDUCATION VOUCHER

Senior Enlisted Personnel (E-7 to E-9) have educational opportunities through the Advanced Education Voucher (AEV) program. Every year a NAVADMIN is released, typically in March, offering qualified, superior performing chiefs, senior chiefs, and master chiefs an opportunity to receive special funding for a Navy-related bachelor's or master's degree.

For bachelor's degree programs, the AEV can provide up to $6,700 per year for a maximum of thirty-six months from the date of signing a letter of acceptance. Total cost cannot exceed $20,000. For master's degree programs, the AEV can provide up to $20,000 per year for up to twenty-four months from signing the letter of acceptance. Total program costs per participant may not exceed $40,000. The Master Chief Petty Officer of the Navy (MCPON) convenes a board annually, usually in June, to select candidates.

Chief petty officers must have no more than seventeen years of time in service (TIS) if applying. Senior chief petty officers may not have more than nineteen years TIS. Master chief petty officers must not have more than twenty-three years TIS. Time in service is computed to October 1 of the year in which the application is submitted.

Navy-related majors for the bachelor's degree option include strategic foreign language, construction management, emergency and disaster management, human resources, paralegal, leadership and management, engineering, information technology, nursing, business administration, and electrical and electronic technology. Other degree programs may be submitted with a request for validation as a Navy-relevant degree. Designation as a Navy-relevant degree is not guaranteed for the bachelor's or master's degree pathway.

Navy-related areas of study for the master's degree option include emergency and disaster management, human resources, project management, engineering and technology, systems analysis, information technology, homeland defense and security, leadership and management, business administration, and education and training management. As with the bachelor's degree programs, other degree programs may be submitted with a request for validation as a Navy-relevant master's degree.

The AEV program cannot be combined with the funding from the TA program. However, senior enlisted personnel who have already been working toward a degree goal using TA or other funding and financial programs are eligible to apply for the AEV program. AEV cannot be used for a lateral degree, meaning that it is not authorized to take courses to earn an additional degree at the same or lower education level that a sailor already possesses. Lower-division courses may be authorized if the courses are required prerequisites on the approved individual education plan. Applications must include endorsements by both the commanding officer and the command master chief.

Due to high year tenure restriction, waivers of the time in service requirement may not be considered. The program is not restricted to degrees available only in a classroom format, but it is strictly an off-duty program. Active-duty members may apply, as well as reservists who are full-time support (FTS). The program is intended for sea-duty personnel about to rotate to shore duty or already serving on shore duty with sufficient time to finish the degree. Consideration can be provided for the program to be completed on sea duty only with special endorsement from the commanding officer and master chief petty officer of the command. Although TA cannot be combined with AEV, sailors may use the GI Bill to offset their school costs.

The Navy College website provides the format for the application letter and the IEP. The IEP must be submitted as a verified degree plan signed by a counselor for the applicable college. All college transcripts must be submitted as enclosures to the application letter. Photos of the candidate in khakis and uncovered must be submitted with the application letter—full frontal and side view.

Application packages should be submitted to:

Naval Education and Training Command
250 Dallas St.
Pensacola, FL 32508-5220

NAVADMIN 072/014 can be found at

https://www.navycollege.navy.mil/aev/aev_home.aspx
https://www.navycollege.navy.mil/aev/aev_faq.aspx#2

NAVAL ACADEMY

There are two pathways into the United States Naval Academy (USNA; http://www.usna.edu/): entrance with an appointment directly after high school or nomination by the secretary of the Navy (SECNAV) while serving on active duty. If applying while in high school, you will need a nomination from your congressman, a senator, or the vice president. The secretary of the Navy is allowed to make Naval Academy appointments for active-duty service members bypassing the congressional nomination process required for civilians. The process for both pathways is highly competitive, and a nomination does not guarantee an appointment will be awarded. According to the Naval Academy, "In a typical year, approximately 4,000 candidates receive nominations. However, only 1,500 appointments will be given out."[2]

If granted an appointment and accepted into the academy, students attend school as active-duty midshipman with the U.S. Navy and spend four years completing their educational and training requirements. At this point, students are commissioned either as ensigns with the Navy or as second lieutenants in the Marine Corps. All students have a five-year obligatory contract of active military service upon completion of the academy.

The USNA focuses primarily on STEM fields of education, which include science, technology, engineering, and math. The academics of the institution are based upon the current and future needs of the U.S. Navy. Students can select majors from twenty-five different degree fields offered by the school. Subjects include, but are not limited to, Arabic, mechanical engineering, political science, physics, and information technology. For a complete list of degrees available to pursue at the USNA, see http://www.usna.edu/Academics/Majors-and-Courses/index.php.

Currently, the needs of the Navy require that at least 65 percent of all majors from the 2013 class and beyond be in STEM disciplines. At the end of their first year at the academy, students will receive assistance in choosing a major course of study. Academic and military advisers will assist students in determining the best route.

The second pathway into the USNA is available to active-duty or reserve sailors and Marines. Each year, there are seats for 170 individuals currently serving to receive nomination to the academy. Nominations begin with commanding officers. Typically, an enlisted person would need to demonstrate exemplary service and show initiative in other areas of his or her life, such as community involvement. Students apply in accordance with OPNAVINST 1420.1 or MARINE CORPS ORDER 1530.11. More information on the application process can be found at http://www.usna.edu/Admissions/Steps-for-Admission/Active-Duty-Service-Applicants.php.

The process is competitive and requires students to be highly prepared. Minimum requirements for test scores for a SECNAV nomination are listed on the website, but acceptance into the academy is more competitive. Candidates testing at minimum levels might be placed in contention for the Naval Academy Preparatory School (NAPS). NAPS is a ten-month preparatory program designed to "enhance midshipman candidates' moral, mental, and physical foundations to prepare them for success at the U.S. Naval Academy."[3] For more information on the preparatory pathway, see www.usna.edu/NAPS/.

The following is an example of a sailor pursing the SECNAV entrance option:

Culinary Specialist Seaman (CSSN) O'Reilly was assigned to the guided missile cruiser USS *Stony Point* (CG-111). He was called to speak with the executive officer of the ship, Commander (CDR) Tidwell. The executive officer was accompanied by Command Master Chief (CMDMC) Stein and his department head, Lieutenant Commander (LCDR) Washington. The executive officer, the department head, and the command master chief wanted to discuss Culinary Specialist Seaman O'Reilly's superior performance during the short time he had been a member of the ship's company. He had quite a number of accomplishments for the first year in the fleet. He:

- completed all important personnel qualification standards months early;
- made significant progress on Enlisted Surface Warfare Specialist qualification;

- completed all advancement requirements for Petty Officer Third Class;
- completed three college courses with grades of A;
- volunteered for Project Handclasp projects overseas;
- received outstanding marks on his evaluations; and
- was selected as Junior Sailor of the Quarter.

His chain of command noticed his leadership qualities and understood how rare they were for someone junior in rank. His fellow junior enlisted personnel followed his example, even volunteering for Project Handclasp community service projects because he did. During an admiral's visit, Culinary Specialist Seaman O'Reilly's performance in the wardroom was noticed. The admiral even mentioned he would like to have someone like O'Reilly working for him. His command also knew that he had performed academically at a superior level during high school prior to joining the Navy, and determined that he was a good candidate for a SECNAV nomination to the Naval Academy.

The Naval Academy offers more than just a college education. It prepares young men and women to serve as commissioned officers in the U.S. Navy and U.S. Marine Corps. Graduates are commissioned as Navy ensigns and Marine Corps second lieutenants upon graduation. The Naval Academy instills the highest standards of honor and integrity as part of the process. Sailors may pursue commissioning as Navy or Marine Corps officers.

OPNAVINST 1420.1B and the annual NAVADMIN message provide requirements, applications procedures, and the nomination process. Requirements:

- U.S. citizenship
- Be at least seventeen years of age but not have passed their twenty-third birthday on July 1 of the year entering the Academy
- Be of good moral character and have no courts-martial conviction or civilian felony conviction
- No record of disciplinary action under the UCMJ, article 15, or conviction by civil court for misdemeanors (except minor traffic violations) within the past three years
- No substantiated drug or alcohol abuse
- Unmarried, not pregnant, and have no incurred obligations of parenthood
- Normal 20/20 vision in each eye, though some degree of visual defectiveness is permitted if it can be corrected to 20/20 with lenses

- Normal color vision
- No extreme tattoos, brands, or unusual body part piercing if visible when wearing regulation swim gear
- No offensive tattoos that threaten good order and discipline
- Physically qualified as determined by the Department of Defense Medical Examination Review Board

Applicants must meet scholastic qualifications:

- Acceptable secondary school transcript with college preparatory subjects and grades indicating college capability
- Four years each of math and English, one year of chemistry
- Physics, history, two years of foreign language recommended
- Precalculus and calculus encouraged
- SECNAV nomination considerations require candidates to score 550 math and 500 English on the SAT or 24 math and 22 English on the ACT. To increase competitiveness, test should be taken within one year. Such minimal scores are not competitive, but they may place a candidate in contention for the Naval Academy Preparatory School (NAPS) based on a "whole person" assessment.

Application procedures and deadlines:

- Apply for USNA preliminary application via www.usna.edu/Admissions/pre-application.
- Submit application request for SECNAV nomination via the chain of command to the CO for endorsement. Use format in OPNAVINST 1420.1B.
- Submit SAT or ACT scores to U.S. Naval Academy.

Upon receipt of a SECNAV nomination request letter, CO will interview the application personally according to the following guidance:

- Ensure that applicants have a thorough understanding of military, academic, and physical rigors of the U.S. Naval Academy.
- Pay special attention to military appearance, leadership potential, professional performance, attitude, and character.
- Ensure that only the best are selected by evaluating military performance, suitability for the program, and potential as a commissioned officer.
- Screen the applicant's high school record.

- Provide an endorsement to the applicant's letter (sample format in OPNA-VINST 1420.1B).

Service members offered an appointment must have a minimum of twenty-four months of obligated service as of July 1 of the entering year. Members who do not meet this requirement must agree to extend their enlistment using NAVPERS 1070/621 (agreement to extend enlistment) or NAVPERS 1070/622 (agreement to recall or extend active duty).

Serving in the U.S. Navy offers many educational opportunities, some of which can lead to commissioning as an officer. Some nations have a tradition of the upper classes serving in commissioned ranks; some only offer commissioning opportunities to those with political connections or access to higher education. In contrast, in the United States, even the premier commissioning source, the Naval Academy, is a possibility for qualified enlisted personnel. If you are qualified and have the necessary dedication, consider pursuing a nomination from the secretary of the Navy. The U.S. Navy is truly a meritocracy.

NAVAL POSTGRADUATE SCHOOL

The Naval Postgraduate Academy is a research university operated by the U.S. Navy. It was started in 1909 as the school of marine engineering at the U.S. Naval Academy. In 1912, it became the Postgraduate Department of the Naval Academy. In 1945, Congress passed legislation to make the school a fully accredited graduate degree-granting institution. In 1951, the school moved to Monterey, California, where the main campus is located.

Today the Naval Postgraduate School is a research university offering master's and doctoral degrees in more than sixty subjects, with some programs offered via distance learning, both online and video tele-education (VTE). The institution houses divisions for business and policy, engineering and applied science, operational and information sciences, and international graduate studies.

The Naval Postgraduate School is mission funded to provide tuition-free education to active-duty Navy and Marine Corps commissioned officers, although in recent years a few opportunities have opened up for qualified enlisted personnel. Seats not filled by Navy and Marine Corps officers are made available for open enrollment to commissioned officers of other branches of the service as well as federal employees and defense contractor civilians under sponsorship of their organization.

Officers who are interested in programs should contact their assignment officers to determine qualification for field of study. Applications can be submitted on the Naval Postgraduate School's website. Many Naval Postgraduate School opportunities are announced through Naval Administrative messages (NAVADMIN).

Qualified enlisted personnel may now apply for the twelve-month master of science in applied cyber operations. Those selected are assigned to Navy-funded education as full-time students under permanent change of station orders to Monterey, California. The program is available to active-duty personnel serving in the information systems technician (IT) rating or cryptologic technician network (CTN) rating.

Qualified candidates must possess a bachelor of science degree in a relevant technical field—for example, computer science, electrical engineering, information or engineering technology. Performance in technical courses, including math, must be high. Eligible candidates include pay grades E-6 through E-9 and are eligible for shore rotation. Those selected must be willing to incur a five-year service obligation.

Other requirements:

- Be within physical fitness assessment (PFA) standards with no failures within the last three years.
- Have no evaluation mark less than 3.0 for the past five years.
- Hold or be eligible for a top secret/sensitive compartmented information (SCI) clearance.
- Possess a conditional letter of acceptance.

Written requests should be forwarded via the service member's commanding officer. Applications should include the following:

- Copies of all undergraduate transcripts.
- Certified copies of last four performance evaluations.
- Command financial screening for assignment to a high-cost-of-living area.
- Member's single-page statement of preparedness and motivation to earn a master's degree and future goals.

For the most current information and requirements, check the latest NAVADMIN and Naval Postgraduate School website at http://www.nps.edu/.

UNIFORMED SERVICES UNIVERSITY
OF THE HEALTH SCIENCES

The Uniformed Services University of the Health Sciences was created by Congress in 1972 and its mission is to train uniformed service health professionals. Located in Bethesda, Maryland, the university comprises the F. Edward Hébert School of Medicine, the Daniel K. Inouye Graduate School of Nursing, and the Postgraduate Dental College.

Graduates of the Uniformed Services University do not incur the financial debt associated with traditional medical schools and graduate programs, but they do prepare to serve in the U.S. Army, U.S. Navy, U.S. Air Force, or Public Health Service. Tuition is waived by the Department of Defense in exchange for a seven-year commitment to serve in uniform. While attending, students receive the pay and allowances of junior officers. Before the first year of school for those coming in from civilian status, all future students are sent to officer training programs with their individual service where they are taught to be future leaders.

The school of medicine and the graduate school of nursing have curriculums similar to civilian schools; however, the program is oriented to preparing graduates to also be productive service officers. Approximately half of Uniformed Service University students have no prior military experience.

F. Edward Hébert School of Medicine

Military applicants compete with civilian applicants on the same level. Those who are on active duty, in one of the military academies, or in ROTC must obtain a letter of approval to apply from your branch of service. The letter must clearly state that approval is granted. A statement on the order of "recommended for approval" is insufficient.

Applicants must take the Medical College Admission Test (MCAT). The average score for those matriculating is 31, with 25 the minimum accepted in past years. The minimum cumulative grade point average (GPA) is 3.0, but 3.6 has been the average grade point average. Online or Internet courses are not accepted as prerequisites. Here is the list of prerequisites and requirements in the application:

Biology with lab (one year)
Inorganic chemistry with lab (one year)
Physics with lab (one year)

English (one year)

Calculus (one semester)

Biochemistry and statistics highly recommended, but not required

MCAT results

U.S. citizenship

At least eighteen years old at time of matriculation, but no older than thirty-six as of June 30 in the year of matriculation

Clinical experience (defined as traditional clinical activity with patients and/or health care professional or paraprofessional)

Letter of approval (only required for enlisted, commissioned, reserve, ROTC, academy, and National Guard applicants)

Graduate programs in biomedical science and public health are open to military and civilian applicants. PhD programs offered in the department:

- PhD degrees in three interdisciplinary programs: emerging infectious diseases, molecular and cell biology, and neuroscience
- Clinical psychology
- Medical psychology
- Environmental health science
- Medical zoology
- Public health

Master's degree programs:

- Public health
- Tropical medicine and hygiene
- Public health
- Health administration and policy
- Military medical history

Daniel K. Inouye Graduate School of Nursing

Students admitted are advanced practice nurses already serving in the military or other federal services. Master of Science in Nursing programs are offered in the following fields:

- Adult gerontology CNS option
- Psychiatric nurse practitioner
- Family nurse practitioner

Doctoral programs are offered in:

- Nursing practice
- Nursing science

Postgraduate Dental College

Open to those serving as doctors of dental surgery or doctors of dental medicine in the U.S. Army, U.S. Navy, or U.S. Air Force. The program offers the master's of science in oral biology for the individual service Dental Postgraduate School: Army Postgraduate Dental School, Naval Postgraduate Dental School, and Air Force Postgraduate Dental School.

If you are interested in pursuing a medical career while remaining in the service, this is a viable option, but it will require preparation. Bachelor's degrees are not awarded through this institution. Programs start at the master's degree level. Completing a bachelor's degree that will enable you to pursue an applicable master's program should be your first concern.

Chapter Six

Cost and Payment Resources

Cost is often a major factor for students when picking a college or vocational program to attend. Active-duty service members should try to attend institutions that fall within the parameters of Tuition Assistance (TA). Veterans should consider GI Bill coverage while researching potential schools. Why pay for school when you have coverage? If you can stay within these parameters, you might come out of your educational experience completely debt free.

The following topics will be covered within this section:

- Financial Goals
- Navy Tuition Assistance
- MGIB
- Post 9/11
- GI Bill Top-Up
- GI Bill Application/Conversion Process
- Transferability
- Yellow Ribbon Program (www.gibill.va.gov)
- VA GI Bill Feedback System
- Federal Student Aid (www.fafsa.ed.gov)
- State-Based Veteran Education Benefits
- Scholarships (Including Dependents)
- Textbook Buying Options
- Free Subject Matter Study Support

FINANCIAL GOALS

Transitioning from the military is a difficult process without also having to worry about finances. Veterans who prepare in advance will have less stress during the process and will be able to focus on their studies more effectively. Having minimal distractions during school will enable veterans to achieve a higher degree of academic success. Successfully educated or trained veterans will be more productive in their future endeavors and able to enrich their surrounding civilian communities.

Bypassing the work option, veterans have three main sources of income while attending school. These sources include:

- GI Bill housing stipend
- Federal Student Aid (Pell Grant)
- Unemployment

If a veteran is able to maximize benefits under each of these three options, he or she will have a good starting base and hopefully not have to worry about daily stressors, such as making rent, gas, and food.

The housing stipend on the Post 9/11 GI Bill typically is not enough to take care of one individual's personal needs, especially because "break pay" money is not paid while the student is not physically in school. This chapter's "Post 9/11" section explains that the housing allowance is prorated, and veterans will most likely not be receiving as much money as they expect.

Federal Student Aid Pell Grant money can be a great benefit for veterans attending school. Think about having an extra $5,730 per academic year to help with education-related expenses above and beyond the GI Bill. How much better off would you be for spending thirty minutes to fill out the FAFSA? The time will be well spent, especially if you are awarded assistance.

Your previous year's tax information is required to fill out the FAFSA, so you need to pay attention upon your initial separation from active duty. If you have recently separated from the military, your tax information may not reflect your current financial situation. For example, if Seaman Smith separated in July 2014 and began college in August 2014, he would submit his 2013 taxes on the FAFSA that reflect his military pay. The main problem is that he is no longer working and receiving this level of pay. In most cases, a veteran's pay is drastically reduced upon separation. If Seaman Smith does not receive an award or does not receive the full amount, he needs to visit his financial aid counselor to have his listed income level readjusted. Hopefully, upon readjustment of his income, he will be eligible for the maximum amount of Pell Grant award. Be aware that Pell Grant money is based on your tax information, so it will fluctuate from person to person depending upon household finances.

The Unemployment Compensation for Ex-Servicemembers (UCX) program may help eligible separating service members rate some level of unemployment. Unemployment will vary state by state because the law of the state determines how much money an individual can receive, the length of time to remain eligible, and any other eligibility conditions. Veterans must have been honorably separated in order to be eligible. Information on unemployment can be located on the website of the U.S. Department of Labor (http://workforcesecurity.doleta.gov/unemploy/uifactsheet.asp).

Contact your local State Workforce Agency (http://www.servicelocator.org/OWSLinks.asp) upon separation to determine eligibility and apply. Make sure to have a copy of your DD-214.

Some military members may receive a service-connected disability percentage; others may not. When you separate from the military, you will be screened by the VA to determine whether you sustained any injuries or diseases while on active duty, or if any previous health-related issues were made worse by active military service. If you receive a minimum rating of 10 percent or higher, you may be eligible to receive a tax-free stipend from the VA every month. Zero percent ratings do not have a monetary stipend attached; however, in the "State-Based Benefit" section of this book, you will see that many states offer benefits that are tied to these disability ratings. For example, in California a 0 percent rating equals free schooling for your children at state-supported institutions. If you receive a percentage rating, this may help with your expenses. Be aware that ratings can take as long as twelve months to be determined, and there is such a thing as no rating.

Make sure to be screened prior to exiting the military. If you are not sure where to find your local VA office, it might even be on the base where you are stationed. The Disabled American Veterans (DAV) and the Veterans of Foreign Wars (VFW) maintain offices at several Marine Corps bases and may assist you as well. Many academic institutions have visiting representatives from these organizations. They will help you with your initial claim if you did not make it while still on active duty. They can also help you submit for a claims adjustment if your medical situation has changed.

NAVY TUITION ASSISTANCE

Years ago I (Robert) worked with an ambitious sailor who actually finished an entire bachelor's degree in only one enlistment using Tuition Assistance (TA), CLEP exams, ACE credits, and NCPACE courses. The majority of her course work was completed using TA. By her third year in the Navy, she had been promoted to petty officer second class, but she never had a chance to compete for petty officer first class for a very good reason: with her completed degree, she applied to, and was selected for, Aviation Officer Candidate School and became commissioned as an ensign.

Most people joining the Navy know about the GI Bill. Many, however, do not learn of the available active-duty benefit until reporting to the first duty station. The Navy also has a generous TA program that is separate from the GI Bill. Navy TA can pay up to $4,000 per year for college or vocational education. Over a four-year enlistment, up to $16,000 can be used, which is like having a second GI Bill just for use while on active duty.

Navy TA can pay up to $250 per semester hour for up to sixteen semester hours of college or $166.67 per quarter hour for up to twenty-four quarter hours. For certain vocational programs, Navy TA can pay up to $16.67 per clock hour—not to exceed 240 clock hours.

Which programs can Navy TA pay for? It can pay for high school diplomas, certificate programs, associate's degrees, bachelor's degrees, and master's degrees. Under current policy, Navy TA cannot pay for doctoral degrees. Navy TA can pay for only one degree (or certificate) per category. In other words, TA would not be able to pay for two associate's degrees, but it could pay for an associate's degree and a bachelor's degree. These rules do not apply to the GI Bill, which can pay for more than one degree in the same category.

Why use Tuition Assistance on active duty? Why not just wait until completion of active service and use the very generous Post 9/11 GI Bill? Here are six reasons:

1. The GI Bill pays for thirty-six months of education, which is technically four years of college (nine months per year × four years = thirty-six). However, presently bachelor's degrees often take more than four years to complete. Statistics on this topic can be found on the National Center for Education Statistics website (http://nces.ed.gov/programs/digest/d12/tables/dt12_376.asp).

2. Some degrees have become more technical in nature and require more courses. If a degree takes more than thirty-six months to complete, GI Bill benefits will be exhausted. Using TA to complete some of the educational requirements while on active duty, especially general education classes, can mean starting at sophomore or even junior level when entering a school as a veteran drawing on GI Bill benefits.

3. Many students have to spend time taking remedial English and math classes, which do not count for degree fulfillment. Some students must take prerequisite courses not actually part of the degree program (e.g., required chemistry classes, because they did not take chemistry in high school).

4. Most students change majors at least once, which may lengthen the time it takes to finish a degree.

5. In recent years, many colleges have faced budget cuts, resulting in reduced offerings of required courses. Sometimes students are forced to stay around campus an extra semester or two while waiting for a course required for graduation to be offered again.

6. If a veteran completed some college using TA, less than thirty-six months of GI funding will be required to finish a bachelor's degree. The veteran would be able to use the GI Bill for even higher education goals such as a master's degree.

TA is not intended to pay for books, computers, tools, and other tangible goods. It can pay tuition and, within the caps ($250 per semester hour and $166.67 per quarter hour), it can pay certain mandatory fees required for course instruction. For example, lab and technology fees are eligible. Navy personnel must receive TA training every two years to remain eligible. Sailors may use TA as long as the course ends before EAOS. Enlisted reservists are also eligible for Tuition Assistance if on orders for 120 days or more of continuous active-duty service.

To grant TA, your chain of command must certify that you:

- Will have enough time to pursue off-duty education.
- Have completed the first year at your first permanent duty station (if serving on initial enlistment, but may be waived by CO).
- Have passed your most recent physical fitness assessment or been medically waived.
- Are recommended for advancement or promotion.

- Have participated in most recent advancement exam if eligible (for enlisted only).
- Have not have received nonjudicial punishment within the past six months.
- Are not pending administrative separation.
- Are not under instruction in initial skills training.
- Are not in Duty Under Instruction (DUINS) status.

Navy College and Virtual Education Center staff will verify that:

- You have completed a Tuition Assistance Brief within the past two years.
- Your academic institution has signed a Memorandum of Understanding for meeting Tuition Assistance requirements.
- Your Web TA application reflects semester, quarter, or clock hours of credit.
- You have established an education plan with your Navy College or Virtual Education Center (VEC) counselor.
- Your courses are on education plan to be approved.
- You have documented counseling from Navy College or the Virtual Education Center before applying for TA the first time.
- An Individual Education Plan (IEP) has been uploaded.

Officers have special rules. For accepting TA, officers must serve two years commencing with the last day of the term for which TA was used. However, the two-year requirement may run concurrently with any other obligated service already incurred. Commissioned officers who are reservists may use TA if ordered to active duty for a minimum of two continuous years of active-duty service.

Processing the TA is now completed online by going to the website https://myeducation.netc.navy.mil/. Log in with your CAC card. Once logged in, you will need to upload your individual education plan or degree plan, which you get from your school's website or by requesting it from the school. A screen will appear with several options including a tab labeled "My Education Plan." Upload your individual education plan or degree plan as a Word or PDF document. Provide Navy College or the VEC with information about the plan you uploaded so they can make required entries that will "unlock" the Web tuition assistance program for your application and processing. They will need to know the school, degree level (associate's, bachelor's, etc.), and major (e.g., general studies, history, criminal justice).

You will need some information at your fingertips for your TA application. Have at the ready:

- E-mail address of the person in your chain of command who will be approving your application
- Complete name of your school
- Course information—name of course, department, and number (e.g., ENG 101: English Composition)
- Starting date and ending date of the term in which you are enrolling
- Credits used by the school—semester, quarter, or clock hours
- Number of credit hours for each course
- Cost per credit hour
- If cost per credit hour not maxed out, any mandatory fees (e.g., lab fee, technology fee)
- Course level—lower level (freshman/sophomore), upper level (junior/senior), graduate, or vocational

For processing after you log in, you will use the "Create Application" option. If you have been using TA, an option will be offered to use the school last used for TA as the default school. If the answer is "no," you will be able to change your school. Important—if you change schools, you will be required to upload a new individual education plan or degree plan.

As part of the application process, you will find your school in block twenty-five with the search feature. You will then use the calendar to select the start date of your school term and the end date. Next, in the appropriate place, put in department and number of your course (e.g., HIST 101) and the complete name of the course (e.g., U.S. History I).

Enter information about the course. There will be blocks to fill in for course level, distance learning or classroom, Web or CD-ROM, quarter or semester hours, number of credit hours, cost per credit hour, and fees. Along the way, you will be asked to verify choices, such as the school indicated in your platform. You should always save your information throughout the application process. By saving, your application information will still be in the system if you are unable to complete it in one sitting. Remember that more than one course can be in your application, but only if the dates coincide at the same school.

Finally, the option to submit your application will be available. Once you submit, the person whose e-mail address you provided as your approving official will receive an e-mail. It will state that your TA application has been submitted, and a link will be provided to review your application and provide approval or disapproval. If the application is disapproved for any reason, you will receive a notification e-mail and will be directed to talk to your chain of command to learn the reason for disapproval. If the application is approved, an e-mail will arrive informing you the command has approved your request and it has been forwarded to the Virtual Education Center (VEC) in Dam Neck, Virginia, for final review. If the TA is not approved by the VEC, you will be notified by e-mail with the reason for disapproval. Once the VEC authorizes you TA, e-mail notification will be received with instruction to go back into the Web TA program, bring up your approved application, and print your voucher. Sign the voucher and provide it to your school as your payment.

Remember, any changes in your education must be reported to the Virtual Education Center. Report to the VEC immediately any changes in term dates, course substitution, errors or correction in course information, cancellation, drop, and withdrawal. After completing a course, always provide a copy of your grade report to the VEC. If the VEC does not receive a grade report, you will be asked to repay your TA.

Tuition Assistance will be repaid if an undergraduate course is failed. For graduate programs, TA is repaid for grades of "D" or "F" at undergrad level, and "C," "D," and "F" for grad courses. Money may have to be repaid if a course is dropped after the school's add/drop date deadline for a full refund. If the course had to be dropped for a military reason such as unexpected deployment, Navy College or the VEC can help you with procedures for having your command submit a letter requesting a waiver so that you will not have to repay the money. Submission of a waiver request, of course, does not guarantee approval.

If you have to delay completing a course, and your school assigned you a grade status of "I" or incomplete, TA money will have to be repaid if the course work is not completed within six months.

Navy College sees the following situation happen frequently:

Petty Officer Second Class Lopez received a letter from the Virtual Education Center (VEC) stating she needed to submit a grade or repayment for the course Algebra I. If she did not submit repayment or a grade, part of her paycheck would be involuntarily withheld for repayment. Petty Officer Second Class Lopez could not understand why she had received the letter because she had never actually taken Algebra I.

Her Navy College counselor was quick to pinpoint the problem after ascertaining the circumstances: Petty Officer Second Class Lopez had applied for TA for Algebra I, but she had never registered for the course. She had assumed no further action was required on her part because she did not use the TA voucher to pay for a course. Petty Officer Second Class Lopez was reminded that she had to inform Navy College or the VEC of any change in her education program, including a decision to not use a TA voucher after it was issued. In the end, the Navy College counselor was able to get Petty Officer Second Class Lopez's TA account to reflect a cancellation of the voucher, resulting in cancellation of debt repayment procedures.

Lesson learned by Petty Officer Second Class Lopez: Keep Navy College informed! Tuition Assistance is a great benefit. Follow the rules, study hard, and make it work for you. To learn more about Navy Tuition Assistance, visit the Navy College website at https://www.navycollege.navy.mil. Contact Navy College or the VEC for further questions.

MONTGOMERY GI BILL (MGIB)

Not all service members have MGIB. When you entered the service, if you elected to opt in to MGIB and paid $100 per month for your first year of service to total $1,200, you might rate MGIB. You must be separated with an honorable discharge as well; that goes for most benefits. Double-check your eligibility on the GI Bill website (http://www.gibill.va.gov).

As of October 1, 2014, MGIB will pay $1,717 per month for up to thirty-six months for school. MGIB can be used for academic degrees, certificate programs, on-the-job training (OJT), correspondence classes, apprenticeship programs, and flight training. Benefits are good for ten years after separation from the military.

Some service members participated in the $600 Buy-Up Program under MGIB. For those who did, an extra $150 per month will be added to their MGIB payments. That amount per month pays you back your $600 investment in four months. Every month after that, you are making money. If you cannot remember if you paid the optional Buy-Up Program, check with PSD. For those who did not pay the money, check with the veterans' representatives at the school you are interested in attending before paying it now. If you select Post 9/11, you forfeit the $600 that it takes to fully fund the Buy-Up. Smaller Buy-Up packages can be bought for prorated amounts. If you rate it and decide to stay under MGIB, you will most likely want to pay the Buy-Up for increased monthly payments. PSD can make the unit diary entry prior to your EAS.

Currently, if you paid into MGIB, remain under MGIB, and exhaust all thirty-six months of the benefit, you may be able to extend out an extra twelve months on Post 9/11. Contact the VA for final eligibility determination on this pathway. This may enable you to save some benefit for a master's degree or a certificate program. The problem is that in most cases, MGIB will not cover all of your bills.

I (Jillian) have only found a few situations in which it makes more sense for the veteran to remain under MGIB instead of opting for Post 9/11. There are two big ones: first, online-only schools, which I do not recommend because you might be missing out on the full housing stipend under Post 9/11; and second, when Marines attend school in a state with a full state-based benefit. The state-based benefit section in this chapter will review both of these circumstances and demonstrate why a veteran might elect to remain under MGIB. Prior to electing either GI Bill, it is best to discuss all available options. Contact your state VA to determine your available state benefits and learn how to use them. Contact the veterans' department at the institution you would like to attend and request guidance. Typically, the veterans' representatives can offer great advice pertaining to the best benefit pathway. They have already blazed the trail and learned for themselves. The VA also offers guidance and can be reached at 1-888-GIBILL-1.

POST 9/11

Post 9/11 is truly an amazing educational benefit available to veterans who rate it. To determine your eligibility, visit the website (http://www.gibill.va.gov). Basically, to rate 100 percent of Post 9/11, you need to meet these criteria:

- Served thirty-six consecutive months after September 11, 2001
- Received an honorable discharge

There are other categories for approval, but, as I (Jillian) have stressed at other points in this book, always check to determine your specific eligibility. In this case, contact the VA at 1-888-GIBILL-1.

The Post 9/11 GI Bill has three financial components built into the program: books and supplies, housing, and tuition.

Books and Supplies

Post 9/11 has a books and supplies stipend. The stipend is prorated at $41.67 per credit hour for a maximum of $1,000 per academic year. A regular full-time student (a minimum of twelve credits per semester) would receive the full $1,000. Anything less than that is prorated until the veteran drops below the 50 percent rate of pursuit mark. At that point, the GI Bill stops paying. The stipend is broken into two payments per academic year and lumped in with the first month of the housing stipend for each semester.

You should take note that $1,000 is not actually a great amount for books. Oftentimes books can run more than $200 per class. Many universities list the approximate costs of textbooks for the school year on their website. For example, California State University, Long Beach (CSULB), estimates books at $1,788 for the 2013–2014 academic year. According to their calculations, $1,000 won't suffice for books. You definitely need to check into other options. The "Textbook-Buying Options" section in this chapter is dedicated to helping you find used or rental books.

Housing

The housing stipend is slightly more complicated. Referred to as the Monthly Housing Allowance (MHA), it is equivalent to the salary for an E-5 with dependents and applies for everyone. That is great if you separated anywhere near E-5, but if you separated as an admiral, you will need to adjust your budget (sorry—that is my bad sense of humor!). *Do not* use an online calculator other than the one offered on http://www.gibill.va.gov, which is actually the U.S. Department of Defense calculator (direct link: https://www. defensetravel.dod.mil/site/bahCalc.cfm). This is the only valid website when it comes to determining your MHA based on the ZIP code of your school. That is right; the MHA is based on the ZIP code of your school, not your abode.

Tuition

Tuition under the Post 9/11 GI Bill can be complicated to explain. I am going to keep it simple. If you follow the most basic of parameters, you will not pay a dime for your schooling. Go outside of these parameters and you run into technical billing questions; in this case, you should contact the school you are interested in attending for further information.

If you are pursuing an undergraduate or graduate degree, plan to attend a state school in the state where you have residency, and finish your degree within the thirty-six months of benefit you have allotted, your schooling should be covered. The thirty-six months is enough for most bachelor's degrees if you stay on track because it equates to nine months of school per year over the course of four years. Traditionally, we do not usually attend school in the summer, although you may if you are interested. If one of these factors changes, so might your bill.

Veterans who decided to attend private school received $19,198.31 for the academic year 2013–2014 (http://www.gibill.va.gov/resources/benefits_ resources/rates/CH33/Ch33rates080113.html). Anything above that amount, and you run the risk of having to pay out of pocket. I state it this way because many schools participate in the Yellow Ribbon Program (http://www.gibill. va.gov/benefits/post_911_gibill/yellow_ribbon_program.html), which might help cover private school costs that come in above the maximum VA allotted threshold or out-of-state tuition charges.

What about out-of-state tuition? Well, it is not covered under Post 9/11. You have chances of getting out-of-state tuition covered under Post 9/11, Yellow Ribbon, and possible state-based benefits. These topics will be covered later in this chapter. Refer to those specific sections for more details.

As stated above, the VA will pay you the full-time housing allowance if you pursue school at the full-time rate. The VA considers twelve credit hours to be full-time. However, if you have no previous college credit and intend to pursue a bachelor's degree, twelve credits per semester will not suffice. Most bachelor's degrees require students to complete 120 semester credit hours of specific subject matter in order to have the degree conferred on them. That equates to fifteen credit hours each semester, or five classes.

The college year runs similar to the high school year: two semesters each year over the course of four years. So 120 semester hours breaks down to fifteen semester hours each semester to total thirty credits each year (freshman year, 30; sophomore year, 30; junior year, 30; and senior year, 30; total: 120). If you follow the VA's minimum guidelines of twelve credits each semester, or four classes, you will run out of benefits at the end of your senior year but only have earned ninety-six semester credit hours, twenty-four credits shy of the 120 required. You will be out of benefits but will not have obtained your degree. The academic counselors at the school you attend will help you with your degree plans. If you need to make changes or have questions, contact them for further advice.

GI BILL TOP-UP

If a sailor attending school while on active duty chooses a school that costs more than the amount allotted under TA, GI Bill Top-Up can be used to top off the TA. The sailor would activate his or her GI Bill and tap into it as a funding resource for the portion of the class not covered by TA. This would affect the sailor's overall remaining benefit amount upon separation from the military.

TA only covers up to $250 per credit hour. If a sailor chooses a school that costs $350 per semester hour and is taking a three-hour class, he or she will be $300 out of pocket after using TA. The remaining amount of money will be his or her responsibility to pay out of pocket. In this case, Top-Up could be used to cover the amount.

Using Top-Up may be necessary in some cases, but, generally, I would avoid the recommendation. Tapping into Top-Up will pull on the sailor's available GI Bill months, thereby reducing the amount of benefits remaining after separation from the military.

Many institutions across the country cost less than or equal to the amount covered under TA. If the institution you are planning to attend is over the $250 threshold and recommending GI Bill Top-Up, please speak to an academic counselor for advice prior to making any final decisions.

Three situations come to mind when I discuss using Top-Up for service members.

1. If the individual is about to run out of TA money, is at the end of his or her degree, and is separating from active duty soon. In this case, it is important to note that the individual will obtain the degree prior to separating and will be able to list the accomplishment on his or her résumé. This enables the veteran to get into the workforce faster.
2. In most master's degree programs, the cost is above and beyond the $250 per credit hour that TA can cover. Completing an advanced degree while still on active duty will be an enormous benefit to separating service members.
3. If the service member is looking to attend a prestigious university and cannot cover the costs out of pocket. In this case, I would typically recommend attending a local community college (many have fully online, fast-paced programs available) for as long as possible prior to

transferring into the university. At least this way, the individual would not be drawing from his or her GI Bill for such an extended period.

For the undergraduate rate of study, try all possibilities prior to looking into Top-Up. Oftentimes, the Pell Grant is a viable option (check the "Federal Student Aid" section). Ultimately, the decision to use Top-Up must be the service member's, but the guidelines above are solid and should be considered prior to making a move.

GI BILL APPLICATION/CONVERSION PROCESS

The application process for the GI Bill is not complicated; however, it does take approximately four to six weeks to receive the Certificate of Eligibility (COE) statement. Make sure to allot time for the wait prior to starting school. If you find yourself in a time crunch, check with your school to see if the institution might take a copy of the submitted application and let you start.

If you have MGIB and you are positive you want to convert to Post 9/11, the process can be done at the same time you activate the benefit. Although there is no need to do so prior to this point, some sailors are more comfortable making the switch while still on active duty.

To activate the GI Bill, you will need to access the Veterans Online Application (VONAPP; see http://vabenefits.vba.va.gov/vonapp/). You can also access it by going to the main GI Bill website (http://www.gibill.va.gov): select the "Post 9/11" link on the right-hand side, select "Get Started" on the left-hand side, select "Apply for Benefits," and, finally, select "Apply Online." You will need three pieces of information before you proceed:

1. Your school's name and address
2. A bank account and routing number (VA is direct deposit)
3. An address where you will be in the next four to eight weeks

The easiest way to prepare for the application process is to be accepted at your intended institution prior to applying to activate your benefit, but you can change the required information later by contacting the VA at 1-888-GIBILL-1.

The VA no longer sends hard checks. Inputting your bank account and routing numbers enables the VA to directly deposit your MHA and book stipend money. You may change this information later if you change your bank.

Your Certificate of Eligibility (COE) will be delivered to the address you list. Sailors living in the barracks might want to send their COEs to their parents' or another reliable family member's address. Just make sure that the individuals located at the listed address keep their eyes open for the document and inform you when it arrives. You will need to take that document to the veterans' representative at your school as soon as you receive it, because it is the school's ticket to receive payment from the VA. This is part of the process for you to receive the housing allowance.

Process of Applying

Upon entering the VONAPP website (http://vabenefits.vba.va.gov/vonapp/), you will be asked if you are a first-time VONAAP user; answer accordingly. Next, you will be asked if you possess an eBenefits Account. I find this to be a difficult way to enter the site. If you select that you do not have an eBenefits account, you will need to create a VONAPP account (this seems to be a much easier pathway!). Be aware that you will need an eBenefits account for all other VA-related concerns, but applying directly through VONAPP will not disrupt that process. Once settled, select the "22-1990 Education Benefits" form to proceed. The VONAPP website will ask you information pertaining to your active-duty tours, prior education and training, upcoming start date for your school and training, pursuit of study (associate degree, bachelor's degree, graduate degree, or apprenticeship or on-the-job training), and so on.

If you are concerned about the questions on the 22-1990 or whether you are making the correct choices, contact the VA at 1-888-GIBILL-1. The veterans' representatives at your intended school are usually good sources of information as well. If you would like to see the required information in advance, check with your base's education center to see if it keeps paper copies of the 22-1990s.

Once you receive the COE, you need to take it (a copy!) to the veterans' representatives at your school. You will also need to send a copy of your DD-214 to your local VA processing center. When you finish filling out and submitting the 22-1990, the main page on the VONAPP will maintain two links (side by side) with required, printable information. One is your submitted application; the other is your local processing center, which is oftentimes not in the same state. Some institutions will also want a copy of your DD-214 for verification purposes.

If you are transferring to a new school, you will need to fill out the 22-1995 form, but only if you are not changing GI Bill chapters. The 22-1995 form can be found on the VONAPP website.

POST 9/11 TRANSFERABILITY TO DEPENDENTS

Active-duty service members may be eligible to transfer their Post 9/11 GI Bill benefits to dependents. The transfer process requires a four-year commitment to stay in the military. If benefits are successfully transferred, certain rules apply while the service member remains on active duty.

To be eligible to transfer benefits, a service member must be eligible for Post 9/11 and:

- Have completed six years of active-duty service and agree to four more years
- Have four years remaining on contract (enlisted) or commit four more years (officer)
- *Or* is precluded by standard policy or statute from serving an additional four years (must agree to serve maximum time allowed by such policy)

Transfer must be approved while service member is still in the armed forces.

In a nutshell, sailors need to have completed the required time in service and have four years left on contract. The best time to complete the process is at the same time as a reenlistment or extension package that gives the individual the required amount of payback time.

To transfer benefits, follow these steps:

- Verify your time in service.
- Visit the website (at http://www.benefits.va.gov/gibill/post911_gibill.asp).
- Click on the "Transfer of Entitlement" option.
- Follow the directions ("Apply Now").
- You will find yourself on the MilConnect webpage and will need to enter your CAC card or Defense Finance and Accounting Services (DFAS) account information.
- Click on the "Go to Transfer of Eligible Benefits" link on the right-hand side.

- Apply the needed information and submit—but you are not finished.
- Obtain a Statement of Understanding (SOU) from the website.
- Fill out all required information and take it to the career counselor.
- Career counselors will verify time in service.
- The commanding officer signs off on the application, and then the document must be routed through PSD.
- Once transfer is approved, eligibility documents for each individual will be found in the Transfer Education Benefits (TEB) website (https://www.dmdc.osd.mil/milconnect/help/topics/transfer_of_education_benefits_teb.htm).

Service members may revoke transferred benefits at any given time. Designated months may also be changed or eliminated through the website while on active duty or through a written request to the VA once separated.

Dependents who have received transferred benefits will need to apply to use the benefits through the VONAPP website (www.gibill.va.gov) in the "Post 9/11, Apply for Benefits" section. Dependents may also print the form (22-1990e) and send it into their nearest VA regional office. The form may be found online (www.vba.va.gov/pubs/forms/VBA-22-1990e-ARE.pdf), and regional offices may be found online (www.benefits.va.gov/benefits/offices.asp).

Eligible Dependents

- Spouse
- Service member's children
- Combination of spouse and children

Dependents must be in the Defense Enrollment Eligibility Reporting System (DEERS).

Spouses

- May use the benefit immediately
- Are not entitled to the MHA while the service member remains on active duty, but are entitled once the service member separates
- Are entitled to the book stipend
- May use the benefit for up to fifteen years from the service member's EAS date, just like the service member

Children

- May use the benefit only after the service member has attained ten years on active duty
- May use the benefit while the parent is on active duty or after separation
- Must have obtained a high school diploma or equivalency certificate, or have turned eighteen
- May receive the MHA while a parent remains on active-duty status
- Are entitled to the book stipend
- Do not fall under the fifteen-year delimiting date; however, benefits must be used prior to turning twenty-six years old

Sailors can commit the required payback time of four years after separating from active duty and dropping into the reserves.

The current contact:

http://www.benefits.va.gov/gibill/post911_transfer.asp;   Navy   Active Duty Navy Personnel Command Customer Service Center: 866-827-5672

YELLOW RIBBON PROGRAM (YRP)

YRP is designed to serve two purposes:

1. Help cover out-of-state tuition prior to the veteran gaining in-state tuition.
2. Cover tuition over the maximum allowable rate for private school.

YRP is not automatic, and there are many stipulations to watch out for prior to determining if the benefit will work for your particular purpose. YRP does not pay the student any money.

Eligibility

- Must rate 100 percent of the Post 9/11 GI Bill
- Active-duty members of the military are not eligible, nor are their spouses; however, children of active-duty members may qualify (if the active-duty parent is eligible for 100 percent of 9/11)

YRP potentially enables veterans to cover costs above and beyond the Post 9/11 GI Bill parameters. Not all schools participate, and a school's participation for one year does not guarantee participation in subsequent years. You do not need to maintain full-time status in order to be eligible for YRP. Summer terms may be eligible as well, but check with your particular institution.

Schools must reestablish their YRP program with the VA every year. This means, and I have seen it happen, that a school may participate one year but not the next. You could be left hanging. For example, a Marine corporal attended a well-known private school in Georgia. The school participated during her first year but not the following years. She was out of pocket roughly $22,000 per year for her school at that point . . . ouch!

Schools may participate on different levels by limiting the number of YRP spots available and the amount of money they offer. This can restrict veterans from considering certain institutions based on financial constraints. Here is a hypothetical breakdown:

- School A participates in YRP with unlimited spots and unlimited money. Therefore, you shouldn't pay out of pocket. But you still run the risk of the school choosing not to participate in upcoming years.
- School B participates with twenty spots and $4,000 per student. Therefore, you may or may not get one of those twenty spots (remember that it is first come, first served!), and the VA will match the $4,000, effectively giving you an extra $8,000 toward tuition (this is a rough explanation of how it works).

You must also check to see how the program at your school is participating. Consider the following hypothetical situation:

- School C: This graduate-level business program participates with seventeen spots and $11,000 per student.
- School D: This graduate-level education program participates with four spots and $6,000 per student.

Notice that different programs within the same school may participate with different amounts of money and numbers of available spots.

Lastly, a school may participate differently at the graduate level than it does at the undergraduate level. See the following example:

- School E participates at the undergraduate level with five spots and $8,000 per student.
- School F participates at the graduate level with three spots and $1,000 per student.

Although it can be complicated to determine the benefit you may be eligible for, the vet reps at the school can usually offer sound advice. You can search YRP participating schools by state (http://www.benefits.va.gov/ GIBILL/yellow_ribbon/yrp_list_2014.asp). However, I always recommend contacting the VA directly for solid confirmation that the school you are applying for does participate and to what degree.

Do not make the mistake of thinking that a small, off-the-beaten-path school might not fill its YRP seats. I (Jillian) spoke with a small community college in Washington State that participates in the YRP, wondering if it often fills its openings. At that time, Washington State did not have a state-based law that gave in-state tuition to out-of-state veterans, but it has since passed legislation, so veterans who meet the qualifications should receive the in-state tuition rate. Prior to speaking to the veterans' representative, I thought it was nice that it had allotted so many spots even though they probably were not needed. I mean, how many out-of-state veterans are relocating to this rural area and need help with out-of-state tuition? I was so wrong! The school had a waiting list for its YRP spots in the double digits. Apparently, although the school is located in a rural area, it is also the closest school to one of the state's main snowboarding mountains and maintains a fairly large veteran population. On the flip side, I was happy to hear that our veterans were getting some much-needed R&R after their military service along with a good education.

If you intend to transfer, you must speak with your new school regarding YRP eligibility. Eligibility at one school does not guarantee eligibility at another. If you take a hiatus from the school where you were enrolled in YRP, you may be dropped for subsequent semesters. Before you make any decisions, talk with your academic adviser and/or veteran department. The more informed you are, the better you can plan.

VA GI BILL FEEDBACK SYSTEM

http://www.benefits.va.gov/GIBILL/Feedback.asp

The VA recently implemented a new system to handle complaints pertaining to issues involving the Principles of Excellence. Educational institutions that abide by the specific guidelines of the program agree to:

- Inform students in writing (should be personalized) about all costs associated with education at that institution
- Produce educational plans for military and veteran beneficiaries
- Cease all misleading recruiting techniques
- Accommodate those who are absent due to military requirements
- Appoint a point of contact (POC) that offers education-related and financial advice
- Confirm that all new programs are accredited before enrolling students
- Align refund policies with Title IV policies (Federal Student Aid)

Schools that participate in the Principles of Excellence program can be found on the VA website: www.benefits.va.gov/gibill/principles_of_excellence.asp.

Complaints should be submitted when institutions participating in the program fall below the set of standards listed above. Complaints can be filed on subjects such as recruiting practices, education quality, accreditation issues, grade policies, failure to release transcripts, credit transfer, financial topics, student loan concerns, refund problems, job opportunities after degree completion, and degree plan changes and subsequent requirements. To file a complaint, visit the website and follow the directions.

FEDERAL STUDENT AID

Free Application for Federal Student Aid (FAFSA[SM])
http://www.fafsa.ed.gov/

TA money and GI Bills are a source of funding, but they are not the only source available. Active-duty and veteran service members can apply for Federal Student Aid and should be encouraged to do so, in order to cover any extra costs they are unable to get funded. For example, TA cannot cover books or supplies. Under the Post 9/11 GI Bill, if a student attends school full-time, he or she will receive $1,000 per academic year toward books and supplies. In most cases, this is not enough to cover book expenses. Federal Student Aid is a viable option to help in these circumstances.

Student Aid can come from the U.S. federal government, states, schools, and nonprofit organizations. Student aid money is usually provided on a first-come, first-served basis. Most students elect to apply for Federal Student Aid through the U.S. Department of Education, but not everyone qualifies. Prior to applying for Federal Student Aid, it is important to understand what it is, how it works, and what you would want to accept.

Federal Student Aid comes in three forms: work study, loans, and grants. Work study might be an option upon separation from the service, but it is not a feasible option for active-duty service members. VA Work Study is a great option for veterans who are interested in making extra money while attending school and keeping their work activity on their résumé full at the same time. More information on VA Work Study can be found in chapter 10 of this book.

Active-duty and veteran students using their GI Bills should not require loans in most cases. In fact, it is best to avoid them at all costs. Typically, active-duty service members have access to TA money, and honorably discharged veterans have access to their GI Bills. Loans have to be repaid with interest, and you should think carefully before accepting them.

The much-discussed federal Pell Grant is the target for most. Pell Grant money does not need to be paid back. The award must be used for education-related expenses, and only undergraduate students who do not already possess a bachelor's degree are eligible. The maximum award amount for the 2014–2015 academic year is $5,730.

Not everyone rates Pell Grant money. The award is based on financial need, cost of school, and rate of educational pursuit. The Pell Grant award amount can change yearly, and the FAFSA[SM] must be reapplied for every academic year. The application will repopulate all of your personal information to help expedite the process.

If a student is awarded Pell Grant money, the amount is sent to the school, and the school pays the student. Federal Pell Grant money is paid in at least two disbursements. Most schools pay students at least once per semester.

If any money is owed toward tuition and fees, schools remove that amount from the Pell Grant award prior to turning the remainder of the money over to the student. Award money is typically turned over to students as a check, cash, or a bank deposit. Most veteran students' tuition is covered by the GI Bill, so most veterans should get to keep the full amount of the award. Remember this prior to choosing an institution that may not be fully covered under Post 9/11 or MGIB.

In order to be eligible to apply for Federal Student Aid, borrowers must meet the following parameters:

- Demonstrate financial need (required by most programs)
- Be a U.S. citizen or eligible noncitizen
- Have a valid Social Security number (exceptions apply)
- Be registered with the Selective Service
- Be enrolled or accepted at a minimum of half-time as a regular student into an eligible degree or certificate program

Federal Student Aid applicants will also need to sign statements stating that the student:

- Is not defaulting on any federal student loans
- Does not owe money on any federal grants
- Will only use aid money for educational-related expenses
- Can demonstrate evidence of eligibility by having a high school diploma, GED, or completed home school program approved by state law

Be sure to research and understand where a student loan is coming from prior to accepting any money. Student loans can be federal or private depending on the source. Federally backed loans and private loans have many differences. Here are just a few of the reasons that federally backed loans can offer greater flexibility than loans from private sources:

- Federal loans can offer borrowers fixed interest rates that are typically lower than private sources.
- Borrowers are given a six-month grace period upon completion of the degree to begin repayments. Often, private school loans will require payments to be made while the student is still attending school.
- Only federally backed loans are subsidized, meaning the government pays the interest for a period of time.
- Interest may be deductible; this is not an option for private loans.
- Federal loans can be consolidated into a Direct Consolidation Loan; private loans cannot.

- Private loans might demand that the individual borrowing the money already have a credit record, but most federal student loans will not perform a credit check.
- Federal loans offer more options for forbearance or deferment.

Federal student loans come in three shapes and sizes: Direct Subsidized Loans or Direct Unsubsidized Loans, Direct PLUS Loans (for advanced education), or Perkins Loans.

According to the U.S. Department of Education, Direct Subsidized Loans have slightly better parameters for students with financial need. Direct Subsidized Loans are only available for undergraduate students, and the amount awarded cannot exceed the financial need. Interest on this type of loan is covered by the U.S. Department of Education while students remain in school at a minimum of half-time and for the first six months after graduation (the grace period).

Direct Unsubsidized Loans demand a demonstration of financial need and are available for undergraduate and graduate school. The amount borrowed is regulated by the school and is based upon the school's costs. Interest is the responsibility of the borrower at all times. If the borrower chooses not to pay interest while in school, the amount accrues and is added into the overall loan and will be reflected in payments when they come due.

Federal PLUS loans are available for graduate or professional degree-seeking students and parents of dependent undergraduate students. Schools must participate in the program for students to be eligible. Loans are fixed at 7.9 percent, and borrowers must not have an adverse credit history. PLUS loans do not require financial need and have payback options in case the student has needs above his or her available benefit levels and parents who will help. For more specific information regarding the types of loans available, see the U.S. Department of Education's Federal Student Aid website (http://studentaid.ed.gov/types/loans/federal-vs-private).

The federal Perkins Loan program offers low-interest student loans for undergraduate and graduate students with exceptional financial need. Part-time and full-time students may be eligible. The interest rate for this loan is only 5 percent. Not all schools participate in the Perkins Loan program, so check with your school's financial aid office to see if it participates. If you are an undergraduate student, you may borrow up to $5,500 per year or $27,500 in total. Graduates and professional-degree students may be eligible for up to $8,000 per year with a possible maximum total entitlement of

$80,000. The money can be applied toward tuition, fees, room and board, and other school charges.

If you plan to apply for Federal Student Aid, you will need access to your taxes from the previous year. For example, if you are applying for student aid for the 2014–2015 school year, you will need your 2013 taxes. The FAFSA^{SM} application opens in January of each year and must be reapplied for each year. Check with your state for possible state-based financial awards and potential deadline dates. For example, California has the CalGrant award. The award is applied for while completing the FAFSA^{SM}; however, the deadline is March 2 of each year. If you are eligible and do not fill out the FAFSA^{SM} and submit required documents prior to this point, you will not be eligible for any state-based assistance if attending a school in California.

If you do not rate any money one year, do not let it deter you from applying in subsequent years. You may rate it at another time because finances can change. If you are under the age of twenty-four but have already served on active duty (or are currently serving), you will not need to enter your parents' tax information on the FAFSA^{SM} (Higher Education Reconciliation Act of 2005). You will enter your personal tax information only.

If you are interested in applying for Federal Student Aid but are unsure how to proceed, contact the financial aid office of your school for further guidance.

Here is a quick checklist for applying for federal financial aid:

- Have your tax information from the previous year on hand.
- Apply on http://www.pin.ed.gov for your PIN number.
- Apply for Federal Student Aid through FAFSA^{SM} (www.fafsa.ed.gov; you will need to list your school).
- Verify your submission with your school's financial aid office.
- Keep an eye out for your financial aid award letter, and monitor your student account on your school's website.
- Hopefully, receive a payment!
- The http://www.fafsa.ed.gov website offers many helpful hints if you get stuck while filling out the FAFSA^{SM}. The application should take twenty to thirty minutes to complete online.

STATE-BASED VETERAN EDUCATION BENEFITS

Aside from the federal GI Bills available for honorably discharged veterans, many states also have state-based benefits to help with education. Some of the benefits work quite liberally; others have stricter guidelines. In some cases, it is possible to double-dip on MGIB and a state-based benefit to maximize monetary intake. Potentially, this can mean more money in the student's pocket or longer-lasting education benefits.

It is extremely important to figure out whether you rate a state-based benefit and how that benefit works before you sign up for your federal GI Bill. In some cases, you can bring in more money monthly by staying under MGIB instead of opting for Post 9/11. If you opt for Post 9/11 and activate your GI Bill, and then find out later that you could have made more money under MGIB, it is too late to do anything. Once the Post 9/11 GI Bill is selected and activated, you cannot go back.

In order to determine what benefits your state offers and whether you are eligible, check with your state's Department of Veterans' Affairs Office (http://www.va.gov/statedva.htm). Oftentimes, the school's veterans' representatives have information on their particular state's education benefits, but always check with the state VA to verify all available benefits, including possibilities other than education.

I list and describe many of the state-based benefits later in this chapter. Remember that states may cancel, change, or add benefits over time. Although I strive to be as accurate as possible, this book was compiled and written in 2014, and things change. Because you are the veteran, you need to double-check what is available at any specific time.

I (Jillian) have found two situations where MGIB might be a better choice than Post 9/11, and I explain them below. Remember that you can always visit with an education counselor on your base for further advice, and a quick phone call to the veterans' representatives at the school can usually tell you which GI Bill veterans are opting for in the same situation.

Two examples that I have encountered with veterans who sometimes prefer to remain under MGIB are veterans who come from a state that has a full state-based education benefit and, in a few rare cases, veterans who choose to attend school fully online. I do not recommend fully online school, because it usually means forgoing a good chunk of housing stipend money.

Here is an example of a veteran who did better by staying under MGIB instead of electing Post 9/11:

Hospital Corpsman Third Class (HM3) Smith enlisted in Illinois. In 2014, after serving four years of honorable service in the Navy, he is about to separate and return home. Hospital Corpsman Third Class Smith is interested in attending the University of Illinois in Champaign and needs to determine his available education options.

Hospital Corpsman Third Class Smith learns about the two federal GI Bills and the Illinois Veteran Grant (IVG) after reading this book. Hospital Corpsman Third Class Smith needs to determine whether he paid into MGIB, which would have been $100 per month for the first year of his enlistment to total $1,200. He believes he did, but he cannot remember for sure. He will double-check with the local Personnel Support Detachment (PSD) to clarify, but he continues to plan as if he did pay the $1,200 into MGIB.

Hospital Corpsman Third Class Smith might also be eligible for Illinois Veterans Grant (IVG). Only the Illinois state VA can determine his eligibility, and he will need to verify with them whether he will be able to use the benefit prior to following through with the details.

IVG will cover the cost of tuition and certain fees for eligible veterans at state-supported universities and community colleges within the state of Illinois. If Hospital Corpsman Third Class Smith does rate IVG, he might do better financially by using it in tandem with MGIB rather than opting for Post 9/11.

Here is the IVG eligibility list from the Illinois State VA (also at http://www2.illinois.gov/veterans/benefits/pages/education.aspx) that I reviewed with Hospital Corpsman Third Class Smith (remember: things change!):

- Veteran must have received an honorable discharge.
- Veteran must have resided in Illinois six months prior to entering the service.
- Veteran must have completed a minimum of one full year of active duty in the U.S. Armed Forces (this includes veterans who were assigned to active duty in a foreign country in a time of hostilities in that country, regardless of length of service).
- Veteran must return to Illinois within six months of separation from the service.

Hospital Corpsman Third Class Smith falls within the above-mentioned parameters, feels confident he will rate the IVG, and proceeds accordingly.

Looking up the MHA stipend for the Post 9/11 GI Bill (https://www.defensetravel.dod.mil/site/bahCalc.cfm), Hospital Corpsman Third Class (HM3) Smith finds that the MHA stipend for the academic year 2014 is $1,179. This tool can also be found by visiting the main Post 9/11 GI Bill webpage (http://www.gibill.va.gov). Champaign, Illinois, is located in a rural, southern portion of the state; hence, the housing allowance under Post 9/11 is on the low side. Hospital Corpsman Third Class Smith feels that this amount is too low and that he could do better if he elects to stay under MGIB, rather than choosing Post 9/11.

Here are his calculations:

- Post 9/11 MHA: $1,179.
- MGIB payments (as of October 1, 2014): $1,717.
- Hospital Corpsman Third Class Smith will rate IVG, which will pay most of his public university's tuition and fees.
- If Hospital Corpsman Third Class Smith pays the $600 buy-up to MGIB prior to separation, it will increase his monthly MGIB payments by an extra $150 per month, so his monthly take-home amount would be $1,867, or $688 more than the $1,179 he would receive under Post 9/11. If none of the amounts changes over the thirty-six months Hospital Corpsman Third Class Smith has allotted, he would take home $24,768 more under MGIB than he would under Post 9/11 over the course of the thirty-six months of benefits.
- One drawback is that IVG can be used for a master's degree as well. If Hospital Corpsman Third Class Smith double-dips on his federal and state-based benefit at the same time, he may not retain any benefits that could have been used for graduate school. That is a personal decision.

Hospital Corpsman Third Class Smith reviews his calculations and realizes that he still needs to verify his IVG with the Illinois state VA and his GI Bill eligibility with the federal VA. He also needs to contact the veterans' representatives at the University of Illinois to discuss which GI Bill the veterans already attending the school have chosen and any recommendations that the vet reps may have for him. Hospital Corpsman Third Class Smith must decide whether he minds depleting both of his benefits at the same time, because tapping into them simultaneously will result in that outcome.

In the case of Illinois veterans who meet IVG requirements, they must decide if the extra payoff they obtain by depleting both benefits at the same time is worth it. Many veterans may want to pursue a graduate degree with that benefit later, whereas others may be more interested in maximizing their benefits immediately. Also remember that Hospital Corpsman Third Class Smith is going to attend a school in a rural area. If you are from Illinois and elect an institution closer to Chicago, your MHA amount will be much higher than the listed amount for University of Illinois in Champaign. In this case, double-dipping is not necessary.

The second instance in which some veterans have opted for MGIB is for online-only school. Under the Post 9/11 GI Bill, veterans only receive $754.50 in MHA (as of academic year 2014–2015) for strictly online school, because you must attend a minimum of one face-to-face class every semester in order to rate the full MHA assigned to the ZIP code of the school. In a few cases, veterans who decide that they can only attend online school may do better by remaining under MGIB and paying the $600 buy-up prior to separation.

In the case of strictly online school, it is difficult to run numbers in this book because too many factors are unknown. Examples of this include tuition charges, MHA attached to the school's ZIP code, and fluctuations in GI Bill payouts.

Here is a hypothetical example:

Hospital Corpsman Third Class Smith decides to attend a fully online academic program. The cost of the school per credit hour is $250. He is taking two classes over an eight-week semester. The total cost for his two classes will be $1,500. The MHA for strictly online school at this time is $754.50 per month. Hospital Corpsman Third Class Smith paid the $600 buy-up program at PSD (Unit Diary entry) before separating. His combined monthly payout under MGIB and the buy-up program for academic year 2014–2015 is $1,867. In the span of his eight-week classes, he will take in $3,734. After paying his $1,500 bill for his two classes (two classes on an eight-week-semester schedule is considered full-time), he is left with $2,234. That is roughly $725 more than what he would take home if he had elected Post 9/11 and only received the $754.50 that is allotted for strictly online school ($2,234 − $1,509 = $725). MGIB, in this case, looks like the better choice.

Other state-based benefits can be a bit trickier. At this time, only some states offer in-state tuition to out-of-state residents. The Student Veterans of America maintains a website where you can check to see whether the state where you are planbing to attend school offers this benefit (http://www.

studentveterans.org/what-we-do/in-state-tuition.html). Some university systems will also grant in-state tuition for veterans. There are always qualifying
criteria you must abide by, so, as I keep saying throughout this book, always
check with the state VA or with the vet reps at the school to verify your
eligibility.

As a veteran, it is important for you to follow through with your own
research on state and federal benefits. States are often updating and adding
benefits for veterans. The monetary amounts attached to the federal GI Bills
change as well. The only way to stay current with the information is to
become fluent with the websites and check back regularly.

STATES THAT OFFER IN-STATE TUITION TO VETERANS

Legislation was recently passed that will give veterans and eligible dependents the in-state tuition rate at all state-based colleges and universities that
continue to accept the GI Bills (https://veterans.house.gov/the-veterans
-access-choice-and-accountability-act-of-2014-highlights). The benefit will
take effect on July 1, 2015. Prior to that time, veterans need to properly
prepare for any charges that may not be covered under their available benefits. For updated information regarding this change, visit the Student Veterans of America website (http://www.studentveterans.org/what-we-do/in-
state-tuition.html).

Here are the websites for the states that currently offer in-state residency
to veterans. Some of these states offer other veteran benefits as well. There
are specific steps (such as registering to vote or getting a driver's license)
tied into eligibility for the in-state tuition, and sometimes it is up to the
school to participate. Check with the veterans' representatives at the institution you wish to attend in order to determine how to begin the process for
that particular state. Keep up to speed with states that change their legislation
by checking the Student Veterans of America website (http://www.
studentveterans.org/what-we-do/in-state-tuition.html).

- Alabama (http://openstates.org/al/bills/2013rs/HB424/documents/ALD0
  0016731/): In-state tuition for veterans who reside in Alabama and were
  honorably discharged within the five years immediately preceding their
  enrollment at a state institution of higher learning. Reservists and service-
  connected disabled veterans are eligible as well.

- Arizona (http://dvs.az.gov/tuition.aspx, (602) 255-3373): In-state tuition for veterans who registered to vote in the state and meet at least one of the following parameters: have an Arizona driver license or motor vehicle registration, demonstrate employment history in Arizona, transfer their banking services to Arizona, change their permanent address on all pertinent records, or demonstrate other materials of whatever kind or source relevant to domicile or residency status.
- California (http://www.calvet.ca.gov/VetServices/Education.aspx, (916) 653-2573): Currently, the state of California offers honorary residency to veterans who were stationed in California for one year prior to separation from the military, separate, and stay in the state to attend an institution of higher education.
- Colorado (http://highered.colorado.gov/Finance/Residency/requirements. html, (303) 866-2723): In-state tuition for qualifying veterans and dependents. Veterans must be honorably discharged and maintain a permanent home in Colorado. Enlisted service members who are stationed in Colorado and receiving the resident student rate (themselves or their dependents) will be able to maintain that rate upon separation from the military if they continue to reside in the state.
- Florida (www.flsenate.gov/Session/Bill/2014/7015/BillText/er/PDF): In-state tuition for honorably discharged veterans at state community colleges, state colleges, and universities.
- Idaho (www.legislature.idaho.gov/legislation/2010/S1367.pdf, (208) 577-2310): In-state tuition for qualified veterans and qualifying dependents. Veterans must have served at least two years on active duty, have received an honorable discharge, and enter a public school within one year of separating from the service. Dependents must receive at least 50 percent of their support from the qualifying veteran.
- Illinois (http://studentveterans.org/media-news/press-releases/128-illinois -passes-in-state-tuition-for-veterans.html, http://www3.illinois.gov/Press-Releases/ShowPressRelease.cfm?SubjectID=3&RecNum=11434): Lately passed by the governor; all veterans using the Post 9/11 GI Bill will be billed as in-state residents at state-supported institutions.
- Indiana (www.in.gov/legislative/bills/2013/SE/SE0177.1.html): Veterans enrolled in undergraduate classes no more than twelve months after honorably separating from the armed forces or Indiana National Guard are eligible for in-state tuition.

- Kentucky   (http://cpe.ky.gov/policies/academicpolicies/residency.htm, (502) 573-1555): In-state tuition for qualifying veterans.
- Louisiana (http://legiscan.com/LA/text/HB435/id/649958): In-state tuition for veterans who served a minimum of two years on active duty and received an honorable discharge. Veterans who have been assigned service-connected disability ratings and either are already enrolled or are applying to enroll in a state institution are eligible as well.
- Maine   (www.mainelegislature.org/legis/bills/getDoc.asp?id=39934): Honorably discharged veterans enrolled in a program of education within the University of Maine system, the community college system, or the Maritime Academy are eligible for in-state tuition.
- Maryland   (http://mgaleg.maryland.gov/2013RS/fnotes/bil_0005/hb0935.pdf): In-state tuition for honorably discharged veterans of the armed forces. Veterans must reside in Maryland and attend a state institution of higher learning.
- Minnesota (http://www.ohe.state.mn.us/mPg.cfm?pageID=1688): In-state tuition at the undergraduate rate for veterans.
- Missouri   (www.senate.mo.gov/13info/BTS_Web/Bill.aspx?SessionType =R&BillID=17138567): In-state tuition for veterans who received honorable or general discharges from the service. Benefit can be used at the state two-year or four-year institutions. Two-year institutions also offer the in-district rate.
- Nebraska   (http://www.vets.state.ne.us/benefits.html): Honorably discharged veterans receive in-state tuition if more than two years have not passed since their date of separation from service. Dependents are eligible as well. Not applicable if the service member is eligible for the Yellow Ribbon Program.
- Nevada   (http://leg.state.nv.us/Session/77th2013/Bills/AB/AB260_EN.pdf): In-state tuition for veterans who were honorably discharged and matriculated no more than two years after their date of separation from the armed forces.
- New Mexico (http://www.dvs.state.nm.us/benefits.html, (505) 827-6374): In-state tuition for qualified veterans, their spouses, and their children.
- North Dakota (www.legis.nd.gov/cencode/t15c10.pdf?20131106152541): In-state tuition for veterans who served 180 days or more on active duty and received an honorable discharge. Dependents who received transferred Post 9/11 benefits may also be eligible.

- Ohio (http://codes.ohio.gov/orc/3333.31, (614) 644-0898): In-state tuition for qualified veterans.
- Oregon (https://olis.leg.state.or.us/liz/2013R1/Measures/Text/HB2158/Enrolled): Honorably discharged veterans who establish a physical presence in Oregon within twelve months of enrolling in school may be eligible for in-state tuition and fees.
- South Dakota (http://legis.sd.gov/): In-state tuition for honorably discharged veterans with at least ninety days of service.
- Tennessee (http://www.capitol.tn.gov/Bills/108/Bill/SB1433.pdf): In-state tuition for veterans discharged within two years who did not receive a dishonorable separation.
- Texas (http://www.statutes.legis.state.tx.us/Docs/ED/htm/ED.54.htm#54.241): In-state tuition for veterans who qualify for federal education benefits. Dependents may qualify as well.
- Utah (http://le.utah.gov/code/TITLE53B/pdf/53B08_010200.pdf, (801) 326-2372): In-state tuition for qualifying veterans at certain schools.
- Virginia (http://lis.virginia.gov/cgi-bin/legp604.exe?000+cod+23-7.4: Veterans released or discharged under conditions other than dishonorable are eligible for in-state tuition.
- Washington (http://www.dva.wa.gov/veterantuitionwaiver.html): Veterans (and their dependents) who served a minimum of two years in the military and received an honorable discharge will be granted in-state tuition as long as they enroll in school within one year of their date of separation from the service.

A few state-based university systems across the country may also offer veterans in-state tuition without a state-based benefit in place. Eligibility rules vary. Verify with the institution before making your final decision. The following is a current list:

- University of Alaska school system: http://www.alaska.edu/bor/policy-regulations/
- Mississippi institutions of higher learning: http://www.ihl.state.ms.us/board/downloads/policiesandbylaws.pdf
- University of Wisconsin school system: http://www.wisconsin.edu/acss/residency/FINALGuidelinesHEOA_ResidencyLegislation4-30-10.pdf
- Kentucky public universities: http://www.lrc.ky.gov/record/11rs/HB425.htm

- University of Iowa school system: http://www.registrar.uiowa.edu/LinkClick.aspx?fileticket=EnXD7AdsnJ0%3d&tabid=94
- University system of Georgia: http://www.usg.edu/policymanual/section7/C453/
- University of Rhode Island: http://www.uri.edu/home/campus/
- University of Delaware: http://www.udel.edu/aboutus/

Many institutions of higher learning have adopted scholarships for disabled veterans. For example, the University of Idaho has the Operation Education scholarship that may provide financial assistance for eligible service-connected disabled veterans and their spouses (http://www.uidaho.edu/operationeducation). Check with the institutions you are interested in attending to obtain information regarding policies or programs that may benefit you.

The following are states with state-based education benefits at this time. Most of the information is taken directly from the state VA websites.

ALABAMA

http://www.va.state.al.us/otherbenefits.aspx
http://www.va.state.al.us/gi_dep_scholarship.aspx

Benefit

- Purple Heart recipients may be eligible to have tuition and fees waived for undergraduate studies.

State residents with service-connected disability ratings of 20 percent or higher may qualify for his or her:

- Spouse: three standard academic years without payment of tuition, mandatory textbooks, or instructional fees at a state institution of higher learning, or for a prescribed technical course not to exceed twenty-seven months of training at a state institution.
- Dependent children: five standard academic years or part-time equivalent at any Alabama state-supported institution of higher learning or a state-supported technical school without payment of any tuition, mandatory textbooks, or instructional fees. Dependent children must start school prior to age twenty-six.

Eligibility and residency requirements for veterans:

- Must have honorably served at least ninety days of continuous active federal military service during wartime, or be honorably discharged by reason of service-connected disability after serving less than ninety days of continuous active federal military service during wartime.
- Permanent civilian resident of the state of Alabama for at least one year immediately prior to (1) the initial entry into active military service or (2) any subsequent period of military service in which a break (one year or more) in service occurred and the Alabama civilian residency was established. Permanently service-connected veterans rated at 100 percent who did not enter service from Alabama may qualify but must first establish at least five years of permanent residency in Alabama prior to application.

Note: If you are a veteran with a PH and MGIB, you may want to stay on MGIB instead of electing Post 9/11.

The following subsection is a breakdown of current payout under MGIB versus Post 9/11 with a veteran using his or her Alabama state benefit under MGIB at a community college.

Northeast Alabama Community College
MGIB currently pays out $1,564/month + $600 (buy-up) = $1,714/month
Total for 4 months = $6,856
MHA under Post 9/11 $957 × 4 months = $3,828

Veterans who qualify for the state-based PH waiver earn $3,028 more in four months under MGIB than if they opted for Post 9/11. Remember that the state pays the school tuition in this case.

CALIFORNIA

https://www.calvet.ca.gov/VetServices/Pages/College-Fee-Waiver.aspx

Benefit

- Dependent children tuition waiver at state-supported schools for service-connected disabled veterans.

The California State benefit has four different pathways for eligibility. They can be confusing. Mainly, they are Medal of Honor recipients and their children, National Guard members, children of veterans with service-connected disabilities (the most common category), and spouses (veteran is totally disabled, or whose death was service connected). Let's discuss the most common category: children. California veterans who rate a 0 percent disability rating or higher may qualify for their children to receive waivers of tuition at state community colleges and universities. Please note that a 0 percent disability rating is an actual rating. Fees for books, housing, parking, and so on are not included in the waiver. The state of California does not care where you enlisted. If you separate, have a service-connected disability, and become a California resident, you may be eligible.

This is a great way to have your children's college expenses covered. Many veterans use the benefit to send their children to state schools to pursue higher education and not worry about the bills. The universities in the state are accustomed to children using this benefit, and the veterans' representatives at the institutions know how to facilitate it for dependent children.

To read a more thorough breakdown of eligibility, check at http://www.calvet.ca.gov/Files/VetServices/Veterans_Resource_Book.pdf.

Eligibility and residency requirements for child for most common pathway:

- Make less than $11,945 per year (changes yearly to reflect cost of living).
- Meet in-state residency requirements determined by school.
- Provide proof of relationship to the veteran.

Benefit

- In-state tuition for veterans. Must be stationed in California for one year prior to separation, separate in the state, and remain in California for school.
- http://www.calvet.ca.gov/VetServices/NonResFeeWaiver.aspx

CONNECTICUT

http://www.ct.gov/ctva/cwp/view.asp?A=2014&Q=290874

Benefit

- Tuition waivers at Connecticut state community colleges and state colleges/universities for eligible veterans.

Only the cost of tuition is waived. Other charges such as books, student fees, and parking are not waived. Students must be matriculated into a degree program.

Eligibility and residency requirements for veterans:

- Be honorably discharged.
- Have served at least ninety days of active military duty during war.
- Be a resident of Connecticut at least one year prior to enrolling in college.
- Be a resident of Connecticut at the time he or she applies for the state benefit.

FLORIDA

http://floridavets.org/?page_id=60

Benefit

- Waiver of undergraduate-level tuition at state universities and community colleges for recipients of the PH and other combat-related decorations superior in precedence to the PH. Waiver covers 110 percent of the required credit hours for the degree or certificate.

Eligibility and residency requirements:

- Veteran must be admitted as a part- or full-time student in a course of study leading to a degree or certificate.
- Must have been a Florida state resident at the time the military action that resulted in the awarding of the PH (or other award) took place and must currently be a Florida state resident.
- Must submit DD-214 documenting PH to school.

ILLINOIS

http://www2.illinois.gov/veterans/benefits/Pages/education.aspx

Benefit

- The Illinois Veterans' Grant (IVG) is a tuition (and certain fees) waiver for undergraduate and graduate studies at state-supported institutions for veterans who served during a time of hostilities.

  Eligibility and residency requirements for veterans:

- Received an honorable discharge.
- Have resided in Illinois six months prior to entering the military.
- Have served a minimum of one year on active duty with the Armed Forces, or was assigned to active duty in a foreign country in a time of hostilities in that country, regardless of length of service.
- Returned to Illinois within six months of separation from the military.

Many Illinois veterans choose to stay under MGIB as opposed to Post 9/11 to fully maximize dollar amounts under their available benefits. If you plan to attend school in a rural area—for example, University of Illinois in Champaign—double-dipping on MGIB and IVG can produce more money on a monthly basis. If you do this, be aware that you will be depleting both state and federal benefits at the same time. That means that you may not have any benefit left for a master's degree later.

If the school you choose is located in a rural area, and the MHA on Post 9/11 is significantly less than the maxed-out MGIB amount (currently $1,564 per month), then double-dipping will be more beneficial.

Here is an example:

Recently Seaman Stevens went to the University of Illinois in Champaign. The MHA for the 2013–2014 school year was $1,047 (http://inquiry. vba.va.gov/weamspub/buildViewOrg.do). Seaman Stevens was an Illinois state resident at enlistment and qualified for the Illinois Veteran Grant. He elected to stay under MGIB, and went to pay the buy-up at IPAC (unit diary entry) prior to his EAS date.

The buy-up option under MGIB increases the monthly payments and must be paid while still on active duty. Buy-up can be paid in different increments, but I recommend the maximum of $600 be paid in order to get

- Received the PH.
- Honorably discharged.
- Veteran entered service prior to June 30, 2011. (*Note*: Be aware that the law changed in 2011; see the text that follows for more information.)

Benefit

As stated above, the law changed in 2011. Here is the difference between the old and new laws:

- Free resident tuition for the children of disabled veterans or PH recipients.
- Benefit includes 124 semester hours of tuition and mandatory fees at the undergraduate rate.
- Benefit can be used for graduate school, but the difference between the undergraduate and graduate rate is the responsibility of the student.

  Eligibility and residency requirements:

- Biological and legally adopted (by age twenty-four) children of eligible disabled Indiana veterans.
- Child must produce a copy of birth certificate or adoption papers.
- Veteran must have served during a period of wartime.
- Veteran must have been a resident of Indiana for a minimum of three consecutive years at some point in his or her lifetime.
- Must rate a service-connected disability (or have died a service-connected death) or have received the PH (demonstration of proof is necessary for either).

  Under the new law, for a veteran who entered service *on or after* July 1, 2011:

- Free resident tuition for the children of disabled veterans or PH recipients.
- Benefit includes 124 semester hours of tuition and mandatory fees for undergraduate study only.
- Benefit is based on the level of disability the veteran rates (see below). Student must maintain a mandatory minimum GPA (see below).
- The program limits the student to eight years.

  Eligibility and residency requirements:

- Biological and legally adopted (by age eighteen) children of eligible disabled Indiana veterans.
- Child must produce a copy of birth certificate or adoption papers.
- Veteran must have served during a period of wartime.
- Must rate a service-connected disability (or have died a service-connected death) or have received the PH (demonstration of proof is necessary for either).
- Student must apply prior to turning thirty-two years old.

Disability rating pro-rated schedule for tuition-taken directly from the website:

- Children of veterans rated 80 percent service-connected disabled or higher by the VA or whose veteran parent is/was a recipient of the Purple Heart Medal will receive 100 percent fee remission.
- Children of veterans rated less than 80 percent service-connected disabled will receive 20 percent fee remission plus the disability rating of the veteran.
- If the disability rating of the veteran changes after the beginning of the academic semester, quarter, or other period, the change in the disability rating shall be applied beginning with the immediately following academic semester, quarter, or other period.

GPA requirements:

- First-year student must maintain satisfactory academic progress.
- Second-, third-, and fourth-year students must maintain a minimum cumulative GPA of 2.5.

MARYLAND

http://www.mdva.state.md.us/state/scholarships.html

Benefit

- Edward T. Conroy Memorial Scholarship

Aid for qualifying veterans or children of veterans to attend part-time or full-time Maryland state school (community college, university, or private career school). Benefit works for undergraduate and graduate school. Award is not based on economic need. The award is for tuition and fees, but it may not exceed $10,100, whichever is less. Award works for five years at the full-time attendance rate (eight years at part-time). More detailed information can be found at www.mhec.state.md.us/financialAid/COARenewal/2013-2014/2013-2014%20conroy%20conditions%20of%20award%20renewal.pdf.

Eligibility and residency requirements:

- Children of veterans who have died or are 100 percent disabled as a result of military service
- Veterans who have a 25 percent or greater disability rating with the VA and have exhausted federal veterans' education benefits
- Be a Maryland resident

Benefit

- Veterans of the Afghanistan and Iraq Conflicts (VAIC) Scholarship Program

Award is 50 percent of tuition and fees and room and board at the in-state undergraduate rate at a school within the University of Maryland system (UMUC and University of Maryland, Baltimore, are exempt from this award). The award shall not exceed $10,400 for the 2013–2014 school year. All undergraduate majors are eligible. Award works for five years at the full-time attendance rate or eight years at part-time. Students must maintain a minimum 2.5 GPA.

Eligibility and residency requirements:

- Have served in Afghanistan (minimum sixty days) on or after October 24, 2001, or in Iraq on or after March 19, 2003 (minimum sixty days).
- Be on active duty, or a veteran (honorable discharge), or the son, daughter, or spouse of the aforementioned group.
- Must attend school part- or full-time and be degree seeking.
- Supporting documentation of relationship to veteran is necessary (birth certificate or marriage certificate).
- Supporting documentation of active-duty status (orders) or DD-214 is necessary.
- Applicant must be a resident of Maryland (active-duty military stationed in the state at the time of application qualify).

MASSACHUSETTS

http://www.mass.gov/veterans/education/financial-assistance/tuition-waivers.html

Benefit

- Waiver of full or partial tuition at state institutions of higher education on a space-available basis for undergraduate study (fees are not included and can be very high). Graduate school waivers are dependent upon each university. Waivers are for degree or certificate programs.

  Eligibility and residency requirements:

- Be a resident of the state for at least one year prior to the start of the school year
- Not be in default of any federal or state loans or financial aid
- Served a minimum of ninety days and received an honorable discharge
- Maintain a minimum of three undergraduate credits per semester and make satisfactory academic progress

MINNESOTA

http://mn.gov/mdva/resources/education/minnesotagibill.jsp
(800) 657-3866

Benefit

- A maximum payment of $1,000 per semester for full-time students and $500 per semester for part-time students. No more than $10,000 per lifetime. Eligible veterans pursuing OJT or apprenticeship programs can receive up to $2,000 per fiscal year.

  Eligibility and residency requirements:

- Veteran must be a Minnesota resident, under the age of sixty-two, and enrolled in a Minnesota institution.
- Have received an honorable discharge.

- Spouse of a disabled veteran (total and permanent) or surviving spouse or child of a veteran who died as a result of his or her service (must be eligible to receive benefits under Chapter 33/35).
- OJT and apprenticeships must be completed with eligible employers (http://www.doli.state.mn.us/Appr.asp).
- Training must be documented, be reported, and last for at least six months.

Veterans must reapply every year. More information and important links can be found on the website.

MISSOURI

http://www.dhe.mo.gov/files/moretheroesact.pdf

Benefit

- Missouri Returning Heroes' Education Act limits Missouri institutions of higher education from charging eligible veterans more than $50 per credit hour.

Eligibility and residency requirements:

- Received an honorable discharge.
- Served in an armed combat zone for more than thirty days after September 11, 2001.
- Veteran was a Missouri resident when he or she entered the service.
- Enroll in an undergraduate degree-seeking program.
- Maintain a minimum 2.5 GPA every semester.

Note: Missouri residents who qualify for this benefit and MGIB should run the numbers before electing Post 9/11. Many of the veterans I (Jillian) counsel choose to stay under MGIB as opposed to Post 9/11 to fully maximize their dollars under their available benefits.

Speak to a counselor at your closest education center on the base, or contact the veterans' representatives at your chosen school for advice. Remember, once you select Post 9/11 you can never return to MGIB, so make an educated decision.

Example: Petty Officer Second Class (PO2) Carlson meets the eligibility requirements as listed above. He will attend Three Rivers Community College in Poplar Bluff, Missouri. The housing allowance under Post 9/11 is $999 per month. The tuition per semester will be $750 (for fifteen credit hours) under his state-based benefit. If he elects to stay under MGIB, he needs to pay the buy-up at IPAC (unit diary entry) prior to his expiration of active obligated service (EAOS), and then he will receive $1,867 per month. After paying his tuition the first month, he will have $1,117 remaining, but every month past that point he will receive $1,867 for the rest of the semester. That means $868 more per month than if he elected Post 9/11. The process would repeat itself every semester. Veterans who elect this option must remember that the book stipend is only received under Post 9/11.

Let's run the numbers:

- Tuition per semester: $750 (verify that you will not need to pay any other large fees)
- MGIB with Buy-Up: $7,468 (based on a four-month semester)
- Minus the tuition for the semester: $6,718
- Minus the book stipend that would be received under Post 9/11: $6,218
- Post 9/11 MHA for the school $999 per month: $3,996
- Including the books and supplies stipend under 9/11 for the semester: $4,496

This amounts to more per semester if the veteran decides to remain under MGIB and also qualifies for the state-based benefit. Remember that under MGIB, you must verify that you are attending school each month.

Petty Officer Second Class (PO2) Carlson elected to stay under MGIB, and he paid the buy-up at IPAC (unit diary entry) prior to his EAS date.

Explanation of the MGIB Buy-Up: The buy-up option under MGIB increases the monthly payments and must be paid while still on active duty. Buy-up can be paid in different increments, but I recommend the maximum of $600 be paid in order to get the maximum monthly increase of $150. After paying the full buy-up amount, the MGIB monthly payments are increased to $1,714. Remember that these amounts will change yearly as the COLA increases.

Always remember to verify eligibility for the state-based benefits and call the veterans' representatives at the school before making any final decisions.

MONTANA

http://wsd.dli.mt.gov/veterans/vetedu.asp

Benefit

• Tuition waivers for eligible wartime veterans who have exhausted all federal education benefits. Award works for undergraduate programs of study for a maximum of twelve semesters. Veteran must make satisfactory academic progress.

   Eligibility and residency requirements:

• Be a state resident.
• Have received an honorable discharge.
• Veteran has not already received a bachelor's degree.
• Served in a combat theater in Afghanistan or Iraq after September 11, 2001 (must have received one of the following: Global War on Terrorism Expeditionary Medal, Afghanistan Campaign Medal, or Iraq Campaign Medal).

NEW YORK

http://www.hesc.ny.gov/pay-for-college/financial-aid/types-of-financial-aid/nys-grants-scholarships-awards/veterans-tuition-awards.html
http://www.hesc.ny.gov/pay-for-college/financial-aid/types-of-financial-aid/nys-grants-scholarships-awards/msrs-scholarship.html

Benefit

• Veterans' tuition awards are available for students attending undergraduate or graduate degree-granting schools, or vocational training programs at the part- or full-time rate.

Award covers the full cost of the undergraduate tuition for New York residents at the State University of New York (SUNY) or the actual amount of the tuition (whatever is the lesser charge).

   "Full-time" is defined as twelve or more credits per semester (a maximum of eight semesters for undergraduate study and six for graduate study). "Part-time" is at least three but fewer than twelve credits per semester (within the same time frames).

The benefit was set at a maximum of $6,195 for the 2014–2015 school year. Veterans who qualify for the state benefit and MGIB may be able to double-dip (there is no double-dipping under Post 9/11, unless the veteran is not eligible for 100 percent).

Vocational programs need to be approved by the state of New York and must be at least 320 clock hours in duration.

Eligibility and residency requirements:

- New York State resident.
- Certain eligible periods of service pertain (mainly if you served in hostilities after February 28, 1961, as evidenced by receipt of an Armed Forces Expeditionary Medal, Navy Expeditionary Medal, or Marine Corps Expeditionary Medal).
- Matriculated in an undergraduate or graduate degree-granting institution in New York State or in an approved vocational training program in New York State.

Benefit

- Military Enhanced Recognition Incentive and Tribute (MERIT) Scholarship: Financial aid for qualifying veterans and dependents of veterans. Award is a maximum of four years (five for approved five-year programs) of full-time study at the undergraduate level. Award works at SUNY or City University of New York (CUNY) schools for the actual tuition and mandatory fees, plus room and board (on campus) and books and supplies. Those who attend school off-campus will receive an allowance. Private school attendees will receive a sum equal to the public school costs.

Eligibility and residency requirements:

- New York residents who died or became severely and permanently disabled (verify degree with the state) while participating in hostilities, or in training for duty in a combat theater.
- Must have occurred on or after August 2, 1990.

NORTH CAROLINA

http://www.doa.state.nc.us/vets/scholarshipclasses.aspx

Benefit

- Scholarships for dependent children of veterans who rate a minimum of 20 percent disability and served during wartime or received the Purple Heart.

Maximum of one hundred awards per year. Award is for eight semesters completed within eight years. It covers tuition, an allowance for room and board, and exemption from certain mandatory fees at public, community, and technical colleges and institutions, or $4,500 per academic year at private schools.

Eligibility and residency requirements:

- Natural and adopted (prior to age fifteen) children of qualifying veterans.
- Be under the age of twenty-five.
- Upon submission of application, student must be a resident of North Carolina.
- Veteran must have entered service in North Carolina, or the applicant must have been born in North Carolina and maintained continuous residency in the state.

OREGON

http://www.oregon.gov/odva/BENEFITS/Pages/OregonEducationBenefit.aspx

Benefit

- The Oregon Veteran Educational Aid Program

Financial aid for veterans who have exhausted all federal education benefits. The maximum award is thirty-six months (award months equal months of service) of $150 per month for full-time students or $100 per month for part-time students. Face-to-face classes, home study, vocational training, licenses, and certificates from accredited Oregon academic institutions are eligible.

Benefits are paid while pursuing classroom instruction, home study courses, vocational training, licensing, and certificates from accredited Oregon educational institutions.

Eligibility and residency requirements:

- Served on active duty a minimum of ninety days and received an honorable discharge
- Be a resident of Oregon
- Served after June 30, 1958

PUERTO RICO

Puerto Rico Public Advocate for Veterans Affairs
Public Advocate for Veterans Affairs
P.O. Box 11737
San Juan, PR 00910-1737
(787) 758-5760

Benefit

- For those attending the University of Puerto Rico and its regional colleges, free tuition for veterans who have exhausted federal benefits before completing a degree. Verify qualifying criteria with the institutions.

SOUTH CAROLINA

http://www.govoepp.state.sc.us/va/benefits.html#ed_assis

Benefit

- Free tuition for children of veterans who have been awarded the PH for wounds received in combat. Award can be used at state-supported schools or technical education institutions.

Eligibility and residency requirements:

- Veteran must have been a resident at time of entry into the military and throughout the service period, or if veteran has been a resident of South Carolina for a minimum of one year and still resides in the state.
- Veteran was honorably discharged.
- Served during a war period.
- Student must be twenty-six years old or younger.

SOUTH DAKOTA

http://vetaffairs.sd.gov/benefits/State/State%20Education%20Programs
.aspx

Benefit

- Free tuition for eligible veterans who have exhausted all federal education benefits they were eligible to receive.

Award is pro-rated on the veteran's qualifying military service (one month for each qualified month of service, for a maximum of four years). Veteran has twenty years from the end date of a qualifying service period to use the entitlement.

Eligibility and residency requirements:

- Veteran must be a resident of the state and qualify for resident tuition.
- Received an honorable discharge.
- Received a U.S. campaign or service medal for participating in combat operations outside the United States (e.g., an Armed Forces Expeditionary Medal).
- Veteran has a 10 percent (or more) disability rating with the VA.

TENNESSEE

http://www.tn.gov/sos/rules/1640/1640-01-22.20090529.pdf

Benefit

- The Helping Heroes Grant for Veterans is available yearly to a maximum of 375 qualifying veterans.

The $1,000 per semester award is given on a first-come, first-served basis to students completing a minimum of twelve credit hours per semester. Award can be applied for until the eighth anniversary of the veteran's separation date, or when the student has received the award for a total of eight semesters.

Eligibility and residency requirements:

- Be a Tennessee resident for one year prior to application.
- Be admitted to an eligible institution of higher education for an associate or bachelor's degree.
- Received an honorable discharge.
- Veteran received the Iraq Campaign Medal, Afghanistan Campaign Medal, or Global War on Terrorism Expeditionary Medal on or after September 1, 2001.
- Not be in default on any federal student aid programs or Tennessee student financial aid programs.
- Veteran does not have a bachelor's degree already.
- Is not in jail (that's right . . . you heard me—stated as such on the website).

TEXAS

http://veterans.portal.texas.gov/en/Pages/education.aspx

Benefit

- Hazlewood tuition waivers at state institutions

Eligible schools can be found on the Public School list at http://www.collegeforalltexans.com/index.cfm?ObjectID=D57D0AC5-AB2D-EFB0-FC201080B528442A. The award covers tuition, dues, fees, and other required charges up to 150 semester hours. The award will not cover room and board, books, student services fees, or deposit fees. The waiver can be used for undergraduate and graduate classes. Teacher certification fees, aircraft flight training courses, and distance-learning classes may also be covered (verify with the school).

Eligibility and residency requirements:

- At the time of entry into the military was a Texas state resident, designated Texas as home of record, or entered the service in Texas.

- Veteran served a minimum of 181 days of active duty.
- Received an honorable discharge and provide proof.
- Exhausted Post 9/11 GI Bill benefits.
- Veteran is not in default on state-guaranteed student loans.
- Must reside in Texas during the semester the exemption is being claimed (new rule started in fall 2011).

Note: Veterans are not able to double-dip with Post 9/11 and Hazlewood at the same time. Texas schools maintain a great amount of control over Hazlewood Act usage at its institutions. In most cases, veterans stay with Post 9/11. The Hazlewood Act's goal is to cover tuition at state-supported institutions if an eligible individual runs out of GI Bill benefit. Always contact the vet reps at your institution of choice prior to making any final decisions.

Benefit

- Legacy Program

Children may be eligible to have unused Hazlewood benefits transferred to them. The award can only be used at state-supported institutions. A list of eligible schools can be found at http://www.collegeforalltexans.com/index.cfm?ObjectID=D57D0AC5-AB2D-EFB0-FC201080B528442A under the Public School list. The award covers tuition, dues, fees, and other required charges up to 150 semester hours. The award will not cover room and board, books, student services fees, or deposit fees.

Eligibility and residency requirements:

- Veteran was a Texas state resident when he or she entered the military, designated Texas as home of record, or entered the service in Texas.
- Child must be the biological child, stepchild, adopted child, or claimed as a dependent in the current or previous tax year.
- Be under the age of twenty-five at the beginning of any term for which the benefit is being claimed (some exemptions may apply).
- Make satisfactory academic progress.
- Provide proof of veteran's honorable discharge.

Benefit

- Combat Tuition Exemption

Dependent children of service members deployed in combat zones receive tuition waivers (fees not exempted).
   Eligibility and residency requirements:

- Child must be a resident of Texas, or entitled to receive the in-state tuition rate (dependents of military personnel stationed in Texas).
- Must be enrolled during the time the service member is deployed in combat zone.
- If out-of-state resident, child may need to provide copy of parent's orders.

UTAH

http://veterans.utah.gov/state-benefits/

Benefit

- Purple Heart recipients are eligible for tuition waivers at state schools.

Award works for undergraduate and graduate programs. Veterans who were eligible for this benefit should be able to complete a bachelor's and master's degree with little or no debt.
   Eligibility and residency requirements:

- Show proof of Purple Heart.
- Be a Utah state resident.

VIRGIN ISLANDS

http://www.militaryvi.org/benefits/

Benefit

- Free tuition is offered for attendance at local public educational institutions and at the University of the Virgin Islands.

This program is for veterans who entered the Armed Forces while residing in the Virgin Islands. Contact the schools for more information.

WASHINGTON

http://www.dva.wa.gov/education.html

Benefit

• Full or partial tuition waivers at state schools for undergraduate education for up to two hundred quarter credits (or equivalent semester credits).

Some schools offer the waiver for graduate programs (check with your institution). Full- or part-time enrollment is eligible. Award may work at some private institutions. Be aware that the tuition may not be fully covered.
  Eligibility and residency requirements:

• Make satisfactory academic progress.
• Have served in a war or conflict fought on foreign soil or in international waters or in another location in support of those serving on foreign soil or in international waters.
• Received an honorable discharge.
• Be a resident of the state.

WEST VIRGINIA

http://www.veterans.wv.gov/Pages/default.aspx

Benefit

• West Virginia Veteran's Re-Education Scholarship Program

Eligible veterans can receive $500 per term (part-time students, $250). Amount cannot exceed a total of $1,500 per academic year. Program funding may be used to cover professional exam costs as well. Eligible veterans may use the scholarship in tandem with the Workforce Investment Act (WIA) and/or Trade Adjustment Act (TAA) if program cost exceeds the amount allocated under the other two programs.

Eligibility and residency requirements:

- Veteran must be a resident of the state.
- Received an honorable discharge.
- Served 181 consecutive days on active duty.
- Eligible for Pell Grant or unemployed.
- Veteran has exhausted all federal GI Bill money possibilities (including Vocational Rehabilitation, if eligible).

WISCONSIN

www.wisvets.com/wisgibill

Benefit

- Wisconsin GI Bill tuition remission benefit program (WI GI Bill)

Remission of tuition and fees at state institutions (University of Wisconsin and Wisconsin Technical Colleges) for eligible veterans and dependents. The award is good for a maximum of eight semesters (or 128 semester credits), undergraduate and graduate education, and professional programs. There are no income restrictions or delimiting periods. Many fees are not covered, such as books, meals, room and board, and online fees. Award cannot be combined with federal benefits.

Eligibility and residency requirements:

- Veteran must have served since September 10, 2001, and entered the service from Wisconsin.
- Must apply for Post 9/11 GI Bill benefits first, if eligible. Talk to an education counselor or the veterans' representatives before you elect which GI Bill you will use.
- Children and spouses of veterans with a combined rating of 30 percent or greater from the VA may be eligible for the award.
- Child must be biological, stepchild, adopted child, or any other child who is a member of the veteran's household.
- Child must be at least seventeen but no older than twenty-six, and a resident of the state.
- Spouse must be a resident of the state for tuition purposes.

- Spouse has ten years from the date of the veteran's VA rating to use the benefit.

The most clearly written information on eligibility for the state education benefits can be found at http://dva.state.wi.us/WebForms/WDVA_B0105_ Wisconsin_Tuition_Programs_WI_GI_Bill_Color.pdf.

The state of Wisconsin does not allow veterans to double-dip on federal and state-based benefits. However, if veterans paid into MGIB and if the MHA under Post 9/11 at the school they want to attend is less than what they would have received under MGIB, the school will reimburse the veteran for the difference. Talk to the veterans' representatives at the institutions for more information.

Benefit

- Veterans Education (VetEd) Reimbursement (www.WisVets.com/VetEd)

Reimbursement grant program. Reimburses veterans after successful completion of coursework (University of Wisconsin locations, Wisconsin Technical Colleges, or a private institution of higher education in Wisconsin or Minnesota) at the undergraduate level only. Reimbursement is prorated based on aggregate length of qualifying active-duty service. Veterans with a minimum of 30 percent of qualifying disability from the VA are reimbursed at 100 percent.

Eligibility and residency requirements:

- Veteran entered active duty as a Wisconsin resident, or lived in Wisconsin for twelve months prior to entering the service.
- If veteran was discharged more than ten years ago, only reimbursement at the part-time rate is possible.
- Exhaust all other benefits first (including WI State GI Bill).
- Maximum income limit applies (annual income of veteran and spouse cannot exceed $50,000, plus $1,000 for each dependent beyond two). Provide proof of income (AGI from current tax return).
- Not already possess a bachelor's degree.
- Not be delinquent on child-support payments.
- Maintain a 2.0 GPA.

WYOMING

http://www.communitycolleges.wy.edu/Data/Sites/1/commissionFiles/
  Programs/Veteran/_doc/statue-19-14-106.pdf
https://sites.google.com/a/wyo.gov/wyomingmilitarydepartment/vete-
  rans-commission/res#TOC-Tuition-Assistance-for-Veterans-and-Sur-
  viving-Dependents

Benefit

• Free tuition and fees for overseas combat veterans.

Award can be used at the University of Wyoming and the state community colleges. Eligible veterans can receive ten semesters of schooling through this benefit.

Eligibility and residency requirements:

• Veteran must have had residency in state for a minimum of one year prior to entering service.
• Home of residence on DD214 states Wyoming.
• Honorable discharge.
• Received the Armed Forces Expeditionary Medal or campaign medal for service in any conflict in a foreign country (list of qualifying medals is found at http://www.communitycolleges.wy.edu/Data/Sites/1/commissionFiles/Programs/Veteran/_doc/expeditionary-medal-list--2-jul-07.pdf).
• Maintain a 2.0 GPA.
• Veteran has eight years from date of acceptance into program to use it.

STATE-BASED EDUCATION BENEFITS BASED ON SEVERE LEVELS OF DISABILITY/OR DEATH

Other states besides those listed above offer education benefits for spouses and/or children. In the case of these states, the veteran must be severely and permanently disabled, or have died while on active duty service (in many cases, in combat or combat-related situations). I am not going to cover the specific details of these benefits, but below you will find a list of the states that offer this benefit and the links to their websites:

Alabama: http://www.va.state.al.us/gi_dep_scholarship.aspx

Alaska: http://www.veterans.alaska.gov/education-benefits.html

Arkansas: http://www.veterans.arkansas.gov/benefits.html#edu

California: https://www.calvet.ca.gov/VetServices/Pages/College-Fee-Waiver.aspx

Delaware: http://veteransaffairs.delaware.gov/veterans_benefits.shtml

Florida: http://floridavets.org/?page_id=60

Iowa: http://www.in.gov/dva/2378.htm

Kentucky: http://veterans.ky.gov/Benefits/Documents/KDVAInfoBook-letIssueAugust2010.pdf

Louisiana: http://vetaffairs.la.gov/Programs/Education.aspx

Maine: http://www.maine.gov/dvem/bvs/VDEB_2.pdf

Maryland: http://veterans.maryland.gov/wp-content/uploads/sites/2/2013/10/MDBenefitsGuide.pdf

Massachusetts: http://www.mass.gov/veterans/education/for-family/mslf.html

Michigan: http://www.michigan.gov/dmva/0,4569,7-126-2362-305076--,00.html

Minnesota: http://www.mdva.state.mn.us/education/SurvivingSpouse DependentInformationSheet.pdf

Missouri: http://mvc.dps.mo.gov/docs/veterans-benefits-guide.pdf

Montana: http://life.umt.edu/finaid/tuition-waivers/mt-veteran.php, http://wsd.dli.mt.gov/veterans/vetstatebenefits.asp

Nebraska: http://www.vets.state.ne.us/waiver.html

New Hampshire: http://www.nh.gov/nhveterans/benefits/education.htm

New Jersey: http://www.state.nj.us/military/veterans/programs.html

New Mexico: http://www.dvs.state.nm.us/benefits.html

New York: http://www.veterans.ny.gov/

North   Carolina: http://www.doa.nc.gov/vets/benefitslist.aspx?pid= scholarships

North Dakota: http://www.nd.gov/veterans/benefits/nd-dependent-tuition -waiver

Ohio: https://www.ohiohighered.org/ohio-war-orphans

Oregon: http://www.ous.edu/stucoun/prospstu/vb

Pennsylvania: http://www.portal.state.pa.us/portal/server.pt/community/ veterans_benefits/11386/disabled_benefits/567417,   http://www.pheaa.org/ funding-opportunities/other-educational-aid/postsecondary-educational-gratuity.shtml the maximum monthly increase of $150. After paying the full buy-up amount, the MGIB monthly payments increase to $1,714. Remember, these amounts will change yearly as the cost of living (COLA) increases.

Seaman Stevens will double-dip on IVG and MGIB. IVG will pay the school tuition, and he will collect $1,714 per month under MGIB as opposed to $1,047 per month under the MHA on Post 9/11. That is a difference of $667 per month. Over the course of a nine-month school year, the veteran earns an extra $6,003—a much better deal all around! But, remember, once you select Post 9/11 you can never return to MGIB, so make an educated decision.

Benefit

• Children of Veterans Scholarship:

  http://www.osfa.uiuc.edu/aid/scholarships/waivers_COV.html

Each county in the state is authorized one scholarship yearly at the University of Illinois for children of veterans of World War I, World War II, the Korean War, the Vietnam Conflict, Operation Enduring Freedom, or Operation Iraqi Freedom. Children of deceased and disabled veterans are given priority. These children can receive four consecutive years tuition-free (undergraduate, graduate, or professional studies) at the University of Illinois (Urbana-Champaign, Chicago Health Sciences Center, or Springfield Campus). See http://www.osfa.uiuc.edu/aid/scholarships/waivers_COV.html.

INDIANA

http://www.in.gov/dva/2378.htm

Benefit

• Indiana Purple Heart Recipients receive free tuition at the resident tuition rate for 124 semester credit hours at state-supported postsecondary schools for undergraduate study only.

  Eligibility and residency requirements:

• Entered service from a permanent home address in Indiana.

South Carolina: http://www.govoepp.state.sc.us/va/documents/ftapp.pdf

South Dakota: http://vetaffairs.sd.gov/benefits/State/State%20Education%20Programs.aspx

Tennessee: http://www.state.tn.us/veteran/state_benifits/dep_tuition.html

Texas: http://www.tvc.texas.gov/Hazlewood-Act.aspx

Utah: http://veterans.utah.gov/category/education/

Virginia: http://www.dvs.virginia.gov/veterans-benefits.shtml

Washington: http://www.dva.wa.gov/dependentstuitionwaiver.html

Wisconsin: http://dva.state.wi.us/Ben-education.asp#Tuition

West Virginia: http://www.veterans.wv.gov/assistance/Pages/default.aspx

Wyoming: https://sites.google.com/a/wyo.gov/wyomingmilitarydepartment/veterans-commission/res

SCHOLARSHIPS

For some reason, sailors are loath to apply for scholarships, but military dependents are always ready and prepared to write. Last year, I helped the dependent daughter of a gunnery sergeant friend with several essays for submission to scholarships. She was awarded close to $15,000 for her first year of college! That was a large pot of easy money to help with school. Sound good? If so, read on.

Although quite a bit of scholarship money is available for veterans, you must be proactive in your pursuit. No one is going to hand you the money without you making an effort. Applying for scholarships is not as difficult as it seems. Oftentimes, you can reuse information, so keep everything you write. Most education centers have financial aid packets available for you to pick up or posted on their websites (e.g., Camp Pendleton, http://mccscp.com/jec). These packets offer a good place to start your search.

Try to remember that the active duty TA money only goes so far. TA does not cover books, tools, computers, and so on. You should run the numbers before you start. For example, California State University, Long Beach (CSULB), estimated the 2013–2014 school year book costs at $1,788. Currently, if a veteran is attending school full-time, the maximum book stipend awarded under the Post 9/11 GI Bill is $1,000 per academic year. That leaves a gap of $788 for the veteran attending CSULB to cover out of pocket. In either case, applying for scholarships is a wise move, although not your only option.

Scholarships come in all shapes and sizes. You will need to determine which scholarships may apply to you. Do not limit yourself to veteran-based possibilities; you can apply for civilian scholarships as well. Most break down into specific categories, such as pursuit of study, age, gender, race, disability, state based, or school based.

When you begin your search, remember that it will take some time to find and determine eligibility. Start by making a quick search on your school's website. Many schools list scholarships specific to their institution right on their own pages. Check with your school's veterans' representatives, the financial aid department, and the local education center for possible scholarship opportunities. Libraries are an underused resource for scholarship opportunities. Check opportunities based on options outside your military experience; then check opportunities based on options in the military community. Prepare the best essay possible, and see if someone in the education center is willing to proofread it for you. Always start far, far in advance. Most scholarships are due during the spring semester in order to pay out for the following fall.

Be very careful of organizations demanding you pay money in order to be eligible for a scholarship. Scholarship information is widely available, and you should not have to pay to find, receive, or complete an application. Most certainly, *never* give any credit card information. If you need help, contact your school's financial aid department.

MILITARY SERVICE-RELATED SCHOLARSHIPS

The following are just a few of the scholarships available to service members. See what might be relevant to you. At the end of the section, several scholarship search sites are listed.

Pat Tillman Scholarship

http://www.pattillmanfoundation.org/tillman-military-scholars/apply/
(480) 621-4074
info@pattillmanfoundation.org

Award amount varies every year. This year's awards per scholar averaged $11,000. That would be money above and beyond your GI Bill. Active duty, veterans, and spouses of both categories are eligible to apply. Applicant must be attending school full-time at a four-year university or college (public or private) at the undergraduate or graduate level. This scholarship is a great opportunity for graduate school students, because options at that level are more difficult to find. Applicant must apply for Federal Financial Aid (FAFSA). Digital files of the applicant's DD214 or personal service record and résumé will be required in order to submit, as well as responding to the two essay prompts. Those who proceed further will need to turn in their financial aid award letter (from attending institution), SAR report from FAFSA, and a photo highlighting the applicable individual's military service. Application opens in January and closes the following month. Check the website for more information.

American Veterans (AMVETS)

http://www.amvets.org/pdfs/programs_pdfs/scholarship_application_
    veteran.pdf
(877) 726-8387

Award amount is $4,000 over four years. Applicant must be pursuing full-time study at the undergraduate, graduate, or certification level from an accredited institution. Three scholarships awarded annually. Application is due by April 15. Applicant must be a veteran, be a U.S. citizen, and have financial need. Required materials include the veteran's DD214, official school transcripts, a completed (and signed) 1040 form, a completed FAFSA application, an essay of fifty to one hundred words addressing a specific prompt (see website), a résumé (see website), and proof of school-based expenses.

American Veterans (AMVETS) National Ladies Auxiliary

http://amvetsaux.org/assets/national-scholarship-application.pdf
(301) 459-6255

Two scholarships at $1,000 each and up to five scholarships at $750 each may be available. In order to be eligible, applicant must be a current member of the AMVETS Ladies Auxiliary or a son or daughter, stepchild, or grandchild or stepgrandchild of a member. Application can be filled out starting in the eligible individual's second year of undergraduate study at an eligible institution. Required documents include a personal essay of two hundred to five hundred words (see website for more information), three letters of recommendation, official transcripts, a copy of the member's membership card, and all required paperwork from the Ladies Auxiliary. Applications are due by July 1.

Military Order of the Purple Heart (MOPH)

http://www.purpleheart.org/scholarships/Default.aspx
http://www.purpleheart.org/Downloads/Forms/ScholarshipApplication
.pdf
(703) 642-5360
scholarship@purpleheart.org

Be aware that this scholarship demands a $15 payment at time of submittal. Applicant must be a Purple Heart recipient and a member of the Military Order of the Purple Heart, or a spouse, widow, child (step and adopted), or grandchild. Student must currently be a high school senior or attending college as an undergraduate student full-time (or attending trade school), and have a minimum 2.75 GPA on a 4.0 scale. Applicant must submit an essay of two hundred to three hundred words (see site for prompt), two letters of recommendation, all other required materials, and the $15 fee (check or money order).

American Legion Auxiliary

http://www.alaforveterans.org/Scholarships/Non-Traditional-Student-
Scholarship/

Approximately five scholarships at $2,000 each are awarded to applicants who are members of the American Legion, American Legion Auxiliary, or Sons of the American Legion. Members must have paid dues for a minimum of two years prior to applying. Applicants must be nontraditional students (going back to school after an absence or starting later in life). Applications are due by March 1.

Veterans of Foreign Wars (VFW)

http://www.vfw.org/Scholarship/
816-756-3390, ext. 220

Twenty-five annual scholarships for VFW members who served or are currently serving in one of the branches, or members of their immediate family. Five scholarships per branch will be awarded at $3,000 apiece. If already separated, the EAS date must have been within thirty-six months before the December 31 annual deadline.

Armed Forces Communications and Electronics Association (AFCEA)

http://www.afcea.org/education/scholarships/undergraduate/military.asp
(703) 631-6100

Three scholarships are available to eligible veterans through the AFCEA: the Military Personnel/Dependents Scholarship, the Afghanistan and Iraq War Veterans Scholarship, and the Disabled War Veterans Scholarship (Afghanistan or Iraq).

The Military Personnel/Dependents Scholarship awards $2,000. Active-duty service members, veterans, dependents, and spouses may apply, but they must be attending a four-year institution (no community college) full-time. Active-duty members and veterans can apply in their first year of school; however, spouses and dependents must be in their second year at minimum.

AFCEA scholarships require certain fields of study, such as electrical, chemical, systems, or aerospace engineering; mathematics, physics, science, or mathematics education; technology management; management information systems; or computer science. Majors of study that support U.S. intelligence initiatives or national security may be eligible as well, if the subjects are applicable to the purpose of AFCEA.

Transcripts and two letters of recommendation from faculty members are mandatory.

Disabled American Veterans Auxiliary

http://auxiliary.dav.org/membership/Programs.aspx
(877) 426-2838 ext. 4020

Life members with the DAV Auxiliary who are attending a college or vocational school full-time can participate in the scholarship program. The scholarship maxes out at $1,500. Part-time pursuit of study may be eligible for $750. Applicants must maintain a minimum of twelve credit hours per semester to remain eligible. Renewals are not guaranteed.

Society of Sponsors of the United States Navy Centennial Scholarship

http://societyofsponsorsofusn.org/scholarship-program/

Applicant must be combat-wounded Iraq or Afghanistan veteran (or spouse) with an associate degree (or equivalent credits), pursuing a bachelor's degree (full-time) leading to a teacher credential. Five $3,000 scholarships will be awarded annually. Applications can be submitted throughout the academic year (August–May) for open enrollment.

Navy and Marine Corps Relief Society

Navy and Marine Corps Wounded Veterans
http://www.nmcrs.org/pages/education-loans-and-scholarships

Navy and Marine Corps wounded veterans of OIF, OEF, Operation New Dawn, or those wounded in operational deployments, major training exercises, or operational mishaps may be eligible for $3,000 scholarships. Applicant must be pursuing a degree in a teaching profession. Spouses of Wounded Warriors may be eligible as well (teaching profession, medical, or medical-related fields only).

MECEP or MECP Programs-LOAN

http://www.nmcrs.org/pages/education-loans-and-scholarships

Active-duty Marines and sailors accepted into the Marine Enlisted Commissioning Education Program (MECEP) or Medical Enlisted Commissioning Program (MECP) may be eligible to apply for a $500–3,000 loan per year through NMCRS. The interest-free loan must be paid back within forty-eight months of commissioning.

SCHOOL-BASED SCHOLARSHIPS

Many schools offer internal scholarships. Speak to the financial aid department of your chosen institution to find out about opportunities. This section demonstrates just a few of the scholarships available around the country.

Florida

Santa Fe College

Jeffrey Mattison Wershow Memorial Scholarship
http://m.sfcollege.edu/development/index.php?section=info/JeffreyMatti-sonWershowMemorial

Applicant must have received an honorable discharge (but can still be on active duty) and must maintain a 2.5 GPA for award renewal. Award amount is $1,600 per year, or $800 per semester. Application demands a thousand-word essay pertaining to student's education (see website) and three letters of recommendation (see website).

Idaho

Idaho State University

Iwo Jima Scholarship
http://www.isu.edu/scholar/forms/IwoJimaAnn.pdf

The Iwo Jima Scholarship may be available to a descendant of World War II veterans (preference for those who served at Iwo Jima). Applicant must have a 3.0 GPA to be eligible, and preference is given to engineering majors. Personal statement and discharge papers are required (see website).

Kansas

Johnston County Community College

Veterans Scholarship
http://www.jccc.edu/financialaid/scholarships/institutional-scholarships/veterans/avetrn.html

This scholarship is designed to assist veterans who are reentering the workforce or higher education after being discharged from active duty or deployment. Funding is available to veterans who have been discharged within six months of the first day of classes of the semester they plan to enroll at JCCC. The scholarship will be applied to tuition and book costs, with no cash going directly to the student. Books must be purchased at the JCCC bookstore.

Dixon Memorial Veterans Scholarship
http://www.jccc.edu/financialaid/scholarships/institutional-scholarships/
veterans/fdixvt.html
913-469-3840

Veteran applying for scholarship must have completed a minimum of nine credit hours prior to submitting application. Applicant must demonstrate need and have at least a 2.5 GPA. Student must be enrolled in a minimum of nine credit hours to receive the $500 award and must have submitted all required documents (see website), including a FAFSA application.

Maryland

Wor-Wic Community College

Salisbury Optimist Scholarship
http://www.worwic.edu/StudentServices/FinancialAidScholarships/
LocalNeedBasedScholarships.aspx

Applicant must be a resident of Wicomico County, Maryland; must enroll at the college within two years of returning from the military; and must demonstrate financial need. A GPA of 3.0 is necessary to apply.

Michigan

Michigan State University

MSU Disabled Veteran's Assistance Program
http://finaid.msu.edu/veterans.asp

New and returning undergraduate veterans with a military-related disability who are Michigan residents and working on their first baccalaureate degree potentially qualify for an aid package that covers all costs.

Minnesota

University of Minnesota Duluth

LaVerne Noyes Scholarship
http://www.d.umn.edu/onestop/student-finances/financial-aid/types/
scholarships/umd-current.html

This scholarship is available to students attending the University of Minnesota Duluth. Applicant must be a direct blood descendant of a military member who served in the U.S. Army or Navy in World War I and died in service or received an honorable discharge. Applicant must demonstrate financial need. Award is $1,000.

New York

Cornell University Law School

Dickson Randolph Knott Memorial
http://www.lawschool.cornell.edu/alumni/giving/endowed_funds/
    scholarships_g-l.cfm

Applicant must be a military veteran enrolled in the law school (see website for more information).

Monroe Community College

Donald W. Holleder Endowed Scholarship
http://www.monroecc.edu/depts/finaid/documents/scholarshipbrochure-
    listing2012_2013.pdf

Applicant must demonstrate financial need, and preference is given to Vietnam veterans and their dependents. Award is for $600 per year.

Hilbert College

Sgt. Martin F. Bogdanowicz Memorial Scholarship
http://www.hilbert.edu/admissions/student-aid/scholarships-grants

Scholarship is for entering freshman veterans (or their children).

Ohio

Cedarville University

James Cain Special Education Award
http://publications.cedarville.edu/academiccatalogs/2008-2009/files/
    assets/basic-html/page270.html

Full-time sophomore, junior, or senior students at the university majoring in special education (intent on teaching kids with special needs) may apply.

Applicant must demonstrate financial need, and preference is given to certain populations, including those who have served in the military.

Texas

Angelina College

Disabled American Veterans Scholarship
http://www.angelina.edu/giving-scholarships/

Applicant must be a descendant of a member of the DAV. Award is $500 per semester for full-time study.

Texas Christian University

Adrienne Miller Perner Scholarship
http://www.dance.tcu.edu/financialaid.asp
(817) 257-7615

Amount varies. Applicant must be a child or grandchild of a career military service member. Applicant must also be female and majoring in ballet. Scholarship is based on talent or community work.

Utah

Westminster College

Doris Edwards Miller Endowed Scholarship
http://www.westminstercollege.edu/pdf/financial_aid_current/
0910schlplist.pdf

This scholarship is available to veterans or their children, but both must demonstrate need. Full-time enrollment is mandatory in order to be eligible for this scholarship (eight at $3,500 each).

SCHOLARSHIP POSSIBILITIES FOR DEPENDENTS

Below is a list of scholarships available for spouses and dependent children. Always check with the Naval Officers' Spouses Club (NOSC) at the base where you are stationed if you are still on active duty with the Navy. The NOSCs usually have scholarship possibilities every year. The National Military Family Association has a list of military bases with officer spousal clubs that offer scholarship opportunities, at http://www.militaryfamily.org/get-info/spouse-education/financial-assistance/spouse-club-scholarships.html.

Ladies Auxiliary VFW

Continuing Education Scholarship
https://www.ladiesauxvfw.org/programs-page/scholarships/

Spouses, sons, and daughters of members may be eligible if they are pursuing a college degree or career pathway at a technical school.

Fisher House

http://www.militaryscholar.org/

Run by the commissaries. A minimum of one $2,000 scholarship is awarded through every commissary location, although more might be possible depending on funding. Award may be used for payment of tuition, books, lab fees, or other education-related expenses. Scholarship is open to children of active-duty, retired, or reserve service members. Applicant must have a minimum of a 3.0 GPA on a 4.0 scale.

The Joanne Holbrook Patton Military Spouse Scholarships

For spouses of active-duty, retired, and reserve service members. Award may be used for tuition, fees, or school room and board. The scholarship offers assistance for GED or ESL, vocational training or certification, undergraduate or graduate degrees, licensure fees, and clinical hours for mental health licensure. Applicants can attend face-to-face schooling or online.

American Legion

http://www.legion.org/scholarships

Samsung American Legion Scholarship

For high school juniors who complete a Boys State or Girls State program. Applicant must also be a direct descendant of an eligible wartime veteran (see website for more information). Scholarship is for undergraduate study only and is based on financial need. It can be used for tuition, books, fees, or room and board. Applicants must have completed a Boys State or Girls State program, be direct descendants or legally adopted children of wartime veterans (must be eligible for American Legion membership), and be in their junior year of high school. Award is up to $20,000 for an undergraduate course of study. Winners are selected based upon academic record, financial need, and participation in community activities. Application requires several mini-essays.

Legacy Scholarship

http://www.legion.org/scholarships/legacy

Eligible applicants are children or adopted children of military members who died while on active duty on or after September 11, 2001; are high school seniors or already graduated; and are pursuing an undergraduate degree.

The Baseball Scholarship

http://www.legion.org/scholarships/baseball
baseball@legion.org

Applicant must have graduated high school, be on a team affiliated with an American Legion post, and be on a 2013 roster filed with the national headquarters. High school transcripts, three letters of testimony, and a completed application must be filed.

National High School Oratorical Contest Scholarship

http://www.legion.org/scholarships/oratorical
oratorical@legion.org

Scholarship money (up to $18,000 for first place) can be used at any college or university within the United States. Scholarship has hundreds of small rewards involved at local levels.

Navy and Marine Corps Relief Society

http://www.nmcrs.org/pages/education-loans-and-scholarships

Children and spouses of active or retired military may be eligible to apply for interest-free loans and scholarships that range from $500 to $2,500. Applicant must be pursuing full-time study and demonstrate financial need. Loans must be paid back within twenty-four months. Scholarships are only available to spouses and children of service members who died on active duty or in retirement.

Department of Michigan-American Legion Auxiliary

http://michalaux.org/

Medical Career Scholarship

Applicants should be daughters, granddaughters, great-granddaughters, sons, grandsons, or great-grandsons of honorably discharged or deceased veterans of specific conflicts (World War I, World War II, Korea, Vietnam, Persian Gulf, etc.) and be living in Michigan. Award is $500 for tuition, room and board fees, books, and so on. Scholarship must be used at a school in Michigan, and applicants must be in their senior year of high school (top quarter of their class) and preparing to enter college. This is a need-based scholarship.

Scholarship for Nontraditional Students

One two-year scholarship of $500 per year will be awarded. Applicant must be the descendant of a veteran, over the age of twenty-two, and attending college or trade school for the first time or attending college after a significantly long break. The award may be used toward tuition and books at a school in the state of Michigan. Entries are due by March 15. Application includes short essays.

National American Legion Auxiliary

Children of Warriors Scholarship National Presidents' Scholarship

Fifteen scholarships were awarded in 2012–2013. Applicants must be daughters or sons, stepdaughters or stepsons, grandsons or granddaughters, stepgrandsons or stepgranddaughters, or stepgreat-grandsons or stepgreat-granddaughters of eligible American Legion members. Applicants should be in their senior year of high school and complete fifty hours of volunteer service. Completed applications and all documentation (includes an essay) are due to the local American Legion Auxiliary Unit by March 1, and winners are announced on March 15.

Spirit of Youth Scholarship

Five awards at $5,000 each for this scholarship. Applicants must be seniors in high school and junior members of the American Legion Auxiliary for the past three years, hold current membership, and continue membership throughout awarding years. A 3.0 GPA is mandatory for individuals applying for this scholarship. Applications are due by March 1; winners are announced March 15. ACT or SAT scores, high school transcripts, four letters of recommendation, a completed FAFSA application, and essays are required.

Marine Corps Scholarship Foundation

http://www.mcsf.org/eligibility
(703) 549-0060

Applicants must be the son or daughter of one of the following:

- Active-duty or reserve U.S. Marine
- Veteran U.S. Marine who has received an honorable discharge, medical discharge, was wounded, or was killed while serving in the U.S. Marine Corps
- Active-duty or reserve U.S. Navy corpsman who is serving or has served with a U.S. Marine unit
- Veteran U.S. Navy corpsman who has served with a U.S. Marine unit and has received an honorable discharge, medical discharge, was wounded, or was killed in the U.S. Navy

Applicants must meet the following eligibility criteria:

- Plan to attend an accredited undergraduate college or vocational/technical institution in the upcoming academic year to pursue a first bachelor's degree or technical certificate. Students attending federal service academies or pursing graduate degrees are not eligible.
- Family adjusted gross income for the 2012 tax year that does not exceed $91,000. Nontaxable allowances are not included in determining adjusted gross income.
- GPA of at least 2.0 (on a 4.0 scale).

Heroes Tribute Scholarship Program for Children of the Fallen

The Scholarship Foundation guarantees scholarships of up to $30,000 over four years ($7,500 a year) to the following:

- Children of Marines and veteran Marines who were killed in the terrorist attacks on September 11, 2001
- Children of Marines and children of Navy corpsmen attached to a Marine unit who were killed in combat after September 11, 2001
- Children of Navy Religious Program specialists attached to a Marine unit who were killed in combat on or after September 27, 2008
- Children of Marines who were killed in training after September 27, 2008

Heroes Tribute Scholarship Program for Children of the Fallen applicants must meet the established eligibility criteria, excluding the income eligibility requirement.

Limited grandchildren eligibility: The Marine Corps Scholarship Foundation administers scholarship programs of several Marine Corps associations that offer scholarships to the grandchildren of their members. To qualify, a student must provide proof of their grandparent's membership in one of the following associations *and* meet the established eligibility criteria. There are no exceptions.

- 4th Marine Division Association of World War II
- 5th Marine Division Association of World War II
- 6th Marine Division Association of World War II
- 531 Gray Ghost Squadron Association
- 3rd Battalion/26th Marines
- Basic Class 3-56 Graduate

Other extremely noteworthy options:

The American Military Retirees Scholarships:

http://amra1973.org/Scholarship/

The Mike Weston Memorial Scholarship Fund:

http://www.pendleton.marines.mil/Portals/98/Docs/SLO/2013%20Weston%20Book%20Scholarship%20description_1.pdf

Federal sites for scholarship searches:

> http://www.careerinfonet.org/scholarshipsearch/ScholarshipCatego-
>   ry.asp?searchtype=category&nodeid=22
> http://studentaid.ed.gov/

Searches:

> https://www.horatioalger.org/scholarships/index.cfm
> http://www.collegescholarships.org/scholarships/army.htm
> http://www.finaid.org/military/veterans.phtml
> www.scholarships.com
> www.collegeboard.org
> http://www.scholarships4students.com/council_of_college_and_
>   military_educators_scholarship.htm
> http://scholarshipamerica.org/
> www.careeronestop.org
> www.collegedata.com
> http://www.finaid.org/scholarships/
> http://fedmoney.org/
> www.militaryonesource.com

TEXTBOOK BUYING OPTIONS

Who knew books could be so expensive? Welcome to college! The cost of books can be out of control. The Post 9/11 GI Bill maxes out at $1,000 per academic year for books and supplies, and often that does not begin to cover the bill. If you are still on active duty, you already know that TA does not cover books.

College books are notoriously expensive. Unlike high school, a year of college requires an incredible number of books. Professors have to find supplemental materials to feed your brain and back up the information with proof. Books are still the most common, easiest way of accomplishing this task.

Now you know why you need them, but not why college books are so expensive. A few reasons come to mind: for example, copyrighted material, specialized material, and online supplements. College books can hold an incredible amount of copyrighted material. Publishers have to cover the copyright fees, as well as all other fees, within the cost of the book. Information within college books is usually quite specialized and often not found elsewhere. This means the books do not have another avenue for sales, which contributes to a highly competitive market, driving up the cost. Many books also have online supplements attached to them, and those fees must be included in the cost.

Last—although I hate addressing this reason, but feel I must—many professors have written books. Can you guess which books could be included in your reading list? Terrible, I agree . . . because professors get royalties just like other authors. Let's think more positively about the situation. These books can be among your most informative and easily organized reference material. Professors often write books based on the knowledge they have derived from their years in the classroom and field experience to help themselves or others teach. Many schools take pride in having such accomplished professors on staff. Speaking from personal experience, being published is no easy feat. This practice may sometimes help a professor cut down on the book expenses for his or her students because the book follows along closely with the class's learning expectations, thereby allowing the student to purchase one book, or at least fewer books than previously necessary.

Although many other reasons contribute to book costs, this is the reason you are reading this section: how to pay for them. The first trip to the bookstore can be excruciating as reality sets in. Do not stress; other options may exist. Because many books top the $100 range (sometimes closer to $200), students should spend as much time as feasible trying to find books from alternate sources.

I still recommend checking the campus bookstore first. Some schools maintain significant used textbook sections. You will need to get to the store as early as possible to take advantage of this possibility; discounted books will be the first ones to leave the shelves. See if you can sell back your books at the end of the semester. Most likely, the store will offer you a greatly reduced amount. Think of it as "a little cash is better than none," and you can roll that money into your textbooks for the following semester.

Next, you can try either renting or buying the books used online. Which path you choose depends on whether you want to keep the books. Personally, because books change every few years and the information in them becomes outdated at such a fast pace, I only kept my French books. The language was not changing, so I figured I would keep them for future reference.

An astounding number of sites on the Internet sell or rent used textbooks. Even some bigwigs have gotten into the game. Amazon has a used textbook section (www.amazon.com/New-Used-Textbooks-Books/b?ie=UTF8&node

=465600) that may suit all of your needs. It enables users to refer friends and earn $5 credits. Although $5 may not seem like much, if you are the first in your group to start referring friends, you could end up with a stash of extra money to help cover your own textbook expenses.

Amazon also allows users to sell back books for Amazon gift cards. If you would prefer to rent (yes, for a full semester!), the site has that option available to users. If you are an Amazon Prime member (payment required: join as a student and receive a discount), you can receive your shipment in two days; otherwise, orders over $25 receive free shipping but will run on regular shipment time frames. Lastly, you can rent or buy Kindle Textbooks for Kindle Fire Tablets, or put the Kindle application on your iPad, Android tablet, PC, or Mac, and read it on your own device. You can rent the eText-books for an amount of time you specify. When you pick a book, Amazon lets you set the return date, although the price goes up the longer you keep the book.

Barnes & Noble offers the same services as Amazon (see www. barnesandnoble.com/u/textbooks-college-textbooks/379002366/). You can receive a check from the store and even get a quick quote by entering some easy information on the website. The eTextbooks offered through B&N can be viewed with a seven-day free trial before purchasing on your PC or Mac (not available for the actual NOOK device or mobile phones). This may come in handy if you are looking for an older version to save money. Make sure you compare the older version against a new version before purchasing. The eTextbooks are viewed through NOOK Study (free app). You can high-light, tag, link, and conduct searches on textbooks downloaded with this app.

If I were currently attending school, I would ask for gift certificates to these two stores for every single holiday. The generosity of family could keep me going with school textbooks for quite some time.

Now, these are not the only two sites to rent or purchase textbooks. Below are a few other possible sources. Always compare prices at different sites to make sure you are getting the best deal possible before you proceed.

- Amazon Student Website: http://www.amazon.com/New-Used-Text-books-Books/b?ie=UTF8&node=465600
- Barnes and Noble: http://www.barnesandnoble.com/u/textbooks-college-textbooks/379002366/
- Compare book prices:

www.bookfinder4u.com
www.textbookrentals.com

- Rent, sell, or buy back books:

  www.chegg.com
  www.campusbookrentals.com
  www.bookrenter.com
  www.valorebooks.com
  www.skyo.com

Here are my last few ideas on this subject. You may be incredibly shocked to learn that sometimes the library is a good place to start. Check out both your college's library and your community library. The book may not be available for rental for the full semester, but if you only need a section or two, copy machines will work nicely. Or befriend someone who has already taken the class and has not returned his or her book, and offer that individual a decent price. Check with the college's bookstore for class reading lists, or send a nice e-mail to the professor to find out the reading list in advance, and then double down on your mission.

FREE SUBJECT MATTER STUDY SUPPORT—MILITARY BASED

This section will be short and sweet. I packed it full of free websites and preparatory programs that can help in your educational pursuits. Often, all it takes is a little extra help, or a different explanation of the same material in order to clear the cobwebs and make progress in a subject. I find the websites listed below to have the best information/explanations to help promote learning.

Peterson's, a Nelnet Company

www.petersons.com/dod

Peterson's is incredibly comprehensive. Pretty much anything you need, you will be able to find on this site. You can continue to use this site upon separation from the Navy. Here is a basic rundown of what you and your dependents (free for them as well) can access on the site:

- SAT/ACT prep
- CLEP prep (see the CLEP section for more info)

- DSST prep (see the CLEP section for more info)
- ASVAB prep
- AFOQT Air Force
- Military flight aptitude prep
- GED prep
- GRE/GMAT prep
- LSAT prep
- NCLEX PN/RN (nursing)
- PRAXIS I and II

This site also has options to help users narrow their searches—for example, by undergraduate and graduate school, vocational-technical school, or Servicemembers Opportunity Colleges (SOC). Under the undergraduate and graduate school search tabs are listed helpful articles that may give you more guidance in your pursuit of an appropriate school, an appropriate program, or preparing for the admissions process, which can be very long and time consuming.

Lastly, on the home page of Peterson's is a link labeled OASC, Online Academic Skills Course. The program is intended to boost the user's reading comprehension, vocabulary, and math abilities. The pre-assessment will determine the user's strengths and weaknesses and help design an appropriate learning plan. As a user progresses through OASC, learning is supported by interactive exercises and quizzes.

eKnowledge Corporation & NFL Players

SAT & ACT test preparation
www.eknowledge.com/military
(770) 992-0900
LoriCaputo@eknowledge.com

This program is a combined effort of the Department of Defense and some patriotic NFL players. eKnowledge Corporation donates SAT and ACT test preparation software to military families and veterans. The software usually runs approximately $200, but it is free for service members and their families. The programs include classroom instruction, interactive learning participation, and 120 classroom video lessons.

Veterans Attending School with the GI Bill-Tutoring Available

Veterans attending school on a GI Bill at one-half time or more in a postsecondary program at an educational institution may be eligible for an extra tutoring stipend from the VA. The VA will pay up to $100 per month for tutoring on top of your regular GI Bill payments. The subject must be mandatory for program completion. Total amount cannot exceed $1,200. Students must need help in the subject, and even if currently receiving a passing grade, they can receive the assistance if the current grade will not count toward program completion.

Under Post 9/11, there is no entitlement charge (deduction of remaining months of benefit). Under MGIB, there is no entitlement charge for the first $600.

http://www.gibill.va.gov/resources/education_resources/programs/tutorial_assistance_program.html

Navy Knowledge Online

https://www.nko.navy.mil/

Navy Knowledge Online (NKO) is discussed in depth in the "Research Tools" chapter. The site is especially beneficial for DSST study material, but it is only accessible by active-duty sailors, as it has recently gone CAC access only.

NON-MILITARY SUPPORTED FREE SUBJECT MATTER HELP

Here is a list of free non-military-related study websites I like to use when I need extra help. I have used all of them at some point and found each beneficial for one thing or another. Hopefully, you will find them constructive too.

Math

Khan Academy (www.khanacademy.org)

The very first website that should be on anyone's list for math is Khan Academy. This is far and away the most amazing math help available without paying for one-on-one tutoring. You can register for the site through Facebook or Google, and it is incredibly easy to use (and of course *free!*).

Videos guide the user through different problems, and discussion question threads allow the user to ask questions. The site offers other subjects besides math. Science and economics, humanities, computer science, and some test prep help are available as well.

Purple Math (www.purplemath.com)

Purple Math offers a wide array of math topics. You can find anything you might need on the site. The main page is a bit jumbled, and many of the links take you to external sites. Stick to the main Purple Math page. The examples are written step-by-step to show you how to proceed for each particular problem.

English

Grammar Bytes (www.chompchomp.com)

I (Jillian) dig this website. The layout is easy to understand without any mumbo jumbo to sort through. Each section has a print tab that organizes the material in a easily printed (no pictures or extra garbage to waste ink!), easily read manner. The subject matter is comprehensive, and the site even contains YouTube videos.

Purdue Owl (http://owl.english.purdue.edu/owl/)

As an English teacher, I love Purdue Owl. Everything I need is on this site. Plus the site offers instructive writing help, such as thesis statement development, dealing with writer's block, and creating an outline to start a paper. If you are in need of American Psychological Association (APA) or Modern Language Association (MLA) formatting help, go to this site. APA and MLA are formatting structures that most higher education classes demand be used in writing papers.

Guide to Grammar Writing (http://grammar.ccc.commnet.edu/grammar/)

This is a no-nonsense website that has all of the basics organized in a user-friendly manner. The Editing and Rewriting Skills section has a checklist that is similar to the one I use when writing and grading papers. The checklist also offers the user links to some of the most common grammatical problems facing writers.

The Grammar Book (www.grammarbook.com)

Another good no-nonsense English grammar website. The explanations are brief and easy to understand. The examples are to-the-point easy to follow. The Quizzes tab also has two sections of comprehensive free activities to test your aptitude.

Citation formatting for APA and MLA references:

http://citationmachine.net/index2.php
https://www.calvin.edu/library/knightcite/

APA format guidance:

American Psychological Association: www.apastyle.org
Purdue Owl: https://owl.english.purdue.edu/owl/resource/560/01/

MLA format guidance:

Cornell University Library: https://www.library.cornell.edu/research/citation/mla
California State University Los Angeles: http://web.calstatela.edu/library/guides/3mla.pdf
Purdue Owl: https://owl.english.purdue.edu/owl/resource/747/01/

Chapter Seven

Prior Learning Credit

Prior learning credit is college credit that is granted for learning that occurred after a student completed high school. Many schools award prior learning credit even though it is not widely advertised. For service members, prior learning credit is often awarded by institutions of higher learning for military training. Schools always demand evidence of the learning that took place. For sailors, that evidence is demonstrated through an evaluation of their Joint Services Transcript. If granted, these credits can result in service members expediting their college degrees. This chapter includes information on the following topics:

- Prior Learning Credit
- American Council on Education (ACE)
- Joint Services Transcript (JST)
- Servicemembers Opportunity Colleges (SOC) and the SOCNAV Agreement
- Subject Matter Proficiency Exams (CLEP/DSST)

PRIOR LEARNING CREDIT

Prior learning credit is often granted for training, learning, and/or knowledge already gained. This type of credit is nontraditional in nature and is awarded by the good grace of the school. Not all schools will consider awarding prior learning credit, although it is becoming more popular. For military personnel, prior learning credit is most often granted after reviewing the service member's Joint Services Transcript (JST).

Colleges often avoid advertising their ability to offer prior learning credit, so it might not be widely detailed on their website. Veterans are often granted credit in this fashion. Contacting the school to determine whether the institution will review your military transcript might get you free credit based upon learning you have already completed. Not every school awards JST-based prior learning credit; however, more institutions are opting to participate every year. Schools that award prior learning credit through military training and learning place value on the knowledge a service member has gained through his service and demonstrate the institutions' capacity for understanding the rigorous demands that active service has placed upon the student.

Why do you care if the school you have chosen awards prior learning credit? Because it will help fast-track your degree. You only have thirty-six months of GI Bill benefits available to use. Think of the flexibility you will gain if you attend an institution that awards prior learning credit. You might be able to save some benefits for a master's degree or certification program, or you could possibly build a small buffer into each semester's class load. Consider the process as a beneficial pathway to helping you achieve your degree.

THE AMERICAN COUNCIL ON EDUCATION (ACE)

The American Council on Education (ACE; www.acenet.edu/higher-education/topics/Pages/College-Credit-for-Military-Service.aspx) works with the Department of Defense (DOD) to translate military training and experiences into potential credit. ACE has evaluated every branch's rate or MOS, formal courses, and mandatory training requirements to determine what might be eligible for academic credit. ACE makes its recommendations, which are reflected in a sailor's JST. Schools that elect to award credit must first determine how to convert the recommendations into credit that their institution offers. Just because your JST reflects ACE recommendations does not mean your school will adhere to the recommendations and award you credit. Remember, prior learning credit is granted at the will of the institution.

ACE credit recommendations are based on nontraditional learning, meaning it was not completed in an academic environment. ACE credit evaluators are professors who are teaching within the field they are assigned to evaluate. These professors understand that learning can be completed through traditional and nontraditional methods, and they take that into account while conducting evaluations of military credit. Evaluations are ongoing in order to maintain a status that accurately reflects current military training requirements. During the evaluations, faculty members review the military coursework length, learning outcomes, and instruction, and then offer credit recommendations that describe the training in a manner that institutions of higher learning can understand and relate to coursework already offered at their school. Not all military training is awarded credit recommendations.

If you are interested in finding out what type of credit is recommended for a particular course or rating, you can search on the ACE website, www. acenet.edu/news-room/Pages/Military-Guide-Online.aspx. You can search by military course numbers, course titles and locations, subject level, or ACE identification numbers.

Familiarize yourself with the website so you can become a better-prepared student. Your school might not award credit through JST evaluation; however, it may be willing to award prior learning credit in another manner. What if you read the class description of a course listed on your education plan and you realize that it is similar to training you completed while in the Navy? You might be able to petition your school for prior learning credit based upon demonstration of the knowledge. That might earn you college credit without you actually attending the class.

The following is a detailed example of how to use the ACE website to find information regarding your training—it will help you become a better researcher.

Navy Counselor Chief (NCC) Drummonds visits the ACE website to learn more about the command career counselor course that he attended in October 1998. He clicks on the "Higher Education Topics" link at the top of the page, then scrolls down to the "Military and Veterans' Program" link located under "Attainment and Innovation." Once on the new page, he clicks on the "Military Guide" on the right-hand side and now finds himself on the search page. Navy Counselor Chief Drummonds will search on the "Courses" tab for his information.

He selects his branch, lists his course, inputs the month and year, and initiates the search. The search produces several results. Navy Counselor Chief Drummonds scrolls down until he finds the correct course. He notices that the dates listed for his course just encompass the dates he attended the course. He clicks on the description and is brought to a page that details the course parameters and learning outcomes.

If Navy Counselor Chief Drummonds would like to search his rating, he would return to the main search page and click on "Search Occupations," choose "Navy Enlisted" under "Occupation," list career counselor under "Occupation Title," and input the time frame (1989) that he completed his occupational training. Only one result comes up during the course of the search. The search results also yield the ACE ID (in this case, NER-NC-002). Searches can also be conducted by the ACE ID number that you can find on your JST.

Before you write a submission request for prior learning credit, always double-check with your academic counselor to determine if the school will consider the request and what is the best way to make the request. Some institutions have very specific pathways that must be completed to be considered for the free credits and fees that must be paid. That said, a generic pathway might resemble something like the following example.

Information Systems Technician Third Class (IT3) Richards was assigned duties as an information technology network technician while he was in the Navy. After separating from active service, he decides to attend ABC University. ABC University does not evaluate JSTs, but the institution is willing to consider prior learning credit if Information Systems Technician Third Class Richards can make a connection between training completed and knowledge earned while on active duty with the Navy and demonstrate that it equates to a specific class that ABC University offers.

Information Systems Technician Third Class Richards looks up the definition of his rating in the Navy on the Navy COOL website, www.cool.navy. mil. This is the exact definition from the site:

> In the area of Network Administration, IT Technicians provide technical assistance to computer system users. They answer questions and/or resolve computer problems for clients IT Technicians provide assistance concerning the use of computer hardware and software, including printing, installation, word-processing, electronic mail, and operating systems. They conduct help desk functions and repair fiber optics and a variety of cables. Additionally, IT Technicians conduct day-to-day operations such as system backups and restores, and add, modify, or delete user accounts. They install operating systems, applications and peripherals, troubleshoot user problems, debug command language scripts, and assist the Information Systems Security Officer (ISSO) in access control security (i.e., passwords, access and control lists, etc).[1]

He also visited the ACE website and searched his occupation. He was rewarded with an entire page description of his occupational specialty that included a description, related competencies, and credit recommendations. ACE lists the following as credit recommendations for an information systems technician third class sailor:

> In the lower-division baccalaureate/associate degree category, 1 semester hour in computer applications, 1 in IT customer service, 2 in network security, 2 in PC repair and maintenance, 2 in computer networks, 1 in navigation, 2 in systems maintenance, 1 in introduction to operating systems, 1 in telecommunications, 1 in network hardware installation, and 2 in introduction to supervision (1/07).[2]

Information Systems Technician Third Class Richards now has a good idea where to start looking at classes his school offers for possible credit matches. He accesses the school's class description link on the website and begins his search under computer science or information technology. He needs to look for coursework that details learning and knowledge similar to what he was taught in the Navy. If he finds a class that meets those requirements, he will need to document his learning and demonstrate the similarities. He will also need to plead his case, demonstrating why he deserves the prior learning credit. Using the descriptions from Navy COOL and the ACE website will help him. Navy COOL and ACE give descriptions of his military specialty, and ACE has already completed significant and widely accepted transfer recommendations. He should also include a copy of the military certificate he was given upon completion of his course. The more documentation you can produce, the better to prove your case.

ACE also completes credit evaluations in sectors that are not related to the military, and it is a well-known organization in the civilian sector with a highly credible reputation. Referencing that organization and demonstrating its recommended credit will give your petition more weight.

The following is a detailed example of how to use the ACE website:

Navy Counselor Chief Drummonds visits the ACE website to learn more about the Command Career Counselor course he attended in October 1998. He clicks on the "Higher Education Topics" link at the top of the page, then scrolls down to the "Military and Veterans' Program" link located under "Attainment and Innovation." Once on the new page, he clicks on the "Military Guide" on the right-hand side and now finds himself on the search page.

Command Career Counselor Drummonds will search on the "Courses" tab for his information.

He selects his branch, lists his course, inputs the month and year, and initiates the search. The search produces several results. Command Career Counselor Drummonds scrolls down until he finds the correct course. He notices that the dates listed for his course just encompass the dates he attended the course. He clicks on the description and is brought to a page that details the course parameters and learning outcomes.

At this point, Command Career Counselor Drummonds can view all of the detailed information that ACE wrote regarding the learning parameters and desired outcome goals of the course. He can use the information in a résumé, or to assist in petitioning his school for prior learning credit if he can match the course description to a class his school offers.

JOINT SERVICES TRANSCRIPT

The Joint Services Transcript (JST; https://jst.doded.mil/) was formerly known as the Sailor and Marine ACE Registry Transcript (SMART). The Army and Coast Guard now use the transcript as well (hence the name change). The JST document compiles the ACE credit-recommended coursework information into a transcript that academic institutions can read. The document endorses a sailor's military experiences as valuable in an academic setting.

If your school recognizes the JST, you will want to send an official copy to the institution for credit evaluation. The official JST can be requested by you, someone at Navy College, or an Education Center if you are stationed at a Marine Corps base. The official request goes to Virtual Education Center, Virginia Beach, and then it is sent to the institution. The requests are free, and you do not need to be on active duty; veterans can use the site as well. If you want to pull your unofficial JST, visit the website, create an account, click the "Transcripts" link at the top of the page, and then choose the "Combo Report."

ACE recommended credit means you might be able to collect free college credit as discussed in the section regarding the organization. Remember that free credit helps you fast-track your degree. That means getting into the workforce faster, saving GI Bill benefit, or simply giving you a small buffer in the number of classes you need to take each semester in order to graduate.

Let's discuss the credit load concerns. Your GI Bill has thirty-six months of benefit available for you to use. That equates to nine months per year over the course of four academic years. That is enough benefit to attain most bachelor's degrees, which require 120 semester credit hours to graduate. But those semester hours are not in random classes. Your academic counselor will build a degree plan for you based upon your academic goals, meaning the degree you want to attain. Upon completion, most classes earn you three credits; some math classes and most sciences will earn you four credits because they often have a mandatory one credit hour lab attached to them. In order to attain your declared degree (if it requires 120 semester hours), your semesters will look like this:

Fall semester freshman year: 5 classes × 3 credits = 15 credit hours
Spring semester freshman year: 5 classes × 3 credits = 15 credit hours

This totals thirty semester credit hours earned for your first year of school. Complete the same process for your sophomore, junior, and senior years. You end up with 120 semester credit hours, and you will have earned your degree.

Here is where it gets tricky. The VA considers twelve credit hours every semester (on a normal sixteen-week semester schedule) to be full-time. Full-time semesters equal full-time housing allowance under Post 9/11. If you only complete the bare minimum according to the VA to maintain your full-time benefits, you will not collect the number of credits you need in order to graduate. Twelve credits per semester will only total ninety-six credits at the end of your senior year of college. You will be out of benefits, but you will not have attained your degree yet.

Because the VA considers four to six classes to be full-time, you could take four classes one semester and six the next to make up the difference. If your school awards JST credit, you may not have this worry. For example, if Seaman Thompson attends ABC University and is awarded fifteen JST credits, he has two choices in building his semester schedules. He could consider those fifteen credits as a full semester and continue along a normal pathway to graduate early, or he could use the free JST credit as a built-in buffer to enable him to build a slightly less intensive semester schedule. He would have the ability to schedule four classes per semester for his first two and a half years, maintain full-time GI Bill benefits, and still be on track to graduate because he will make up the missing fifteen credits with the free JST credit he was awarded.

Options abound, but only you can determine the best pathway for your life. Discuss your needs with an academic counselor at the school and consider all applicable pathways before you decide. Most of the sailors I work with opt to fast-track their educations. They use the JST credit they are awarded to fill semesters in order to graduate early. This is most beneficial, as it can save you benefits toward another pathway such as a master's degree or a certification.

Typically, when attending college, students have three different types of credit they must earn: general education, core, and elective. General education credits include math, English, history, arts, health, natural science, social and behavioral sciences. Core credits include all classes specific to your particular major—for example, business classes if you are a business major. Elective credits are your free choices. They give you a well-rounded education. Your educational pathway will demand a certain number of elective credits depending upon your major course of study. Choosing a major that is heavy on core classes, such as engineering, will reduce the number of elective credits.

JST credit is typically applied to the free-choice elective credits section. Although each school determines what it accepts and how the free credit will be applied, some schools offer rating-related degrees that enable JST credit to be applied to core credits. The overall value of a sailor's JST will depend upon his desired educational pathway at an institution that is open to accepting military credit, his chosen Navy rating, and completed training. Typically, the longer you are in the military, the more JST credit you are able to pick up. Remember, because acceptance of the JST is at the discretion of each institution, some schools will not accept any JST credit. Ahhh . . . the horror!

As a counselor, I (Jillian) cannot recommend that you search out schools based on how many free JST credits the institution will award you for your military training. In fact, I would be skeptical of an institution that made big promises. The point in attending school is to get an education, to feed your brain. Choose a school that fits all of your needs, not just the need to finish fast.

Learning to read the JST is not an exciting task, but it will make you a better-informed student. If you have already pulled your transcript, find it and follow along. The JST is divided into the following six sections.

1. Military Course Completions

2. Military Experience

The "Military Course Completion" and the "Military Experience" sections host all of the training and courses the service member completed during his active-duty service. The military course ID, the ACE identifier, course title, location, description, credit areas, dates taken, and ACE credit recommendations are listed in this section. You can search by the military course ID and the ACE identifier on the ACE website to access more detailed information.

The "Description" section gives a quick rundown of the specific areas of academic course work that ACE is recommending. The "ACE Credit Recommendation" section lists the number of credit hours ACE recommends for the breakdown of each course. The section marked "Level" will have an L, U, or V listed. The L stands for lower-level credit or anything at the freshman or sophomore level of college. The U stands for upper-division credit or anything at the junior or senior level of college. The V is for vocational education.

3. College-Level Test Scores

The "College-Level Test Scores" section lists any CLEP, DSST, or DLPT exams the service member completed while on active duty and the scores received.

4. Other Learning Experiences

This section houses all of the training the service member completed that does not receive credit for one or more of these reasons: ACE has not evaluated the specific course, attendance dates are missing, the course might have been evaluated but not for the dates the service member attended, or ACE did not evaluate the course at the location the service member attended. This section also lists any training that might receive credit but currently does not due to a mistake in the transcript updating process. This will be demonstrated by 4,2 codes listed together instead of one single separate code.

5. The Summary

The "Summary" section is the part of the transcript the schools are going to review. This section breaks down all of your potential credits and houses all of your juicy stuff! Everything you completed while on active duty that ACE recommends for credit is listed in this section. The credits and levels are listed as well as the Servicemember Opportunity College (SOC) category code, which details the subject areas where SOC recommends credit. For example, recruit training breaks down into Personal Fitness and Personal Community Health credits.

The following demonstrates the credit recommendation breakdowns per category:

- Personal Fitness = 1 S, L, Physical Education
- Personal Community Health

6. Academic Institution Courses

This section lists all of the classes a service member took using the active-duty Tuition Assistance benefit. If any degrees have been completed and run through the sailor's military record, they will also be listed in this section.

If you notice that any training is missing on your JST, contact your local Navy College to seek assistance in facilitating corrections. Remember, if it isn't on your JST, your school will not be able to see it; hence, you might miss some credit.

The Joint Services Transcript is not strictly for academic credit or degree completion. The JST can be used in many different areas such as employment and skills documentation, state credential verification, and résumé development. If you are putting together a résumé, you can reference your JST for work history. The Fleet and Family Services Centers on the bases have credentialed résumé writers. Their help is free for service members and their dependents. Be sure to bring your JST and VMET (https://www.dmdc.osd.mil/tgps/) with you if you schedule an appointment.

SERVICEMEMBERS OPPORTUNITY COLLEGES AND THE SOCNAV SERVICEMEMBERS OPPORTUNITY COLLEGES (SOC)

SOC was created to assist active-duty service members and their spouses in their pursuit of education. SOC operates in collaboration with higher education associations, the Department of Defense (DOD), and active and reserve components of the military. The Defense Activity for Non-Traditional Education Support (DANTES) manages the contract that is funded through the

DOD. The group aims to improve higher education opportunities for active-duty military members.

Service members often face roadblocks when pursuing higher education during their active-duty time. The SOC Consortium tries to eliminate many of these roadblocks by working with educational institutions and creating higher degrees of flexibility. The point is to facilitate military degree completion as opposed to simply compiling course credits. The program is available to family members as well.

Attending SOC schools can benefit active-duty members and veterans. SOC schools will look at a service member's JST (https://jst.doded.mil) and possibly award prior learning credit based on experience. More information on the JST can be found elsewhere in this chapter.

Not every school participates in the SOC Consortium. Currently, about nineteen hundred schools are enrolled with available associate, bachelor's, and graduate-level programs. Consortium members offer their students reasonable transfer credit, reduced academic residency, credit for training (JST), and credit for testing programs such as the College-Level Examination Program (CLEP) or DSST (formerly "DANTES Subject Standardized Tests"). Find more information regarding these topics at the SOC Consortium website (http://www.soc.aascu.org).

Service members already enrolled in a school can search for the school's status on the website. For example, if Seaman Jones is enrolled in Old Dominion University in Virginia for a bachelor's degree and wants to find more information about its affiliation with SOC, Seaman Jones should start on the SOC website.

Seaman Jones clicks on the "SOC Consortium" tab on the main website page, then clicks a search by either state or school name. Upon finding "Old Dominion," he clicks the tab and is taken to the school's website. Sometimes the link will take users directly to the SOC information page for the school. Other times, the link will go directly to the school's main page, and a search will need to be conducted to find the desired information.

In the case of Old Dominion, Seaman Jones needs to search. He did not find the "Military/Veterans" tab clearly labeled on the main page, so he writes *military* in the search bar and clicks to search. He then selects the "Military and Veterans" option and scrolls down until he finds the "Service Affiliations" tab; clicking on that tab produces information regarding Old Dominion's Navy partner programs and a small description of the Servicemembers Opportunity College program. Seaman Jones decides to contact the military department to verify its SOC status and how it will help him facilitate degree completion while on active duty.

Many SOC schools also maintain rating-related degrees. Rating-related degrees enable sailors to maximize their military experiences and use them to facilitate college degrees. These degrees consist of pre-negotiated credit aligned with specific rates. Choosing a school with a rating-related degree for which you qualify might enable you to save time and money. Remember that it limits the subject area you will study. More information regarding rating-related degrees can be found in chapter 5.

The SOC website has numerous search options. Students can search for schools, review the "Frequently Asked Questions" sections, and read *The Military Educator*, which is the newsletter of the Commission on Military Education and Training (CMET) (it is distributed by SOC). The newsletter provides information on programs and services pertaining to the DOD Voluntary Education Program.

SOCNAV AGREEMENT

SOCNAV stands for the Servicemembers Opportunity Colleges Navy agreement. This is juicy information, so pay attention! SOCNAV schools are selected by the Navy to offer associate and bachelor's degrees to sailors and their dependents. If your school awards the SOCNAV, you definitely want to request one. You should complete the agreement by the end of your first six credits.

The SOCNAV agreement has two major benefits:

1. It protects your degree plan.
2. It may lock in JST credits.

Let's talk about the SOCNAV and how it can lock in your degree plan. Petty Officer First Class (PO1) Bailey attended XYZ community college, which was a SOCNAV-awarding institution. He went to the JST website and requested his official transcript be sent to his school, declared for an associate degree in business, and received an official degree plan. Before he completed five classes (according to Navy TA rules), he requested and received a SOCNAV.

Fast-forward toward the end of his degree. He has three classes left to take. The school notifies him of a change to the business degree plan, which means instead he now needs to complete six classes before the school will consider him for graduation. After he produces a copy of his SOCNAV agreement, the school is required to honor that initial agreement. This means he cannot be forced to participate in classes he is not prepared to take. The SOCNAV holds the petty officer and the school to the initial degree plan to which both had agreed through the SOCNAV.

This is not a common occurrence. Schools do periodically change degree plans, but not typically so often that you need to worry about it.

The SOCNAV may also help you lock in free JST credits your school awarded you, in case you need to transfer. This pathway can be sticky. As I state in the JST section of this chapter, credit awarded at one school may not be honored at another. Just as transferring regular academic credit is at the discretion of the school to which you are transferring, so are JST credits.

The possibility exists that you could receive free JST elective credits from your school, transfer, and lose them all. For example, when Chief Stevens attended ABC Community College, the school awarded him twenty-one JST elective credits. He locked in a SOCNAV, finished the associate degree while on active duty, and after separation tried to transfer to a four-year university that did not participate in the SOCNAV agreement. The university would not honor the twenty-one JST credits he was awarded through ABC Community College. He was aware beforehand that this might happen, and he might have to make up those credits. He was not upset because he still owned the associate degree and was able to list it on his résumé. If you are aware that in a transfer situation you might have to play catch-up, you will be a well-informed student and better able to prepare in case this does occur.

Remember that awarding of JST credit is up to the schools. But if you transfer from one SOCNAV-awarding school to another SOCNAV-awarding school, you will be guaranteed a smooth transfer of all credit including any freebie JST you were awarded. When schools agree to award the SOCNAV, they agree to the guaranteed transfer process.

This pathway is easy to facilitate for sailors who remain on active duty. Transferring from one SOCNAV institution into another SOCNAV institution is an easy process, and very often sailors pursue this pathway to fast-track their degrees. Trouble begins when sailors try to transfer college credit before completing a bachelor's degree. Others do not finish the associate while on active duty, but hope upon separation to transfer all traditional credit and JST credit without trouble. Unfortunately, this is not always easy, and sailors will most likely have makeup work to complete.

Sailors do not need to attend two different schools in order to facilitate degree completion. Often, large four-year institutions also offer associate degrees if the sailor prefers to start with a two-year degree. Other sailors might decide to begin working directly on a bachelor's degree.

The list of SOCNAV-awarding associate and bachelor's degree institutions is not enormous, but it is growing rapidly. Check the list at http://www. soc.aascu.org/socnav/Default.html. Even if your school is not on the list, you should contact the institution to enquire if it will evaluate your JST for prior learning credit.

SUBJECT MATTER PROFICIENCY EXAMS

Subject matter proficiency exams allow students to earn college credit by taking tests as opposed to sitting through the traditional class. The exams enable students to save money and time, prepare on their own time line, and fast-track their degrees. All of these reasons are incredibly important for veterans who have to maintain a class load specified by the VA if they want to continue with full benefits.

The Navy College Offices on naval bases offer the College Level Examination Program (CLEP) and the DANTES Subject Standardized Tests (DSST). The first exam in every subject is free to active duty. If a service member fails and would like to test again, he or she will need to wait six months and pay a fee (roughly $100). Retirees, dependents, and separated sailors can test for the $100 fee as well (be aware that test costs can increase in the future).

The very first thing students should do prior to taking CLEP or DSST exams is to verify with their school that the institution accepts these exams and in which subjects. There is no point in taking exams for no reason. Many colleges and universities do accept subject matter proficiency exams, but they limit the amount of credit awarded through this pathway, and sometimes they limit which subjects they accept.

After verifying exam acceptance through your school, look at http://www. petersons.com/dod. The Peterson's website maintains free study material for all of the CLEP and DSST exams offered on the bases. Now it is time to study, study, study! After all, who wants to pay to test again?

Once you have determined you are ready to test, contact the Navy College at the base and book an appointment. If the local center offers computerized testing, you will receive instant results for all exams except for the English essay component.

CLEP has thirty-three tests available in six different subject areas: English composition, humanities, mathematics, natural science, social sciences, and history. The exams cover material typically learned during the first two years of college. The College Composition exam is 120 minutes, but all other exams are 90 minutes. Most exams are multiple choice, although some, including the College Composition, have essays or other varieties of questions. CLEP essays are scored by CLEP or the institution giving the exam. If CLEP holds responsibility for scoring, essays are reviewed and scored by two different English composition professors. The scores are combined and then weighted with the multiple-choice section. Exams usually match college classes that are one semester in duration.

The DSST exam program has thirty-eight available tests. DSST exams cover lower- and upper-division classes. This is beneficial for students who have deep knowledge of certain subjects, as it will enable them to test further along the degree pathway. Testing further into a specific subject area may also enable a student to participate in classes that can usually only be accessed after prerequisites are completed. Two tests include optional essays, "Ethics in America" and "Technical Writing." Essays are not scored by DSST; they are forwarded to the institution that the test taker designates on his or her application and graded by the college or university. DSST exams are offered only for three-credit courses.

As I (Jillian) stated earlier, you will benefit greatly as a veteran using your GI Bill if you take and pass CLEP or DSST exams while still on active duty, because during that time you can test for free. Veterans should still consider paying for the exams; it could get you into the workforce faster.

Veterans who take and pass subject matter proficiency exams may reap two major benefits: build a buffer to the required semester credit load and graduate early.

The VA demands that students maintain a minimum of twelve credit hours per semester in order to rate the full housing and book stipend. Twelve credits equal four classes. Maintaining four classes per semester is not a difficult course load; however, if your goal is a bachelor's degree and you have no previous college credit, you will need to take five classes (which typically equal fifteen credit hours) every semester. Most bachelor's degrees demand 120 credit hours of predetermined courses (found on your degree plan) in order to graduate. Twelve credit hours each semester will come to ninety-six credit hours, which are not sufficient to graduate, and you will be out of monthly benefits. If you can add some CLEP or DSST scores into each semester, you will have reduced your required course load.

Reaching graduation early can be a boost to many veterans, especially those with families. Veterans who have completed CLEP or DSST credit may be able to combine those exams with their JST credit and finish their degrees in less than the four years normally required. This enables students to get into the workforce faster or save GI Bill benefits for graduate school, certificate programs, and so on.

ACE also recommends credit for Defense Language Proficiency Tests (DLPTs). The Defense Language Institute Foreign Language Center (DLIFLC) is a school that select Marines may attend to become proficient in foreign languages. The DLIFLC produces the DLPTs that the DOD uses for military and other select personnel. These exams might be taken while on active duty if you speak a second language. DLPTs score the test takers' reading, listening, and real-life proficiency in a foreign language. In some cases, sailors can receive extra pay on a monthly basis depending upon their scores, the language tested, their current assignment, and possibly the test taker's MOS. If you took a DLPT while on active duty but cannot remember your score, you can check your JST (https://jst.doded.mil). The ACE policy regarding DLPT credit can be found online (http://www.dliflc.edu/academiccreditfo2.html). Ask your school if the institution awards credit for DLPT exams. If you speak a second language and you are still on active duty, contact the local Navy College for more guidance regarding DLPT testing policies. For study materials, visit the DLIFLC website (http://www.dliflc.edu).

Sailors with families are always looking for ways to pursue higher education at a faster pace, ways that offer the least interruption to their working careers while they complete their degrees. This is a reasonable desire: They have families and need to maximize their income-earning potential. Passing CLEP, DSST, or DLPT exams while on active duty can have a major impact on the amount of time these sailors must spend in the classroom later. Often, they take several CLEPs on active duty even if they do not elect to take classes until after they separate from the service. Both planning for long-term goals and accomplishing what is possible at the moment give sailors good insight into their future academic pathways and help with time management.

Chapter Eight

Troops to Teachers

Troops to Teachers (TTT) is a U.S. Department of Defense (DOD) program that may help eligible service members pursue a career as a teacher in the public K–12 school system.

The program has two pathways:

1. Counseling pertaining to credentialing pathways and resources to help the service member or veteran achieve success.
2. Financial support to help obtain a credential (note that this pathway incurs a three-year payback commitment).

The thought process behind TTT is to empower service members and veterans to pursue secondary careers as public school teachers while filling teacher shortage needs, especially in subjects such as math and science. The program aims to service schools that maintain populations of low-income families with highly qualified teachers.

Although TTT does not train veterans to be teachers, the counselors give guidance and direct eligible personnel toward appropriate credentialing programs. I (Jillian) am a credentialed English teacher and have a few ideas that I will go into in more depth in this chapter.

At this time, education in this country is taking a beating. Many states have experienced massive teacher furloughs and big pay cuts. Very few areas in this country are facing teacher shortages. Hopefully, this will change in the future, but there are no guarantees. Look into all possible options to protect your future—for example, private schools, community colleges (maybe a different education pathway!), teaching abroad (sounds like fun, right?), on-line teaching, and charter schools, just to name a few.

Any resource should be looked into as a possible information-gathering activity, including TTT. Check in with your state's chapter (http://troopstoteachers.net/Portals/1/National%20Home%20Page/stateoffices.pdf) to determine what it can offer you. Almost every state has a chapter. If your state does not, check with the national TTT department at (850) 452-1242 or (800) 231-6242 or via e-mail at ttt@navy.mil.

TTT can be used by eligible personnel while still on active duty; however, you must be within one year of retirement. The program does not participate in job placement, but the website offers the links to each state's teacher job bank for self-directed searching. If you are a veteran and have already exhausted your GI Bill, TTT may give you the money you need to pursue a teacher credential.

Before you follow through on your decision to be a teacher, read below and check the TTT website (http://www.dantes.doded.mil/Programs/TTT_GettingStarted.html) for some good advice.

THOUGHTS FOR TEACHER CREDENTIALING

Teacher-credentialing programs are next to impossible to do while on active duty. They always require some form of student teaching, ranging from six weeks to a full semester. If you are on active duty, would like to be a teacher, and do not have a bachelor's degree in an applicable subject, that should be your first goal.

Always contact the state credentialing authority first. You need to determine an appropriate pathway based on the information the state gives you. Usually, state governments maintain this information on their websites. A quick Google search should lead to that site. Second, research the schools in that particular state to determine the academic pathways they follow to obtain a teaching credential and/or bachelor's degree that leads in that direction. I work with many sailors who attend their community colleges back home online while on active duty. Check the Department of Defense Memorandum of Understanding website (http://www.dodmou.com) to see if your school is eligible for Tuition Assistance.

If you are unable to attend a school in your desired state, make an appointment at your local education center to find an available equivalent pathway in your current location, or complete your own search on the College Navigator website.

You can always consider the time you have left while on active duty. Maybe a better pathway for you if you are just getting started would be to attend a local community college and begin working toward the credit you will need in order to finish at a school back home. You cannot go wrong by starting with general education classes: math, English, arts and humanities, social and behavior sciences, and sciences.

If this is the case, contact the four-year university you are interested in attending and obtain a degree plan for its recommended academic pathway, and then bring that plan with you to meet the education counselor. He or she will help you find a college you can attend while on active duty that will enable you to fulfill the prescribed parameters. Typically, a state community college will provide you with the safest transfer credit. After you find a local school to attend, you will need to contact the future school and ask about transferability of the credits. Many schools have strict transfer guidelines that you must abide by.

Many teacher-credentialing programs take more time than just a bachelor's degree, but some do not. Check with the schools in the state where you want to earn a credential to determine the proper pathway. You might prefer to complete a master's degree with an attached credentialing program. Typically, a master's degree will earn you more money as a teacher. You may receive an extra yearly stipend, get pushed up the pay scale because it is college credit beyond a bachelor's degree, or even receive a combination of both.

Both GI Bills only afford you thirty-six months of benefits, so you may not have enough to finish a full bachelor's degree and credentialing program. Think ahead! Whatever you accomplish while you are still on active duty leaves less to do after you separate. This pathway will save you time, money, and potentially some GI Bill benefits to use toward a master's degree later. Many of the clients I have worked with prefer to finish their bachelor's degree while on active duty (if possible), and then use their GI Bill for a master's degree and/or a credentialing program after separation.

If you are a veteran and have already exhausted your GI Bill, TTT may give you the money you need to pursue a teacher credential.

Chapter Nine

Vocational Pathways

Oftentimes, sailors tell me (Jillian) that they are not interested in traditional education and are disappointed that the GI Bill will not be able to help them after they separate. But the GI Bills will cover an array of education options, not just the traditional sort. Learning a trade or a skill while using a GI Bill is possible, and many sailors prefer pursuing an apprenticeship or OJT training program instead of a strictly academic pathway. In fact, many continue down the same pathway they were on while on active duty. The USMAP may also be an available benefit if you are still on active duty.

In this chapter, we will consider:

- OJT/Apprenticeship Programs
- GI Bill
- United Services Military Apprenticeship Program (USMAP)

ON-THE-JOB TRAINING (OJT)
AND APPRENTICESHIP PROGRAMS

On-the-Job Training (OJT)

What is OJT, you ask? Well, OJT is designed to help hire and train employees who do not already possess the required knowledge for the position. The method is commonly used to increase productivity and develop an employee's skill base. Training is hands-on, typically somewhere between six months and two years, and is usually done at the worksite as opposed to a classroom setting for traditional education. Typically, a mentor is assigned to each individual (mandatory for the GI Bills) within the program in order for training to be planned and implemented more effectively. Some potential fields of employment for OJT are heating and air conditioning, law enforcement, welding, electrical work, and auto mechanics. Be aware that OJT is not an apprenticeship program. OJT does not have an instruction portion that requires you to attend classes.

Employers and employees reap numerous benefits from participating in OJT. Employers training employees using OJT promote a good public image through their commitment to the community, help create a more skilled workforce, and see immediate return on their investment because the employee is trained to specific company-driven standards. Employees benefit by earning wages as they learn a new skill, gaining job experience immediately, developing a new marketable skill set, and earning certifications or journeyman standing. Productivity is increased on both sides as training progresses, as does trust as relationships develop through teamwork.

If you were recently hired at a new job, and your employer does not currently participate in OJT programs with the VA, contact the State Approving Agency (http://www.nasaa-vetseducation.com/Contacts.aspx) to determine if it is possible to facilitate your OJT with the GI Bill. The State Approving Authority within each state approves OJT programs within its borders. If you are looking for a program that is VA approved, contact the same website, or search for participating employers at http://inquiry.vba.va.gov/weamspub/buildSearchInstitutionCriteria.do.

Apprenticeship Programs

Like OJT, the GI Bill can be used toward apprenticeship training. Apprenticeships are programs lasting a specific amount of time while you work under a tradesman before you earn the same status. Apprenticeship programs are common in trades that are skill based, such as welding and electrical work. Oftentimes, skilled trades require formal licensure, which is obtained partly by working under a journeyman within the field.

Apprenticeship programs can last anywhere from one to six years depending upon the technical field. Assessments throughout the program, mandatory testing, and work inspection conducted by a master tradesman are part of the apprenticeship process. Formal classroom training is part of an apprenticeship. Classes typically include general education, such as math and English, and classes pertaining to technical theory and applied skills. State-man-dated licensing for many fields, such as plumbing, can demand numerous study hours and formal preparation prior to testing.

Apprenticeship is only the starting point; journeyman and master trades-man are the following two steps. Apprentices are overseen by a journeyman or master tradesman, who ultimately is responsible for your work at that time. The goal, over time and with continuing education, is to reach journey-man or master tradesman status. High-level tradesman status leads to higher pay.

The U.S. Department of Labor's (DOL) website has a wealth of informa-tion regarding apprenticeship programs (http://www.doleta.gov/oa/). The site explains how registered apprenticeship programs train skilled workers to meet the needs of American industry in fields such as energy and telecom-munications. The DOL site has links to search for state apprenticeship agen-cies, all approved apprenticeship programs, and state-based program spon-sors.

Last week I spoke with a sailor who had separated from the service and was back home in Wisconsin. He was interested in an electrician program and was wondering if I could help. I found him a contact through the State of Wisconsin Department of Workforce Development website (https://dwd. wisconsin.gov/apprenticeship/trades/construction_electrician.htm) and ex-plained how to use his GI Bill for the training. Contacts can also be found on the National Association of State Approving Agencies website (http://www. nasaa-vetseducation.com/Contacts.aspx). This sailor had no idea that he would be able to access GI Bill benefits for an apprenticeship program and was happy he made the call.

Participants in registered apprenticeship programs receive pay starting from the first day of the program, and this pay will grow over time as the apprentice learns more skill. Many programs have mandatory college classes, usually at the local community college, built into the program. Typically, these classes are paid for by the employer. Participants in apprenticeship programs often finish without any education debt. Completing a registered apprenticeship program earns participants certification that is recognized across the country, making them highly portable career fields. According to the DOL, "In the U.S. today, some 37,000 program sponsors, representing over a quarter million employers, industries and companies, offer registered apprenticeship training to approximately 440,000 apprentices. These training programs serve a diverse population which includes minorities, women, youth, and dislocated workers."[1]

Apprenticeship programs are found in a broad range of industries, including construction, manufacturing, public utilities, health care, and the military (read the "USMAP" section). Apprentice-able occupations come in all shapes and sizes, including airfield management, automobile mechanic, welder, and cabinetmaker. Major companies such as UPS, CVS, Simplex-Grinnell, Werner Enterprises, and CN (railways) provide apprenticeship opportunities.

Green technology has a bright future for growth. Areas such as recycling in the green technology field have some of the fastest-growing apprenticeship programs. Wind turbine technicians, hydrologists, and toxic waste cleanup specialists are all in demand.

GI BILLS AND TRAINING

Either the Montgomery GI Bill (MGIB) or Post 9/11 may be used for OJT. If you rate both, double-check with the institution within which you plan to work to determine the best pathway, or contact the VA directly (1-888-GIBILL-1).

The Post 9/11 GI Bill pays a scaled monthly housing allowance (MHA) if you are accepted into an eligible OJT or apprenticeship program. You will earn wages as well from the company training you, although normally wages are low while participating in OJT because both OJT and apprenticeship pay are usually not a percentage of (or related to) journeyman pay.

Post 9/11 payments for apprenticeship programs are:

- 100 percent of your applicable MHA for the first six months of training
- 80 percent of your applicable MHA for the second six months of training
- 60 percent of your applicable MHA for the third six months of training
- 40 percent of your applicable MHA for the fourth six months of training
- 20 percent of your applicable MHA for the remainder of the training

As your wages increase, the GI Bill payments decrease. A maximum of $83 per month for a book stipend can also be received during training.

MGIB payments as of October 1, 2014, are:

- First six months: $1,287.75
- Second six months: $944.35
- Remaining training time: $600.95

The VA maintains rules pertaining to how OJT must be run and whether a program is or can be eligible. For example, the length of the OJT program should be equivalent to what is normally required (for civilians), and the program must encompass the knowledge and skills demanded for the position. Participants should earn wages equal to a civilian partaking in the same program, and starting wages should be set with consideration of the previous experience of the participant. All records of the program need to be kept adequately and orderly to verify training with the VA.

Using the GI Bill for OJT purposes is not allowed while on active duty, nor can spouses who have had GI Bill benefits transferred to them participate.

Most states list the available OJT and apprenticeship programs for residents on the state government website. Look through the DOL section as well as the state VA website. You can also contact your VA Regional Office for help (http://www2.va.gov/directory/guide/map_flsh.asp). On the National Association of State Approving Agencies (NASAA) website (http://www.nasaa-vetseducation.com/), under the "Programs" tab, you can search approved education and training programs, which include universities, certificate programs, flight school, correspondence school, and OJT-approved programs. You can also access the approved license and certification programs and approved national exams lists.

USMAP

The United Services Military Apprenticeship Program (https://usmap.cnet.navy.mil) is an apprenticeship opportunity for active-duty Marines, sailors, and Coast Guard members. The DOL oversees the "Certificate of Completion" for the program, which is nationally recognized. The program enables service members to demonstrate and translate to potential civilian employers, in civilian terms, the skills and knowledge they learned while working in their Military Occupational Specialties (MOSs) or ratings.

Let's talk about apprenticeships for a minute. Registered apprenticeship programs certify occupational expertise. Apprenticeship completion demonstrates participants' industry-focused skills. Completed programs can help with career advancement and wage increases. The apprenticeship technique has been used in the United States for many decades. Workers who complete apprenticeships are considered more qualified and can demand higher wages.

In turn, this enables employers to develop a more productive, qualified staff that has been trained to industry standards.

To sign up for USMAP, go to the website listed above and follow the directions. To be eligible, you must:

- Be serving on active duty
- Hold a high school diploma or GED
- Hold an eligible rating or Naval Enlisted Classification (NEC) code
- Be a graduate of "A" School, "C" School, appropriate military school, or equivalent civilian education
- Have enough time in service remaining on contract

If a sailor entered or "struck" for the rating through on-the-job training without benefit of "A" or "C" School, normally the sailor is not eligible for USMAP. The exception is equivalent civilian education for the occupation. In such a circumstance, approval can be requested from the USMAP desk in Pensacola.

If you need help, contact your command career counselor. Also, find out who in your work center or department has completed USMAP. Sometimes the best advice comes from those who have already completed the program. Occasionally, the gentleman in charge of USMAP in Pensacola will even visit a base and brief sailors.

The website is easy to navigate, and many of your questions can be answered in the "Help" section under the "Frequently Asked Questions" tab. To see if you have a certificate available under your rating, go to https://usmap.cnet.navy.mil, click on "Trades," and then click on "Navy Rate." Many ratings have more than one certificate available, and some have special requirements as well. Initially, find the one that best suits your daily job; however, if you are eligible, you can try to complete all of them, but you may be enrolled in no more than one at a time.

Let us look at a few examples.

The culinary specialist rating has more than one USMAP option from which to choose. The trade a culinary specialist selects would normally be the sailor's primary job. Six different certificates are listed for the rating. Most require six thousand hours for completion; however, one option requires four thousand hours and another only two thousand. Five options list an N for Navy; one lists an M for Marine Corps. Sailors can choose Navy or

Marine Corps options if duties include most of the tasks associated with the USMAP trade.

For some ratings, several USMAP trade options have additional requirements for training or Naval Enlisted Classification (NEC) codes—for example, the hospital corpsman rating. Members of the hospital corpsman rating fulfill a variety of medical duties while serving with both the Navy and the Marine Corps. This rating has thirteen different USMAP options, but not all of them are open to all graduates of hospital corpsman "A" school.

Examples:

0842N—Nurse Assistant is open to anyone who graduates from hospital corpsman "A" school.

0844N—Pharmacist Assistant is only open to hospital corpsman personnel who have completed Pharmacy Technician School and serve as pharmacy technicians.

0168N—Electromedical equipment repairer applicants must hold Naval Enlisted Classification Code 8410, 8478, or 8479.

When checking your rating requirements, you will note that each certificate is broken down into sections of required hours. Please do not discard the certificate if your job does not currently include hours in that field. Contact USMAP for further advice at (850) 473-6157 or USMAP@navy.mil if you need further assistance.

Now that you know whether you qualify and which certificate you are going to complete, let's discuss how the program works. First, it is free and does not require any extra class time! Excited yet? You should be. Basically, the entire program only requires you to log the hours you are already working. USMAP will even backdate a thousand hours for every year you have served in pay grade E-4 and above (paid status only, not frocked), not to exceed 50 percent of your required amount.

Here are two hypothetical situations.

Hospital Corpsman Second Class Jackson has been in the Navy for five years. In addition to completing the required hospital corpsman "A" school, he is a graduate of field medical service school, which provided him with the qualification to serve with Marine Corps units. It also made him eligible for the emergency medical technician USMAP option (0730N), requiring six thousand hours.

Hospital Corpsman Jackson was promoted to hospital corpsman third class (E-4) after serving one year and six months in the Navy, but he was not paid as E-4 until reaching two years of service. He has served a total of three years in the Navy, but he can only receive one thousand hours of retroactive credit out of the total requirement of six thousand hours for time actually paid as E-4. Frocking times does not count. At the end of every week, Hospital Corpsman Jackson will have his leading petty officer sign off on his weekly logs. He will keep a hard copy in a folder if needed for future reference. Twice a year Hospital Corpsman Jackson will have a chief petty officer or higher sign off on his paperwork. Hospital Corpsman Jackson will send this semiannual documentation to USMAP in Pensacola. There, his biannual logs will be recorded. When he attains the six thousand hours needed for the program, the USMAP desk in Pensacola will send him his certificate. The entire process is incredibly easy as long as he remembers to track hours and consistently send them to Pensacola.

Hospital Corpsman First Class Weinstein has also signed up for emergency medical technician (0730N). He has served fifteen years in the Navy, of which twelve years of service have been in a pay status of pay grade E-4 and above. Of the six thousand required hours, he may receive retroactive credit on three thousand hours, 50 percent of the hours required.

Upon completion of a program, you will have documented evidence of your work (that civilians can actually understand), including a nationally recognized federal apprenticeship completed and ready to list on your résumé. Even if you do not stay within the same field (rating) upon separating from the Navy, the certification can go on your résumé to demonstrate your high level of experience and help supplement your education and training sections. And it was free!

The USMAP certificate is widely recognized. Participating in programs such as this can help you demonstrate to command your eagerness to learn and improve your skills. Proving your skills with a completed apprenticeship may give you a leg up during your civilian job hunting.

For more information on apprenticeships, check the Department of Labor's website (http://www.doleta.gov/oa/). The direct link to the DOL USMAP site is http://www.doleta.gov/OA/usmap.cfm.

If you need more motivation. . . . In 2012, the DOL published the results of a study designed to determine the benefits of participating in a registered apprenticeship (RA; see http://wdr.doleta.gov/research/FullText_Documents/ETAOP_2012_10.pdf). The study demonstrated that individuals who had participated in an RA program earned higher wages than those who did not.

According to the study, "Over a career, the estimated earnings of RA partici-pants earn an average of $98,718 more than similar nonparticipants."[2]

Still don't understand how it can help? This true story might give you more insight.

Some years ago three sailors in the engineman rating left the Navy at the same time. All three were assigned to the same ship in San Diego; two were enginemen first class and the third was an engineman third class. All three sailors applied to one of the local shipyards. All three were hired. So far, so good—until a couple of weeks later. The two higher-ranking sailors visited their former career counselor to see if they could retroactively complete USMAP. They were not happy with their new employment. It seems that the engineman third class had completed USMAP during his enlistment. The union contract stated anyone who had completed a Department of Labor apprenticeship had to be hired at a higher level of pay and responsibility. The former engineman third class was now assigned as their foreman. What a turn of events! Unfortunately, this was a case of "too bad, so sad." There is no provision to retroactively complete USMAP once separated. Their only recourse was to complete the civilian version of the DOL apprenticeship program, which was going to take more than five years.

What else can the United Services Military Apprenticeship Program do to help you? It can help a sailor become more competitive for promotion to E-7, E-8, and E-9. Tiebreakers are often sought for selection boards that have so many qualified candidates. The tiebreaker can be an extra achievement such as the USMAP Program. It can also help applicants be more competitive for selection to commissioned officer programs such as limited duty officer and chief warrant officer.

USMAP completion can help in the quest for a civilian job, especially if pursing a civilian occupation related to the Navy rating. As a sailor, I (Rob-ert) completed the USMAP option for the occupation of counselor while still in the Navy. The USMAP certificate was one of the tiebreakers the selection board used to promote me from E-6 to E-7. Upon leaving active duty after twenty-four years of service, I used the USMAP certificate to apply for counseling positions and received jobs offers for drug and alcohol counselor, financial management counselor, and education counselor with the military, which was the job I chose.

Chapter Ten

VA Programs

The VA has several little-known programs available for veterans. The following programs I (Jillian) reference often during my counseling appointments. Always check your eligibility because many stipulations apply, such as the disability rating for vocational rehabilitation. The following programs are discussed in this chapter:

- Veterans Upward Bound (VUB)
- Vocational Rehabilitation
- VA Work Study
- GI Bill Tutorial Assistance

VETERANS UPWARD BOUND (VUB)

Veterans Upward Bound (VUB; http://www.navub.org/) is a U.S. Department of Education program that assists and promotes veteran success within higher education. The free program aids veteran students who have not been to school for a long time, or simply need a refresher by assisting in academic preparation. The programs are conducted on college campuses. "The primary goal of the program is to increase the rate at which participants enroll in and complete postsecondary education programs."[1]

VUB participants may receive academic skills assessment and refresher courses to enhance their college-level skills. The courses consist of subjects such as math, science, English, computers, and foreign languages. Veteran education services may also be available—for example, assistance completing college admissions applications or GI Bill applications, academic advising, tutoring, or cultural field trips.

In order to qualify, veterans must:

- Have completed a minimum of 180 days of active service, or have been discharged prior to that point because of a service-connected disability *or* have been with a reserve component that served on active duty on or after September 11, 2001, for a contingency operation
- Have any discharge other than dishonorable
- Be low income (based upon family income and number of household dependents) *or* be a first-generation college student (parents do not have degrees)

To find a VUB program in a specific state, check http://www.navub.org/VUB-Program-Information.html and contact the program director. Information about the program can also be found on the Department of Education's website, http://www2.ed.gov/programs/triovub/index.html.

VOCATIONAL REHABILITATION

VA Vocational Rehabilitation (Voc Rehab; http://www.benefits.va.gov/vocrehab/) may assist service-connected veterans with job training, job skills, education, or employment accommodations. Voc Rehab counselors will work with individuals to determine career interests, skills, and existing abilities. They will help participants find jobs, on-the-job training, or apprenticeship programs. Formal education through an institution of higher learning might also be a necessary component to the retraining program. Veterans with severe disabilities can seek assistance through Voc Rehab to find help for independent living.

Eligible service members must meet the following parameters:

- If still on active duty, must be expecting to receive an honorable discharge, becoming service connected at a minimum of 20 percent
- Veterans must receive a discharge that is anything other than dishonorable, and receive a VA service-connected rating of 10 percent or higher or a memorandum rating of 20 percent or higher.

After a veteran receives a service-connected rating, he or she must apply for Voc Rehab and schedule an appointment with a counselor. The vocational rehabilitation counselors (VRCs) will complete an evaluation to determine final eligibility. If eligible, the VRC and the veteran will work together to determine the appropriate retraining pathway for the desired career outcome.

To apply for Voc Rehab, visit the VONAPP website (under the "Apply for Benefits" tab) on eBenefits and fill out Vocational Rehabilitation Form 28-1900. eBenefits: https://www.ebenefits.va.gov/ebenefits-portal/ebenefits.portal.

WORK-STUDY

VA Work-Study is a part-time work program available to veterans who currently attend school at the three-quarter pursuit rate or higher. The program offers an opportunity for veteran students to earn money while pursuing education. Work-Study payments are tax free. Participants work within a community of peers and build skills for résumés. All services rendered within the program relate to work within the VA. Eligible participants may not exceed 750 hours of VA Work-Study per fiscal year.

Selected participants receive the federal minimum wage or state minimum wage, depending on which is greater. Sometimes, positions at colleges or universities are paid an extra amount by the school to make up the difference in pay between the institution and the VA Work-Study program.

Students are placed in a variety of positions depending upon availability, institution of attendance, and local VA facilities, such as Department of Veterans Affairs (DVA) regional offices or DVA medical offices. Priority may be given to veterans who have disability ratings of 30 percent or higher. Selection depends on factors such as job availability and a student's ability to complete the contract prior to exhausting his or her education benefits. Positions can include processing VA documents, assisting in VA information dispersal at educational institutions, and working at a local VA facility.

Veterans must be using one of the following programs in order to be eligible:

- Post 9/11 (including dependents using transferred entitlement)
- Montgomery GI Bill (MGIB) active or reserve
- Raising the Educational Achievement of Paraprofessionals (REAP) participants
- Post–Vietnam Era Veterans' Educational Assistance Program
- Dependents' Educational Assistance Program

- Dependents who are eligible under Chapter 35 may use Work-Study only while training in a state
- Vocational Rehabilitation participants

   To apply for VA Work-Study, visit the VA link at http://www.vba.va.gov/pubs/forms/VBA-22-8691-ARE.pdf or check with your local processing center at http://www.gibill.va.gov/contact/regional_offices/index.html.

GI BILL TUTORIAL ASSISTANCE

If you are a veteran and you are having trouble in one of your classes, tutorial assistance is available under MGIB and Post 9/11. Veterans eligible for this assistance have a deficiency in a subject or prerequisite subject that is required for his or her degree plan. The assistance is a supplement to your selected GI Bill. To be eligible, you must be pursuing education at a 50 percent or greater rate, have a deficiency, and be enrolled in the class during the term in which you are pursuing tutoring.

   The cost cannot exceed $100 per month or the cost of the tutoring if less than $100. If the eligible student is under MGIB, there is no charge to the entitlement for the first $600 of tutoring received. If the eligible student elected the Post 9/11 GI Bill, there is no entitlement charge.

   VA Form 22-1990t, "Application and Enrollment Certification for Individualized Tutorial Assistance," must be completed by the eligible student, the tutor, and the VA certifying official to apply for the benefit. The form must be signed, dated, and filled out either monthly or after a combination of months.

   More information can be found on the VA website, http://www.benefits.va.gov/gibill/tutorial_assistance.asp. For application and enrollment certification for individualized tutorial assistance, see http://www.vba.va.gov/pubs/forms/VBA-22-1990t-ARE.pdf.

Chapter Eleven

Random Service Member and Spousal-Based Programs/Organizations

Many programs are available for veterans and dependents to assist in education and career development. Some of the programs are volunteer-based; others are run on set schedules through institutions of higher learning. Several sailors I (Jillian) know have gone through the programs listed in this chapter, and all speak highly of their experiences.

In this chapter, we will discuss:

- Programs available for active-duty, veterans, and dependents
- Military Spouse Career Advancement Accounts (MyCAA)
- General advice for spouses

PROGRAMS AVAILABLE TO ACTIVE-DUTY, VETERANS, AND DEPENDENTS

I (Jillian) have run across a few organizations and programs that sailors have found especially beneficial over the past few years. I am sure many more wonderful programs are available, but these are the few I use almost daily. Usually, we discuss the organizations that have been around for a while, such as the Veterans of Foreign Wars (VFW), Disabled American Veterans (DAV), and American Veterans (AmVets), mainly because the organizations have very established, credible programs.

Volunteering is a great way for veterans to continue to serve after they leave the service and build skills for their résumés. Staying active with others in the community can give veterans a sense of purpose. Many service members I counsel enjoy volunteering after separating from the service and sometimes while still on active duty.

Oftentimes the younger sailors I work with prefer some of the newer organizations. Mostly, they cater more specifically to Iraq and Afghanistan veterans, such as Iraq and Afghanistan Veterans of America (IAVA). Team Rubicon and The Mission Continues are interesting possibilities for those interested in hands-on participation; the programs handle disaster relief and community building.

The first few organizations listed in this section offer services and programs for veterans. The last few are volunteer-based organizations.

Syracuse University Institute for Veterans and Military Families (IVMF)

http://vets.syr.edu/

Syracuse University, partnered with JPMorgan Chase & Co., has several programs available through the IVMF to assist transitioning Post 9/11 service members with future career plans depending upon their interests and pursuits. Many of the programs consist of free online courses that users can access from any location at any time to promote veteran preparedness and understanding of the civilian sector. Other courses are offered in a face-to-face format that lasts roughly two weeks, and they are now available in several different locations. IVMF offers courses for veterans, active duty, active-duty spouses, and disabled veterans.

The programs currently offered by IVMF include the following:

- EBV: Entrepreneurship Bootcamp for Veterans with Disabilities
- EBV-F: Entrepreneurship Bootcamp for Veterans' Families (caregivers and family members)
- V-WISE: Veteran Women Igniting the Spirit of Entrepreneurship for veteran women, female active duty, and female family members
- E&G: Operation Endure & Grow for guard and reserve members and family
- B2B: Operation Boots to Business: From Service to Startup for transitioning service members
- Veterans' Career Transition Program (VCTP): Great program for active duty to gain industry-level certificates in high-demand career fields.

Entrepreneurship Bootcamp for Veterans with Disabilities (EBV)

http://ebv.vets.syr.edu/

EBV is designed to help post-9/11 veterans with service-connected disabilities in the entrepreneurship and small business management fields. Syracuse University, Texas A&M, Purdue University, UCLA, University of Connecticut, Louisiana State University, Florida State University, and Cornell University currently participate in EBV. EBV promotes long-term success for qualified veterans by teaching them how to create and sustain their entrepreneurial ventures (http://ebv.vets.syr.edu/). All costs associated with EBV are covered by the program, including travel and lodging.

Entrepreneurship Bootcamp for Veterans' Families (EBV-F)

http://ebv.vets.syr.edu/families/

Entrepreneurship Bootcamp for Veterans' Families is offered through Syracuse University's Whitman School of Management and the Florida State University College of Business. The cost-free (including travel and lodging) one-week program assists family members in their pursuit to launch and maintain small businesses.

Eligible spouses include the following:

- A spouse, parent, sibling, or adult child who has a role supporting the veteran (health, education, work, etc.)
- A surviving spouse or adult child of a service member who died while serving after September 11, 2001
- An active-duty service member's spouse

V-WISE

http://whitman.syr.edu/vwise/

Veteran Women Igniting the Spirit of Entrepreneurship is a joint venture with the U.S. Small Business Administration (SBA). The program helps female veterans along the entrepreneurship and small business pathway by arming them with savvy business skills that enable them to turn business ideas into growing ventures. Business planning, marketing, accounting, operations, and human resources are covered. The three-phase approach consists of a fifteen-day online course teaching the basic skills pertaining to being an entrepreneur, a three-day conference with two tracks (for startups or those already in business), and delivery of a comprehensive listing packet that details the community-level resources available to participants.

Eligible participants are honorably separated female veterans from any branch of the military from any time. Female spouses or partners of veteran business owners are eligible as well. Hotel rooms and taxes are covered, but other fees apply, such as travel.

Endure & Grow

http://vets.syr.edu/education/endure-grow/

Operation Endure & Grow is a free online training program open to National Guard, reservists, and their family members. The program has two tracks, one for startups and the other for those who have been in business for more than three years. The tracks are designed to assist participants in creating a new business and all related fundamentals, or to help an operating business stimulate growth.

Operation Boots to Business: From Service to Startup (B2B)

http://boots2business.org/

B2B is a partnership with the Syracuse University Whitman School of Business and the SBA. The program goal is to train transitioning service members to be business owners through three phases. Phases 1 and 2 are taken while the service member is still on active duty, preparing to transition to the civilian world and attending the Transition Readiness Seminar (TRS). The third phase is accessible if veterans elect to continue and consists of an intensive instructor-led eight-week online "mini"-MBA.

Active-duty service members and their spouses or partners are eligible to participate in B2B during the separation process. The entire B2B program is free. Speak to your career planner about electing the Entrepreneurship Pathway during TRS.

Veterans' Career Transition Program (VCTP)

http://vets.syr.edu/education/employment-programs/

The VCTP offers numerous classes for career training and preparation. Many of the courses lead to high-demand industry-level certifications. This free online program is available to eligible post-9/11 veterans. The program is geared to help veterans understand corporate culture in the civilian business world. VCTP is a three-track program that includes professional skills, tech, and independent study tracks.

The professional skills track aims at training veterans in "soft" skills—mainly how to prepare for and implement job searches by conducting company research and creating cover letters and résumés. Foundations for advanced-level courses in Microsoft Office Word, Excel, PowerPoint, and Outlook can be achieved within this track. If a veteran participates in this track, he or she becomes an official Syracuse University student and receives a non-credit-based certificate upon completion.

The tech track is geared to prepare participants for careers in operations or information technology (IT). Industry-level certifications are offered in this level, and, where applicable, VCTP will cover exam fees. Participants also become Syracuse University students and receive non-credit-awarding certificates upon completion. Certificates include proficiency in subject areas such as Comp TIA (Server+, Network+, and A+), Oracle Database 11G, CCNA with CCENT certification, and Lean Six Sigma Green Belt.

The independent study track hosts a large library of online coursework. Coursework includes subject matter pertaining to professional and personal development, leadership, IT, and accounting and finance. Coursework is determined by veterans' demands and learning needs. Students will not be considered Syracuse University students.

American Corporate Partners (ACP)

http://www.acp-usa.org/
http://www.acp-advisornet.org

American Corporate Partners is a New York City–based national nonprofit organization founded in 2008 to help veterans transition from active duty into the civilian workforce by enlisting the help of business professionals nationwide. Through mentoring, career counseling, and networking possibilities, ACP's goal is to build greater connections between corporate America and veteran communities. ACP has two available programs: ACP Advisor-Net, which is open to service members and their immediate family members; and a one-on-one mentoring program for post 9/11 veterans. ACP Advisor-Net is an online business community that offers veterans and immediate family members online career advice through Q&A discussions. The mentoring program connects employees from ACP's participating institutions with veterans or their spouses for mentoring options, networking assistance, and career development. More than fifty major companies are participating in ACP's mentoring program, and success stories and videos are available on ACP's website (http://www.acp-usa.org).

Hiring Our Heroes

http://www.uschamber.com/hiringourheroes

The U.S. Chamber of Commerce Foundation launched Hiring Our Heroes in 2011 to help veterans and spouses of active-duty service members find employment. The program works with state and local chambers as well as partners in the public, private, and nonprofit sectors. Hiring Our Heroes hosts career fairs at military bases. The program offers transition assistance, personal branding, and résumé workshops.

Google for Veterans and Families

http://www.googleforveterans.com/

Google offers a wide range of help for active-duty and veteran military members. It has tools to help families stay in touch during deployments, record military deployments, explore life after service (including résumé-building opportunities), and connect with other veterans.

Vet Net on Google+

VetNet was launched by the U.S. Chamber of Commerce's Hiring Our Heroes program, the IVMF, and Hire Heroes USA as a partnership program. The program is set up similar to the TRS with different pathways designed to help transitioning service members find a more tailored approach to their specific needs. VetNet has three different pathways depending upon your goals: basic training, career connections, and entrepreneur. The site hosts live events and video seminars designed to provide information from those who have gone before them and to generate group discussions about civilian career and entrepreneur challenges. You can find many VetNet videos on YouTube.

Iraq and Afghanistan Veterans of America (IAVA)

http://iava.org/

IAVA offers service members another way to maintain the brotherhood while actively participating in an organization that promotes veteran well-being. The nonprofit, nonpartisan organization is strictly for veterans of the Iraq and Afghanistan campaigns. IAVA actively generates support for veteran-based policies at the local and federal levels while assisting members through programs related to health, employment, education, and community resources. Its aim is to empower veterans who will be future leaders in our communities.

IAVA sponsors several academic and career-related programs for its members. Many of the Marines I work with have sought out IAVA for assistance. One active-duty gunnery sergeant I worked with was accepted to the Culinary Command program offered through IAVA's Rucksack. Culinary Command is a six-week, intensive, top-tier culinary arts program in New York with all costs covered, including travel and accommodations. Many other interesting programs are available for participation, including the War Writer's Campaign (my personal favorite). Programs are offered for online or on-the-ground participation depending upon members' needs.

The Mission Continues

http://missioncontinues.org/

The Mission Continues promotes community service and brotherhood through fellowships with local nonprofit organizations. The program empowers veterans to achieve post-fellowship full-time employment or pursue higher education while continuing a relationship with public service. Fellowships last for six months at twenty hours per week, and fellows receive a living stipend. The program also aims to bridge the military-civilian divide and allow veterans to connect with the community to feel a sense of belonging.

Team Rubicon

http://teamrubiconusa.org/

Team Rubicon unites veterans in a shared sense of purpose through disaster relief assistance by using the skills they have learned in the military. Volunteering veterans reintegrate into society and give back to communities in desperate need. Veterans are the perfect group of trained individuals to cope with the destruction seen in many places hit by natural disasters because many of the circumstances are similar to the conditions that service members were trained to handle while on active duty. Team Rubicon uses the combat skills that many veterans have already cultivated to facilitate greater momentum during disaster relief operations.

The Veterans Posse Foundation

http://www.possefoundation.org/veterans-posse-program

The Veterans Posse Program aims to support veterans who are interested in attending bachelor's degree programs at prestigious institutions across the country. The program creates cohorts of veterans and prepares them to matriculate into select schools. For example, the Veterans Posse Program is currently looking for twenty veterans who are interested in Vassar College or Wesleyan University. Selectees will attend a month-long, all-inclusive, pre-college summer training program in New York City designed to foster leadership and academic excellence. Vassar and Wesleyan guarantee that selectees' full tuition will be covered even after GI Bill and the Yellow Ribbon Program funding runs out.

Warrior-Scholar Project

http://www.warrior-scholar.org

The Warrior-Scholar Project is a two-week intensive program designed to promote veteran academic success. Through classes, workshops, discussions, and one-on-one tutoring sessions, veterans are taught how to transition into higher education, challenged to become leaders in their classes at their institutions, and prepared to overcome challenges and embrace new learning experiences. Yale, Harvard, and the University of Michigan host the program. Be aware that some cost is involved with this program.

Student Veterans of America (SVA)

http://www.studentveterans.org/

The SVA organization is a nonprofit designed to help veterans succeed in higher education. Groups of student veterans on school campuses across the country have gotten together to create member chapters. The goal of these chapters is to help veterans acculturate to college life by offering peer-to-peer support. Chapters organize activities and offer networking opportunities. SVA develops partnerships with other organizations that also aim to promote veteran academic success. Through these partnerships, the SVA has helped to create several new scholarship opportunities. Check the website for more information.

MILITARY SPOUSE CAREER ADVANCEMENT ACCOUNTS (MYCAA)

https://aiportal.acc.af.mil/mycaa

Military One Source facilitates the MyCAA program. The program offers $4,000 to eligible spouses of active-duty military members to be used for education, either traditional or nontraditional. MyCAA is good for an associate degree, a certification, or a license.

The program cannot be used toward a bachelor's degree, but it can be used for programs after a spouse receives a bachelor's degree. For example, I (Jillian) used the program for a supplementary teaching credential offered through the University of California, San Diego, after completing a master's degree in education when I qualified through my husband's rank.

MyCAA aims to increase the portable career skills of active-duty service members' spouses by developing their professional credentials to help them find and maintain work. Military One Source counselors can help eligible spouses find specific programs or schools that participate in the program. Counselors can also help spouses identify local sources of assistance, such as state and local financial assistance, transportation, and child care. They can also help with employment referrals.

Eligible spouses must be married to active-duty service members in the following ranks:

- E1–E5
- O1–O2
- WO1–CWO2

MyCAA will *not* cover the following:

- Prior courses
- Books, supplies, student activities, and the like
- Pre-payment deposits
- Audited courses or internships
- Nonacademic or ungraded courses
- Courses taken more than one time
- College-Level Examination Program (CLEP) or DSST exams
- Associate of arts degrees in general studies or liberal arts
- Personal enrichment courses
- Transportation, lodging, and child care
- Course extensions
- Study abroad

To apply, visit https://aiportal.acc.af.mil/mycaa or call (800) 342-9647 to speak with a Military One Source Counselor.

GENERAL ADVICE FOR SPOUSES

Unfortunately, besides MyCAA, no other direct financial assistance is available for spouses to pursue their education. If spouses are just beginning their education and willing to attend the local community college, MyCAA will typically cover an associate degree, depending upon the cost of the school. Many community colleges offer associate degrees fully online, which may also offer spouses with children more flexibility.

Past the associate degree, scholarship options (see the "Scholarship" section in chapter 6) and, in a few cases, transferring GI Bill benefits from the active-duty spouse are the best bets. Many universities and colleges offer tuition discounts to spouses of active-duty service members but usually not enough to fully alleviate the financial burden.

Spouses should also apply for Federal Student Aid through the Free Application for Federal Student Aid (FAFSA). More information on Federal Student Aid can be found in chapter 6, "Cost and Payment Resources." Many spouses receive all or a portion of the Pell Grant money (see the "Federal Student Aid" section in chapter 6), which does not need to be paid back.

Spouses are entitled to receive in-state tuition rates at state schools in whatever state they are stationed with their active-duty service member. The Higher Education Opportunity Act (H.R. 4137) signed into law on August 14, 2008, guarantees this benefit. This law eliminates all out-of-state tuition fees and at least eases the financial burden of pursuing higher education. Be aware that many schools will want to see a copy of the service member's orders to verify in-state tuition.

Some states offer low-income tuition waivers to residents, usually through the state-based community colleges. Because spouses are eligible for in-state tuition (so are active duty), they may be eligible for this type of waiver as well.

For example, California offers the Board of Governor's (BOG) Fee Waiver (see http://home.cccapply.org/money/bog-fee-waiver) through the state community colleges. Many spouses stationed in California with their active-duty service member are attending community colleges in California and receiving this waiver, and they do not pay to attend school. In fact, many sailors receive this waiver as well and are not bound by the rules of Tuition Assistance.

Always check with the local community colleges first if you are a spouse and are just getting started. In most cases, it is hard to beat their low tuition rates and the flexible class offerings. Community colleges typically also offer vocational programs at drastically reduced prices when compared to private institutions. They should be your number one starting point!

The Officers' Spouses' Clubs on the different bases offer scholarships for enlisted Navy dependents. If you can write an essay and watch the deadline dates, that is usually a decent option for a funding source. As a last resort, you may want to discuss GI Bill transferability with an education counselor at your base. Just remember, if you go that route, that those are benefits your active-duty spouse will not have later. For more information regarding eligibility and the process to transfer the GI Bill, see "Cost and Payment Resources" (chapter 6).

Transferring the GI Bill to a spouse so that he or she can use it while the service member is on active duty is not my first goal in most cases. Spouses are not eligible for the housing stipend while the sailor is still actively serving, but children are eligible. For example, consider the following case.

A sailor transfers his GI Bill to his spouse while still on active duty. She uses the benefit to attend California State University, San Marcos (CSUSM). Although she will receive the book stipend, she will not receive the housing allowance. Her school is paid for, and she has some extra money for books.

Another sailor transfers his GI Bill to his daughter. His daughter attends the same institution and receives the book stipend as well as the housing stipend, which is currently $2,052 per month. At the end of a nine-month school year, the monthly stipend totals $18,468. That is the amount of money the spouse did *not* get while using the benefit. Now consider the same monthly amount (even though it receives cost-of-living adjustments) over a four-year bachelor's degree: $73,872.

For this reason, only in very few circumstances do I recommend that spouses use transferred GI Bill benefits while the sailor is still on active duty. Obviously, this does not take into account different variables. For example, maybe the couple does not plan to have children, maybe the sailor has attained the maximum level of education he or she is interested in pursuing, or maybe the children are very young and the spouse has no other resources. In the end, the decision is personal and all outlets should be pursued.

Appendix 1

Commonly Used Acronyms

AA: associate of arts

AAS: associate of applied science

BA: bachelor of arts

BOG WAIVER: Board of Governors Waiver

BS: bachelor of science

CC: community college

CHEA: Council for Higher Education Accreditation

COE: certificate of eligibility

FAFSA: Free Application for Federal Student Aid

FSA: Federal Student Aid

FY: fiscal year

GPA: grade point average

IAVA: Iraq and Afghanistan Veterans of America

JST: Joint Services Transcript

MA: master of arts

MD: medical doctor

MGIB: Montgomery GI Bill

MOS: Military Occupational Specialty

MS: master of science

MSEP: Midwest Student Exchange Program

OJT: on-the-job training

PCS: permanent change of station

PHD: doctor of philosophy
SOC: Servicemembers Opportunity Colleges
SOCMAR: Servicemembers Opportunity Colleges Marine Corps Agreement
SVA: Student Veterans of America
TA: Tuition Assistance
TAD: Temporary Additional Duty
TAP: Transition Assistance Program
VA: Veterans Administration
VET REPS: Veterans Representatives
VONAPP: Veterans Online Application
VOTECH: vocational technical
YRP: Yellow Ribbon Program

Appendix 2

Websites

ACCREDITING BODIES

- Middle States Association of Colleges and Schools: http://www.msche.org/
- New England Association of School and Colleges: http://cihe.neasc.org/
- North Central Association of Colleges and Schools: http://www.ncahlc.org/
- Northwest Commission on Colleges and Universities: http://www.nwccu.org
- Southern Association of Colleges and Schools: http://www.sacscoc.org/
- Western Association of Schools and Colleges, Accrediting Commission for Community and Junior Colleges: http://www.accjc.org
- Western Association of Schools and Colleges, Accrediting Commission for Senior Colleges and Universities: http://www.wascweb.org/

RESOURCE WEBSITES

- ACT: http://www.act.org
- American Corporate Partners (ACP): http://www.acp-usa.org/, www.acp-advisornet.org
- American Council on Education: http://www.acenet.edu
- American Psychological Association (APA): http://www.apa.org

- Army COOL: http://www.cool.army.mil
- Board of Governors Waiver, California: http://www.icanaffordcollege. com/?navId=10
- Bureau of Labor Statistics: http://www.bls.gov/ooh/
- California Board of Governors (BOG) Waiver: home.cccapply.org/ money/bog-fee-waiver
- Career One Stop: http://www.careeronestop.org/EducationTraining/ KeepLearning/GetCredentials.aspx
- CareerScope: www.gibill.va.gov/studenttools/careerscope/index.html
- Cash for College: http://www.calgrants.org/index.cfm?navid=16
- College Navigator: http://nces.ed.gov/collegenavigator/
- Council for Higher Education Accreditation (CHEA): http://www.chea. org/search/default.asp
- DANTES Kuder: http://www.dantes.kuder.com/
- Defense Language Institute Foreign Language Center (DLIFLC): http:// www.dliflc.edu
- eKnowledge Corporation & NFL Players: http://www.eknowledge.com/ military
- Expeditionary Warfare School and Command and Staff: https://www. tecom.usmc.mil/cdet/sitepages/masters_credit.aspx
- Federal Student Aid: http://www.fafsa.ed.gov/
- GI Bill information: http://www.gibill.va.gov
- Google for Veterans and Families: http://www.googleforveterans.com/
- Grammar Book: http://www.grammarbook.com
- Grammar Bytes: http://www.chompchomp.com
- Guide to Grammar Writing: http://grammar.ccc.commnet.edu/grammar/
- Hiring Our Heroes: http://www.uschamber.com/hiringourheroes
- Institutional Accreditation Search: www.ope.ed.gov/accreditation/, http:// www.chea.org/search/default.asp, http://nces.ed.gov/collegenavigator/
- Iraq and Afghanistan Veterans of America (IAVA): http://iava.org/
- Joint Services Transcript: https://jst.doded.mil/
- Khan Academy: http://www.khanacademy.org
- Know Before You Enroll: http://www.knowbeforeyouenroll.org
- Make the Connection: http://maketheconnection.net/
- Midwest Student Exchange Program: http://msep.mhec.org/
- Military Spouse Career Advancement Accounts (MyCAA): https:// aiportal.acc.af.mil/mycaa
- Mission Continues: http://missioncontinues.org/

- My Next Move for Veterans: http://www.mynextmove.org/vets/
- National Association of Credential Evaluation Services: http://www.naces.org/
- Naval Academy: http://www.usna.edu/
- Naval Reserve Officers Training Corps (NROTC) Program: http://www.nrotc.navy.mil/
- Navy College: https://www.navycollege.navy.mil/
- Navy COOL: http://www.cool.navy.mil
- NavyKnowledge Online (NKO): www.nko.navy.mil
- NCPACE: https://www.navycollege.navy.mil/ncp/ncpace.aspx#o
- O*NET OnLine: http://www.onetonline.org/
- Peterson's: http://www.petersons.com/dod
- Purdue Owl: http://owl.english.purdue.edu/owl/
- Purple Math: http://www.purplemath.com
- Rating-related degrees: https://www.navycollege.navy.mil/ratings.aspx
- SAT: http://www.collegeboard.org
- Servicemembers Opportunity Colleges: http://www.soc.aascu.org/
- SOCNAV: http://www.soc.aascu.org/socnav/
- States' Departments of Veterans Affairs Offices: http://www.va.gov/statedva.htm
- State workforce agencies: http://www.servicelocator.org/OWSLinks.asp
- STEM in the Navy: http://www.navy.com/stem.html
- Student Veterans of America: http://www.studentveterans.org
- Student Veterans of America In-State Tuition Map: http://www.studentveterans.org/what-we-do/in-state-tuition.html
- Syracuse University Institute for Veterans and Military Families (IVMF): http://vets.syr.edu/
- Team Rubicon: http://teamrubiconusa.org/
- Troops to Teachers: http://www.dantes.doded.mil/service-members/troops-to-teachers-faq/index.html
- United Services Military Apprenticeship Program (USMAP): https://usmap.cnet.navy.mil
- University of San Diego's Veterans' Legal Clinic: http://www.sandiego.edu/veteransclinic/
- U.S. Department of Defense Memorandum of Understanding: http://www.dodmou.com
- U.S. Department of Education—national accrediting agencies: http://ope.ed.gov/accreditation/

- U.S. Department of Education College Affordability and Transparency Center: http://collegecost.ed.gov/
- U.S. Department of Labor apprenticeship information: http://www.doleta.gov/oa/
- U.S. Department of Labor's career search tool: http://www.mynextmove.org/
- U.S. Department of Labor unemployment information: http://work forcesecurity.doleta.gov/unemploy/uifactsheet.asp
- U.S. Department of Veterans Affairs (VA): http://www.va.gov
- VA Chapter 36 educational support counseling: http://www.gibill.va.gov/support/counseling_services/
- VA Vet Centers: http://www.vetcenter.va.gov/index.asp
- VA Vocational Rehabilitation: http://www.benefits.va.gov/vocrehab/index.asp
- VA Work Study Local Office Search: http://www.gibill.va.gov/contact/regional_offices/index.html
- VA Yellow Ribbon Program: http://www.gibill.va.gov/benefits/post_911_gibill/yellow_ribbon_program.html
- Veterans On-Line Application (VONAPP): http://vabenefits.vba.va.gov/vonapp/
- Veterans Posse Foundation: http://www.possefoundation.org/veterans-posse-program
- Veterans Upward Bound: http://www.navub.org/
- Vet Net on Google+: http://www.vetnethq.com/
- Warrior-Scholar Project: http://www.warrior-scholar.org

APA FORMAT GUIDANCE

- American Psychological Association: http://www.apastyle.org
- Purdue Owl: https://owl.english.purdue.edu/owl/resource/560/01/

CITATION FORMATTING

- Citation Machine: http://citationmachine.net/index2.php
- KnightCite: https://www.calvin.edu/library/knightcite/

MLA FORMAT GUIDANCE

- California State University, Los Angeles: http://web.calstatela.edu/library/guides/3mla.pdf
- Cornell University Library: www.library.cornell.edu/resrch/citmanage/mla
- Purdue Owl: https://owl.english.purdue.edu/owl/resource/747/01/

Appendix 3

Benefits by State

STATES CURRENTLY WITH IN-STATE TUITION LEGISLATION

Alabama: http://openstates.org/al/bills/2013rs/HB424/documents/ALD0 0016731/

Arizona: http://dvs.az.gov/tuition.aspx

California: http://www.calvet.ca.gov/VetServices/Education.aspx

Colorado: http://highered.colorado.gov/Finance/Residency/requirements. html

Florida: http://www.flsenate.gov/Session/Bill/2014/7015/BillText/er/PDF

Idaho: http://www.legislature.idaho.gov/legislation/2010/S1367.pdf

Illinois: http://www2.illinois.gov/veterans/benefits/pages/education.aspx

Indiana: http://www.in.gov/legislative/bills/2013/SE/SE0177.1.html

Kentucky: http://cpe.ky.gov/policies/academicpolicies/residency.htm

Louisiana: http://legiscan.com/LA/text/HB435/id/649958

Maine: http://www.mainelegislature.org/legis/bills/getDoc.asp?id=39934

Maryland: http://mgaleg.maryland.gov/2013RS/fnotes/bil_0005/hb0935. pdf

Minnesota: http://www.ohe.state.mn.us/mPg.cfm?pageID=1688

Missouri: http://www.senate.mo.gov/13info/BTS_Web/Bill.aspx?Session Type=R&BillID=17138567

Nebraska: http://www.vets.state.ne.us/benefits.html

Nevada: http://leg.state.nv.us/Session/77th2013/Bills/AB/AB260_EN.pdf

New Mexico: http://www.dvs.state.nm.us/benefits.html

North Dakota: www.legis.nd.gov/cencode/t15c10.pdf?20131106152541

Ohio: http://codes.ohio.gov/orc/3333.31

Oregon: https://olis.leg.state.or.us/liz/2013R1/Measures/Text/HB2158/ Enrolled

South Dakota: http://legis.sd.gov/

Tennessee: http://www.capitol.tn.gov/Bills/108/Bill/SB1433.pdf

Texas: http://www.statutes.legis.state.tx.us/Docs/ED/htm/ED.54.htm#54. 241

Utah: http://le.utah.gov/code/TITLE53B/pdf/53B08_010200.pdf

Virginia: http://lis.virginia.gov/cgi-bin/legp604.exe?000+cod+23-7.4

Washington: http://www.dva.wa.gov/veterantuitionwaiver.html

STATES CURRENTLY WITH STATE-BASED EDUCATION BENEFITS

Alabama: http://www.va.state.al.us/gi_dep_scholarship.aspx

Alaska: http://www.veterans.alaska.gov/education-benefits.html

Arkansas: http://www.veterans.arkansas.gov/benefits.html#edu

California: https://www.calvet.ca.gov/VetServices/Pages/College-Fee-Waiver.aspx

Connecticut: http://www.ct.gov/ctva/cwp/view.asp?A=2014&Q=290874

Florida: http://floridavets.org/?page_id=60

Illinois: http://www2.illinois.gov/veterans/benefits/Pages/education.aspx

Indiana: http://www.in.gov/dva/2378.htm

Maryland: http://www.mdva.state.md.us/state/scholarships.html

Massachusetts: www.mass.gov/veterans/education/financial-assistance/ tuition-waivers.html

Minnesota: http://mn.gov/mdva/resources/education/minnesotagibill.jsp

Missouri: http://www.dhe.mo.gov/files/moretheroesact.pdf

Montana: http://life.umt.edu/finaid/tuition-waivers/mt-veteran.php

New York: http://veterans.ny.gov/

North Carolina: http://www.doa.state.nc.us/vets/scholarshipclasses.aspx

North Dakota: http://www.nd.gov/veterans/benefits/nd-dependent-tuition -waiver

Oregon: www.oregon.gov/odva/BENEFITS/Pages/OregonEducation Benefit.aspx

South Carolina: www.govoepp.state.sc.us/va/benefits.html#ed_assis

South Dakota: http://vetaffairs.sd.gov/benefits/State/State%20Education%20Programs.aspx

Tennessee: http://www.tn.gov/sos/rules/1640/1640-01-22.20090529.pdf

Texas: http://veterans.portal.texas.gov/en/Pages/education.aspx

Utah: http://veterans.utah.gov/category/education/

Virgin Islands: http://www.militaryvi.org/benefits/

Washington: http://apps.leg.wa.gov/RCW/default.aspx?cite=28B.15.621

West Virginia: http://www.veterans.wv.gov/Pages/default.aspx

Wisconsin: http://www.wisvets.com/wisgibill

Wyoming: https://sites.google.com/a/wyo.gov/wyomingmilitarydepartment/veterans-commission/res

Appendix 4

Navy College Contact Information

Atsugi, Japan:
DSN (315) 264-4148
Commercial 81-467-63-4148
E-mail: ncoatsugi@fe.navy.mil

Bahrain at Manama:
DSN (318) 439-9094
Commercial 973-1785-9094

Bethesda:
DSN (312) 295-2014
Commercial (301) 295-2014

Bremerton (Kitsap):
DSN (312) 439-4282
Commercial (360) 476-4282

Charleston:
DSN (312) 794-4493
Commercial (843) 764-4493

Coronado:
DSN (312) 526-4922
Commercial (619) 556-4922
nco.coronado@navy.mil
http://www.cnic.navy.mil/regions/cnrsw/installations/navbase_coronado/
about/navy_college.html

Corpus Christi:
DSN (312) 861-3236
Commercial (361) 961-3236

Everett:
DSN (312) 727-3159
Commercial (425) 304-3159

Fallon:
DSN (312) 890-4104/4108
Commercial (775) 426-4104/4108

Fort Worth:
DSN (361) 861-3236
Commercial (361) 961-3236

Great Lakes:
DSN (312) 792-4681
Commercial 847-688-4681 ext. 216
nco_great_lakes@navy.mil

Guam at Marianas:
DSN (315) 339-8291
Commercial 1-671-339-8291

Guantanamo Bay:
DSN (312) 660-2227
Commercial 011-5399-2227

Gulfport:
DSN (312) 868-2785

Commercial (228) 871-2785
https://www.cnic.navy.mil/regions/cnrse/installations/ncbc_gulfport/ffr/
navy_college.html

Jacksonville:
DSN (312) 942-2475
Commercial (904) 542-2475

Key West:
DSN (312) 483-2408
Commercial (305) 293-2408/2075
http://www.keywestnavalhousing.com/template.php?name=educational&
PHPSESSID=10de382fe09722011116083192b292e0

Kings Bay:
DSN (312) 573-4527
Commercial (912) 573-4574

Lemoore:
DSN (312) 949-3857
Commercial (559) 998-3857

Little Creek:
DSN (312) 253-8279
Commercial (757) 462-8279

Mayport:
DSN (312) 270-6341
Commercial (904) 270-6341

Millington:
DSN (312) 882-5290
Commercial (901) 874-5290

Misawa:
DSN (315) 226-2458
Commercial 011-81-176-77-2458

Naples:
DSN (314) 626-6681
Commercial 011-39-081-568-6681

New London:
DSN (312) 694-5203
Commercial (860) 694-5203

New Orleans:
DSN (312) 678-3779
Commercial (504) 678-3779

Norfolk:
DSN (312) 564-9250
Commercial (757) 444-7453

Patuxent River:
DSN (312) 757-4100
Commercial (301) 757-4111

Pearl Harbor:
DSN (315) 473-4766
Commercial (808) 473-5705

Pensacola:
DSN (312) 922-4510
Commercial (850) 452-4510

Rota:
DSN (314) 727-2798/2785
Commercial 011-34-956-82-2798/2785

San Diego:
DSN (312) 526-4922
Commercial (619) 556-4922

Sasebo:
DSN (315) 252-3511
Commercial 011-81-956-50-3511

Sigonella:
DSN (314) 624-4514
Commercial 011-39-095-56-4514

Souda Bay:
DSN (314) 624-4514
Commercial 011-39-09556-4514
si.navycollege@eu.navy.mil
http://www.cnic.navy.mil/regions/cnreurafswa/installations/nsa_souda_bay/
about/installation_guide/navy_college.html

Tinker AFB:
DSN (312) 339-7861
Commercial (405) 739-7861

Ventura County:
DSN (312) 351-8362
Commercial (805) 989-8362

Whidbey Island:
DSN (312) 820-3027
Commercial (360) 257-3027

Yokosuka:
DSN (315) 243-5058/8131
Commercial 011-81-6160-43-5058/8131

Notes

2. ACTIVE-DUTY AND VETERANS' EDUCATIONAL CONCERNS

1. Kimberly Griffin and Claire Gilbert, "Easing the Transition from Combat to Classroom," The Center for American Progress, http://www.americanprogress.org/wp-content/uploads/issues/2012/04/pdf/student_veterans.pdf (last modified April 2012; accessed June 2, 2013).

4. WHAT SHOULD I LOOK FOR IN A SCHOOL?

1. "For Profit Higher Education: The Failure to Safeguard the Federal Investment and Ensure Student Success," Health, Education, Labor, and Pensions Committee, U.S. Senate (last modified July 30, 2012).

2. Sandy Baum and Jennifer Ma, "Trends in Higher Education 2012," College Board, http://advocacy.collegeboard.org/sites/default/files/college-pricing-2012-full report_0.pdf (accessed July 12, 2013).

3. "Independent Colleges and Universities: A National Profile," National Association of Independent Colleges and Universities, http://www.naicu.edu/docLib/20110317_NatProfile-Final4.pdf (last modified March 8, 2011).

4. "Naval Reserve Officers Training Corps," U.S. Navy, http://www.nrotc.navy.mil/about.aspx (last modified June 27, 2011; accessed March 12, 2014).

5. Judith Eaton, "An Overview of U.S. Accreditation," Council for Higher Education Accreditation, www.chea.org/pdf/Overview%20of%20US%20Accreditation%202012.pdf (last modified August 2012).

5. UNIQUE NAVY-BASED PROGRAMS

1. David Beede, Mark Doms, Beethika Khan, David Langdon, and George McKittrick, "STEM: Good Jobs Now and for the Future," http://www.esa.doc.gov/sites/default/files/reports/documents/stemfinalyjuly14_1.pdf (accessed May 7, 2014).
2. U.S. Naval Academy, "Frequently Asked Questions," http://www.usna.edu/Admissions/FAQ.php (accessed May 6, 2014).
3. U.S. Naval Academy, "Naval Academy Preparatory School," http://www.usna.edu/NAPS/ (accessed May 6, 2014).

7. PRIOR LEARNING CREDIT

1. "IT±Information Technology Network Technician," Navy COOL, https://www.cool.navy.mil/enlisted/desc/it_it_nt_spec_desc.htm (accessed May 9, 2014).
2. "Occupation Exhibit," American Council on Education, http://www2.acenet.edu/militaryguide/ShowAceOccupations.cfm?ACEID=NER-IT-002 (accessed April 9, 2014).

9. VOCATIONAL PATHWAYS

1. "Registered Apprenticeship: A Solution to the Skills Shortage," U.S. Department of Labor, Employment and Training Administration, http://www.doleta.gov/oa/pdf/fsfront.pdf (accessed February 2, 2014).
2. "Registered Apprenticeship: A Solution to the Skills Shortage."

10. VA PROGRAMS

1. "Veterans Upward Bound Program," U.S. Department of Education, http://www2.ed.gov/programs/triovub/index.html (last modified September 27, 2013).

Bibliography

American Council on Education. "Military Guide Frequently Asked Questions." Accessed December 13, 2013. http://www.acenet.edu/news-room/Pages/Military-Guide-Frequently-Asked-Questions.aspx.

———. "Occupation Exhibit." Accessed April 9, 2014. http://www2.acenet.edu/militaryguide/ShowAceOccupations.cfm?ACEID=NER-IT-002.

Baum, Sandy, and Jennifer Ma. College Board. "Trends in Higher Education 2012." Accessed July 12, 2013. http://trends.collegeboard.org/sites/default/files/college-pricing-2012-full-report_0.pdf.

Beede, David, Mark Doms, Beethika Khan, David Langdon, and George McKittrick. "STEM: Good Jobs Now and for the Future." Accessed May 7, 2014. http://www.esa.doc.gov/sites/default/files/reports/documents/stemfinalyjuly14_1.pdf.

College Board. "Veterans and College Admissions: FAQs." Accessed January 12, 2014. https://bigfuture.collegeboard.org/get-in/applying-101/veterans-college-admission-faqs.

———. "Why Community College." Accessed January 11, 2014. http://professionals.collegeboard.com/guidance/college/community-college.

Council for Higher Education Accreditation. "The Fundamentals of Accreditation." Last modified September 2002. Accessed February 10, 2014. http://www.academic.umn.edu/provost/reviews/gen_institutional/fund_accred_20ques_02.pdf.

Council of Regional Accrediting Commissions. "Regional accreditation and student learning: Principles for good practice." Last modified May 2003. http://www.msche.org/publications/Regnlsl050208135331.pdf.

Defense Activity for Non-Traditional Education Support. "Troops to Teachers." Last modified July 2, 2013. http://www.dantes.doded.mil/Programs/TTT.html.

Eaton, Judith. Council for Higher Education Accreditation. "An Overview of U.S. Accreditation." Last modified August 2012. www.chea.org/pdf/Overview%20of%20US%20Accreditation%202012.pdf.

Federal Trade Commission. "Choosing a Vocational School." Last modified August 2012. http://www.consumer.ftc.gov/articles/0241-choosing-vocational-school.

Griffin, Kimberly, and Claire Gilbert. Center for American Progress. "Ease the Transition from Combat to Classroom." Last modified April 2012. Accessed June 2, 2013. http://www.americanprogress.org/wp-content/uploads/issues/2012/04/pdf/student_veterans.pdf.

Kleinman, Rebecca, Annalisa Mastri, Davin Reed, Debbie Reed, Samina Sattar, Albert Yung-Hsu Liu, and Jessica Ziegler. Mathematica Policy Research. "An Effectiveness Assessment and Cost-Benefit Analysis of Registered Apprenticeship in 10 States." Last modified July 25, 2012. http://wdr.doleta.gov/research/FullText_Documents/ETAOP_2012_10.pdf.

Kurtzleben, Danielle. *U.S. News and World Report.* "Apprenticeships a Little-Traveled Path to Jobs." January 13, 2013. Accessed March 4, 2013. http://www.usnews.com/news/articles/2013/01/13/apprenticeships-a-little-traveled-path-to-jobs.

Maryland Higher Education Commission. "The Importance of Accreditation." Last modified November 14, 2011. www.mhec.state.md.us/highered/colleges_universities/accreditation.asp.

National Association of Independent Colleges and Universities. "Independent Colleges and Universities: A National Profile." Last modified March 8, 2011. http://www.naicu.edu/docLib/20110317_NatProfile-Final4.pdf.

National Skills Coalition. "On-the-Job Training Recommendations for Inclusion in a Federal Jobs Bill." Last modified January 2010. http://www.nationalskillscoalition.org/assets/reports-/nsc_issuebrief_ojt_2010-01.pdf.

Navy COOL. "IT—Information Technology Network Technician." Accessed May 9, 2014. https://www.cool.navy.mil/enlisted/desc/it_it_nt_spec_desc.htm.

Peterson's. "Colleges and Universities: Choosing the Right Fit." Accessed June 3, 2013. http://www.petersons.com/college-search/colleges-universities-choosing-fit.aspx.

State of California Employment Development Department. "Workforce Investment Act." Accessed January 23, 2014. http://www.edd.ca.gov/jobs_and_Training/Workforce_Investment_Act.htm.

U.S. Department of Education. "Accreditation in the United States." Last modified February 12, 2014. http://www2.ed.gov/admins/finaid/accred/accreditation_pg2.html. http://professionals.collegeboard.com/guidance/college/community-college.

———. "Career Colleges and Technical Schools—Choosing a School." Last modified June 18, 2013. http://www2.ed.gov/students/prep/college/consumerinfo/choosing.html.

———. "Federal Versus Private Loans." Accessed December 13, 2013. http://studentaid.ed.gov/types/loans/federal-vs-private.

———. "Learn about Your College and Career School Options." Accessed May 15, 2013. http://studentaid.ed.gov/prepare-for-college/choosing-schools/types. www.help.senate.gov/imo/media/for_profit_report/PartI.pdf.

———. "Veterans Upward Bound Program." Last modified September 27, 2013. http://www2.ed.gov/programs/triovub/index.html.

U.S. Department of Labor. "Unemployment Compensation for Ex-servicemembers." Accessed September 12, 2013. http://workforcesecurity.doleta.gov/unemploy/ucx.asp.

———. "Unemployment Insurance." Accessed September 12, 2013. http://www.dol.gov/dol/topic/unemployment-insurance/.

U.S. Department of Labor, Employment and Training Administration. "Registered Apprenticeship: A Solution to the Skills Shortage." Accessed February 2, 2014. http://www.doleta.gov/oa/pdf/fsfront.pdf.

U.S. Department of Veterans Affairs. "On-the-Job Training and Apprenticeship." Last modified December 3, 2013. Accessed February 18, 2014. http://www.benefits.va.gov/gibill/onthejob_apprenticeship.asp.

———. "Tuition Assistance Top Up." Last modified December 5, 2013. http://www.benefits.va.gov/gibill/tuition_assistance.asp.

U.S. Marine Corps, Air Station Beaufort. "Go to College after the Marine Corps." Last modified November 8, 2012. http://www.beaufort.marines.mil/News/NewsView/tabid/14981/ Article/133935/go-to-college-after-the-marine-corps.aspx.

U.S. Military Apprenticeship Program. "Program Information." Last modified October 31, 2013. https://usmap.cnet.navy.mil/usmapss/static/genInfo.jsp.

U.S. Naval Academy. "Frequently Asked Questions." Accessed May 6, 2014. http://www.usna. edu/Admissions/FAQ.php.

———. "Naval Academy Preparatory School." Accessed May 6, 2014. http://www.usna.edu/ NAPS/.

U.S. Navy. "Naval Reserve Officers Training Corps." Last modified June 27, 2011. http:// www.nrotc.navy.mil/about.aspx.

U.S. Senate, Health, Education, Labor, and Pensions Committee. "For Profit Higher Education: The Failure to Safeguard the Federal Investment and Ensure Student Success." Last modified July 30, 2012.

Index

accreditation: bodies' standards of, 43; of career colleges, 37–38; financial aid and, 43; of institutions, 13, 43–46; national, 37, 38, 44–45; programmatic, 45; regional, 34, 44; regulating, 43; of votech schools, 37–38; websites of, 46
ACE. *See* American Council on Education
ACP. *See* American Corporate Partners
ACT. *See* American College Testing
active-duty Marines, 42
active-duty sailors: deployment of, 32; educational needs of, 11–17; flexibility needs of, 12; Navy College offices for, 3, 29; programs for, 205–213; TA for, 4, 92–93; transitioning off, 4
admissions: acceptance and, 55; ACT and, 58–61; application for, 49–54; application requirements for, 7, 8, 42; early, 16; flexible, 36; into four-year institutions and universities, 47; personal statement for, 50–53; process, 33, 48–58; required documents for, 8; requirements for, 6, 31, 46–48; sample essays for, 53–54; SAT and, 58–61; school selection during, 49; into state-based community and technical schools, 46–47; time-line restrictions during, 7; into votech and career colleges, 47–48
Adrienne Miller Perner Scholarship, 156

Advanced Education Voucher (AEV), 78–80
AFCEA. *See* Armed Forces Communication and Electronics Association
AFQT. *See* Armed Forces Qualification Test
Alabama: benefits in, 122–123; in-state tuition in, 118; websites for, 122, 146
Alaska, 146
Amazon, 163–164
American College Testing (ACT), 6, 30; admissions and, 58–61; preparation for, 60; scores, 42, 47, 58, 59, 72–73, 83; websites of, 58
American Corporate Partners (ACP), 209–210
American Council on Education (ACE): on credits, 172–173; websites of, 172, 173–174, 175–176
American Legion, 157
American Legion Auxiliary, 150
American Military University, 65
American Veterans (AMVETS), 14, 149
American Veterans National Lady Auxiliary, 149–150
AMVETS. *See* American Veterans
Angelina College, 156
apprenticeships: at CC, 5, 32–33; options for, 25, 26; Post 9/11 GI Bill for, 194; programs for, 192–194; two-year

About the Authors

Jillian Ventrone is a higher education counselor for service members aboard a federal installation, working with combat veterans and their families to help them transition to education or to other professions.

Robert Blue is a higher education counselor for service members and their families aboard a military base. He has served in this capacity on various bases for two branches of the uniformed services. Additionally, he served as an educational services officer and career counselor while serving in the U.S. Navy.